D1260866

Father Mateo Speaks to Priests

Mateo Crawley-Boevey, SS.CC.

Father Mateo
Speaks to Priests

on *Priestly Perfection*

Translated from the French by
FRANCIS LARKIN, SS.CC.

NP

The Newman Press · Westminster, Maryland
1960

Nihil obstat: WILLIAM DAVIS, SS.CC.
Imprimi potest: WILLIAM J. CONDON, SS.CC.
                 Provincial
                 January 25, 1960
Nihil obstat: EDWARD A. CERNY, SS., S.T.D.
                 Censor librorum
Imprimatur: FRANCIS P. KEOUGH, D.D.
                 Archbishop of Baltimore

                 November 14, 1960

Copyright © 1960 by THE NEWMAN PRESS
Library of Congress Catalog Card Number: 60–14830
Printed in the United States of America

OCLC: 2659057

Foreword

I HAVE always considered it one of the special graces of my life to have known Father Mateo. This foreword is written with a deep feeling of gratitude to Almighty God for the gift of a life like that of Father Mateo and for the incalculable influence for good which his apostolate has exercised over many years.

Father Mateo has been called the Apostle of the Enthronement of the Sacred Heart. And this indeed he is, pre-eminently so. He is also in a most special way the Apostle of priestly sanctity, a theme which he was bidden to preach to his fellow priests by the Holy Father himself. Some of the fruits of that preaching will be found in this precious volume.

Father Mateo seems to have made his own the special mission of St. Thérèse of the Child Jesus, to eliminate the erroneous idea concerning the extraordinary character of sanctity, and to show that sanctity does not demand that one's life be in any way out of the ordinary, but that the common ordinary life of the average good Christian can lead to the highest sanctity, provided it is transformed into an act of the love of God. This teaching he applied with special emphasis to the life of the priest.

Here he had one great consuming passion: to convince every priest that priestly holiness and priestly zeal are in direct proportion to the most sublime act of the priestly life, the celebration of the Holy Sacrifice of the Mass. *Qualis Missa talis Sacerdos et Apostolus* was the inscription which he invariably wrote on pictures of the Sacred Heart that he would distribute to priests at the retreats which he preached to them. Here is the "master-idea" of the preaching of Father Mateo, it seems to me. Ardently promoting the cause of the Sacred Heart in every possible way, he would constantly point to the Mass as the perfect means of being transformed into Christ. In the Mass Father Mateo finds the best means of promoting the truth that sanctity is for everyone, and that it is within the reach of the ordinary person, and that the door is open to all who observe nothing singular in their lives.

One other comment needs to be made. Father Mateo throughout his entire life has vigorously combated every form of Jansenism. His preaching of confidence and trust, based on the solid and orthodox doctrine of the Church concerning devotion to the Sacred Heart of Jesus and to the Immaculate Heart of Mary, was always an outstanding part of the retreats, triduums, and sermons which he gave to priests, religious, and lay people alike. Where the love of the Sacred Heart burns in the heart, no amount of suffering, no amount of the magnitude of evil, can rob the heart of the confident joy in the ultimate triumph of that love. Father Mateo insisted that priests need much encouragement in their work, especially in trying to save souls despite themselves. He constantly pointed to the true doctrine of the Sacred Heart as the unfailing source of encouragement in that confident joy which can come only from living in the Heart of Jesus.

While the printed pages of this little volume cannot bring to life the extraordinary gift for moving men which vibrated in every word and gesture of Father Mateo's sermons, it is my sincere hope that many priests will capture something of his enthusiasm and will be kindled with a spark of the great fire which burned in his heart as he delivered these talks with all the ardor of his own priestly heart, and thus be brought closer to the perfection of the priestly Heart of Jesus Himself.

ALBERT CARDINAL MEYER
Archbishop of Chicago

Letter of Pope Pius XII to Father Mateo

From the Vatican,
June 27, 1942

SECRETARIATE OF STATE
OF HIS HOLINESS

No. 51822

DEAR REVEREND FATHER:

The enthusiastic report about your ministry in the United States of America, particularly retreats preached to the clergy, which your filial communication furnished His Holiness, did not fail to fill the heart of the Venerable Pontiff with a lively consolation.

He Himself cherishes too true and encouraging a memory of His journey throughout distant America, made some years prior to His elevation to the See of Peter, not to hold a special paternal interest in the apostolic enterprises which are under way there with so much success and effectiveness.

Hardly had He assumed the tiara, when one of His first acts was the memorable Encyclical *Sertum Laetitiae*, due to the 150th anniversary of the Catholic Hierarchy in the United States. In it He granted to this great portion of the Church of Jesus Christ His highest rank of nobility and engaged the American people "who by nature are given to great undertakings and to liberality" to the enduring victories of Faith and the Christian name.

Therefore the Holy Father is not surprised at the warrants of satisfaction and hope which you found so plentiful in your work among priests and students for the priesthood. He does not tire in contemplating the ardor with which the "I thirst" of the Sacred Heart, whose zealous messenger you are, is embraced throughout your priestly retreats.

Doubtless, in this way, the Holy Spirit prepares excellent and providential aids for God's Kingdom, who by fulfilling the papal recommendations regarding the intellectual and theological training of the clergy, its intelligent discipline and its devotion to charitable works, may be the most meritorious makers of both the spiritual and temporal welfare of their country.

Enough has been said, Reverend Father, to prove how His Holiness regards you for so salutary an apostolate, what wishes He entertains for your good health, and what prayers He offers up for the moral and the religious advancement of the great country where Divine Providence has directed your steps. To attest His Fatherly trust in you and at the same time to draw down the choicest favors, the Sovereign Pontiff sends you His heartfelt Apostolic Benediction.

With personal wishes and compliments, I beg you, Reverend Father, to accept my sentiments as unreservedly dedicated in Our Savior.

(Signed) L. CARD. MAGLIONE

Father Mateo Crawley-Boevey, SS.CC.

Letter of Pope Pius XII to Father Mateo

From the Vatican,
June 13, 1956

SECRETARIATE OF STATE
OF HIS HOLINESS

No. 377195

REVEREND FATHER:

The International Headquarters of the Work of the Enthronement recently published the text of the *Sacerdotal Retreat* which you preached twenty years ago to French missionaries in Japan. In your name, a copy of this work was presented to the Sovereign Pontiff who received this homage with lively satisfaction.

Immediately following the Encyclical in which he wished, in a solemn manner, to remind Christians throughout the world of the incomparable place of the cult of the Sacred Heart in Christian life, it is particularly pleasing to the head of the Church to congratulate and thank the one who, for so many years, and with such tireless zeal, has been the world-wide apostle of this devotion. And what else is this *Sacerdotal Retreat* but an invitation to priests to draw from the Heart of our Lord the secret of their sanctification and of success in their apostolate?

It gives His Holiness great pleasure to grant you the

consolation of realizing, in the evening of your life, that your apostolate is so fully in accord with these sublime teachings of the Vicar of Jesus Christ. With a paternal wish that this little volume which you offered him today be spread far and wide and thus carry the echo of your voice to a great many of your brothers in the priesthood, the common Father of all sends you as a pledge of his constant good will, the Apostolic Blessing.

Together with my sincere thanks for the copy of the book which you sent for my personal use, kindly accept the assurance of my sentiments of devotedness in our Lord.

/s/ A. DELL'ACQUA
Subst.

Father Mateo Crawley-Boevey, SS.CC.

Note: *Sacerdotal Retreat* referred to in this letter is the title of the French text from which the present translation was made. Cf. the appendix for the text of *Haurietis Aquas*. (Translator)

Preface

FATHER MATEO'S name is well-known to most American priests because of the clergy retreats he preached in the United States from 1940 to 1944, and because of the Enthronement of the Sacred Heart and Night Adoration in the Home which he founded. Many priests know him too from reading *Jesus the King of Love*, or from his other writings.

Few priests have influenced family life on a world-wide scale as has this South American Father of the Sacred Hearts. Since 1907, the year he was cured at Paray-le-Monial, where he received a mission directly from the Sacred Heart, he has preached everywhere the "Social Reign of the Sacred Heart through the Enthronement of the Sacred Heart in the Home." We say "everywhere," for the whole world has been his mission field. Untiringly, preaching many times a day, he has brought the message of the merciful love of the Sacred Heart to almost every country in Europe, the Orient, North and South America.

Millions of families have been affected by his earnest sermons or his eloquent writings. In the United States alone, it is estimated that over a million families have had the Sacred Heart of Jesus enthroned in their homes and some 300,000 individuals and families are making Night Adoration in their homes. Given the social influence of religion in the home, the impact on public life of Father Mateo's apostolate for the sanctification of the family can scarcely be over-estimated.

But it is in the field of clergy retreats that Father Mateo has made his greatest contribution to the advancement of the Kingdom of Christ here on earth. Few, if any, priests have given as many retreats to priests in as many countries as has Father Mateo. In Spanish (his native tongue), French, English, Italian, and Portuguese he has preached the doctrine of priestly sanctity to the clergy (both secular and regular) of almost every nationality. This was especially true when he was invited by many bishops and vicars-apostolic of the Orient to conduct retreats to missionaries from many lands throughout the Far East. From 1935 to 1940, he preached almost unceasingly in Japan, Korea, Manchuria, China, Indochina, Malaya, India, Ceylon, the East Indies, the Philippines and Hawaii. To native priests unfamiliar with European languages he preached full retreats in Latin, no mean feat!

Before leaving Japan, the missionaries urged him to leave with them a summary of the doctrine of priestly holiness which he had preached to them. This he did in a book published in French under the title of *Retraite Sacerdotale.* As the author remarked in his preface: "This book is a summary of my retreat. I say 'summary,' for naturally I had to omit certain conferences and also certain facts of a personal nature, necessary for a retreat but better omitted from a publication, for *scripta manent et . . . volant.*"

This book was first published in 1936. In 1956, on the occasion of the centenary of the extension of the Feast of the Sacred Heart to the universal Church, it was reprinted and a copy sent in Father Mateo's name to Pope Pius XII. It merited the splendid tribute to the veteran priest found in the letter printed in this volume.

As Father John d'Elbee, SS.CC., former Superior General of the Fathers of the Sacred Hearts, remarked in his preface to the 1956 edition: "A remarkable fact about Father Mateo, the world apostle of the Sacred Heart of

Jesus, is the gift which he received from heaven profoundly to move his audiences, whether the masses or the elite, and the 'elite of the elite,' priests.

"In the last years of his life, especially, he preferred to preach to priests. This is quite understandable. 'The priest,' he says, 'is, immediately after Mary, the divine masterpiece of grace, of dignity and power.' He adds, 'Unfortunately this thought does not move us as it should, for we are too accustomed to hearing ourselves called other Christs.'

"The entire book is filled with this supernatural thinking. In these pages will be found the essential principles of the evangelical doctrine preached by Father Mateo, and, we might add, his priestly soul. In them is contained the substance of all he has said and written.

"How many bishops and priests have told us, 'My interior life, in fact my whole life, was transformed as a result of an unforgettable retreat preached by Father Mateo. What a debt of gratitude I owe him!' "

Father Mateo (Edward) Crawley-Boevey, SS.CC., was born on November 18, 1875 in a little town near Arequipa, Peru. His father, a member of an aristocratic English family, was a banker, an Anglican, converted when he married a devout Peruvian Catholic of Spanish descent. The family moved to Valparaíso Chile about 1881. Here Edward studied at the College conducted by the Fathers of the Sacred Hearts, and later became a priest in this Congregation, of which Father Damien was a member. He was appointed professor, and in 1903, director of a school of law which developed into the Catholic University of Valparaiso.

In 1906 an earthquake destroyed the law school, and as a result, Father Mateo's health broke down.

Ordered by his doctors to travel in Europe, he went to
Rome, where with the help of Cardinals Merry del Val
and Vives, he obtained a private audience with Pope St.
Pius X. Having explained his plan for enthroning the
Sacred Heart in the home, he requested permission to
preach it. To his surprise, he was "commanded" to devote
his life to this "work of social salvation." Soon, he was in
Paray-le-Monial, where on August 24, 1907, he was restored
to health upon entering the chapel of apparitions. The
same night in "a sudden illumination," he saw clearly the
Enthronement of the Sacred Heart in the home, the social
cell, which was to be made the basis for a world-wide crusade for the establishing of the "Social Reign of the Sacred
Heart of Jesus."

This was the providential beginning of Father Mateo's
long career. Often handicapped by infirmities of various
kinds, he managed to keep going, claiming that preaching
about "the King of Love" was the best possible tonic for
him. This has been verified by American priests who heard
him preach fiery sermons even though he was 65 when he
came to this country. Often, at the opening of a conference,
he would be too weak to begin at once. At the end, he was
an entirely different man, seemingly transformed by the
very fact of talking about the Sacred Heart.

Father Mateo's active career came to an end in 1946
while preaching in Canada. Forced into a hospital ("the
Sacred Heart never consulted me about this!") by a serious
ailment, he remained a patient until February, 1956, when
he recovered sufficiently (and unexpectedly) to fly back to
Valparaíso. During these long years, he was very active with
his pen, having many articles published in various languages. Among these are his unique *Rosary Meditations*
(New York: Benziger Brothers, Inc.); *The Holy Sacrifice
of the Mass* (National Enthronement Center, Washington
17, D.C.); and *Bethany of the Sacred Heart* (chapter fifteen of this book).

The present volume was translated from the French. This was no easy task, for Father Mateo has a style peculiar to himself. The translator has endeavored to retain the smoothness of the original French, while keeping in mind the literary tastes of American priests. Whether he has succeeded is quite another matter.

Several conferences not contained in the French edition, but taken from Father Mateo's English notes, have been added. The chapter on the Enthronement, originally published under the title of *Bethany of the Sacred Heart*, was also included, though it was not preached as such.

FRANCIS LARKIN, SS.CC.

Note: Father Mateo died on May 4, 1960, in the Sacred Hearts College, Valparaíso, Chile, at the age of eighty-five. The concluding words of his last article, "On Priestly Vocations," are significant: "The Lord is my witness that my only desire is to transform my last days into a thrice-holy Mass, and thus be consumed slowly for Him, the Victim, Mediator and Pontiff, and through this immolation of love to glorify the Blessed Trinity by redeeming many priestly souls. Thy Kingdom come!" In his spiritual testament he requested that after his death Masses be offered, not for him, but for the Reign of the Sacred Heart for his intentions. "In this way," he said, "*defunctus adhuc loquitur.*"

On the occasion of his death, His Holiness, Pope John XXIII, sent the following letter to the Superior General of the Fathers of the Sacred Hearts:

Segretaria di Stato
di Sua Santita

li 16 Mai, 1960
Dal Vaticano

Very Reverend Father:

His Holiness received your recent letter in which you apprised him of the death of Father Mateo Crawley-Boevey. He wishes me to transmit to you his paternal and heartfelt condolences and to assure you of his prayers for the repose of the soul of this illustrious religious. The Holy Father is quite familiar with the role played by Father Mateo in the diffusion of the cult of the Sacred Heart, whose tireless apostle he had been during his entire life. Moreover he is pleased to think that the sad loss sustained by your religious family will be compensated by the presence in Heaven—it is permitted to believe this—of a new and powerful protector.

The Holy Father was also edified by the attitude manifested by the regretted deceased in his last hours. He has no doubt that your Congregation, following the example of Father Mateo, will continue to labor for the greater glory of the Sacred Heart. For this intention he most willingly imparts to you and to all the members of your Institute, a special Apostolic Blessing.

Kindly accept, Reverend Father, the assurance of my devotion in our Lord.

✝A. Dell'Acqua
Subst.

Grateful acknowledgment is made to Benziger Brothers, Inc., for permission to use material from *The Raccolta*.

Contents

Father Mateo Speaks to Priests

Thy friends have been exceedingly honored,
O God. . . . Be saints.

1. Priestly Perfection

THE masterpiece of moral creation and of the omnipotence and the love of God was without doubt the Immaculate Virgin. She stands apart, unique. The uncreated beauty of our Lord poured into her soul the goodness and grandeur of God as far as they can be reproduced in a mere creature. "Thou art all-fair, O Mary!"

But immediately after Mary comes the priest, the divine masterpiece of grace, of dignity and of power.

Unfortunately this thought does not move us as it should, for we are too accustomed to hearing ourselves called *Alter Christus*. Yet this title is far from being a merely conventional one, like so many worldly titles. On the contrary, it corresponds to a divine reality, for we are in truth *Christs*. As one father of the Church puts it, "The priest is something midway between a human and divine nature!" St. Clement goes even further when he calls the priest, "After God, an earthly God." This would seem to be an exaggeration were it not for the fact that it has as its doctrinal basis the sacerdotal character itself and, as an overwhelming argument, our priestly powers.

The altar and confessional leave no room for error or even for exaggeration, for the powers of consecration and absolution infinitely surpass all created powers. I have no trouble understanding the reason for the astonishment of the Jews when they heard Jesus saying to the paralytic, "Rise, thy sins are forgiven thee." They were perfectly right in arguing, "Who can speak thus without blaspheming, except God alone?" No one save God can pronounce the sacred formula which we ourselves use in the confessional, without blaspheming.

We can go even further: at the altar we command our Lord Himself and He obeys.

This brings to mind another cause of scandal for the Jews and even for some of the disciples: at Capharnaum Jesus declared He would give His flesh as food and His blood as drink. Imagine their reaction had they even remotely suspected the undreamed of miraculous privilege of our daily Mass! In truth the priest is "an earthly God, after God—Thy friends have been exceedingly honored, O God!"

But even in the priesthood there is a scale of values. Take, for example, the case of the first apostles. Even though our priesthood is the same as theirs, still it seems quite evident they received greater marks of our Lord's trust than we, for friendship is measured by the amount of trust placed in one's friends.

The apostles, however, were the advance guard and the pioneers of the message of redemption; they were the first ambassadors of the Great King. By the very fact that they were first in honor, they were also first in dangers, the first to receive the violent reaction of the pagan society they were trying to conquer. They fulfilled their privileged role as objects of the opposition and hatred of the pagans very well: of the twelve apostles, eleven were martyrs.

Everything I have just said, consoling because true, is

merely the introduction to a lesson I now wish to point out for the greater glory of the Sacred Heart of Jesus.

Reasoning simply but doctrinally, I assert that to such supernatural dignity of character, of power and of mission, must correspond an equal depth of interior life, of priestly holiness. If then, by the power and the mission conferred upon me, I am truly an *Alter Christus*, I must also be one by my mode of life. Otherwise, if I were permitted to be simply an upright man, an ecclesiastical functionary, and not a saint, then God for the first time would have made a monstrosity. He would have upset the balance of the priesthood: there would be a chasm between our virtue and our power. In this hypothesis, the priest would be of heaven because of his sacerdotal character, and of this earth because of a perfectly legitimate easygoing life of mediocrity. Such want of equilibrium never has been and never could be the work of the Lord.

Hence, He who made me a priest must necessarily have willed to give me, together with my ordination, all the means I need to become a true priest, a well-balanced priest in the full sense of the word.

A Christ who works miracles of grace, but who is not a miracle of grace himself, is not the authentic Christ God wants him to be.

I will now sum up all our dignity and all our power as priests in the celebration of the Holy Sacrifice of the Mass. And I affirm: if Holy Mass is a divine reality—the most divine of all realities—if I really have the power of transubstantiation, of officially offering to the Father the divine Victim, through Christ, with Christ, and in Christ, then it necessarily follows that such a marvelous and divine sacrifice must in itself have the power to sanctify me. To have the power to offer Mass, and not to have the means nor the duty to become a saintly priest are ideas and terms which are mutually exclusive. Therefore, *because I officially offer the Holy Sacrifice, I must be a real saint!*

~~~

To what has already been said, we can add the argument of our mission, of our calling. The wisdom, the justice, the love of God which have launched us on a sea full of the gravest responsibilities, must necessarily have given us more than we need to carry out our redemptive mission.

But note well, this mission of ours does not consist alone or principally in the necessary parish or church administration, but rather in the solid, supernatural, spiritual life of the priest. Moreover, this deep, interior holiness of life will be the soul of all our activities, and will prevent us from becoming mere ecclesiastical functionaries.

Mary, Joseph, and John the Baptist had to be spiritual giants because of their lofty mission, and this strict rule also applies to us. You have never seen and you never will see the "miracle in reverse" of someone to whom our Lord has confided a certain mission, but of whom He has not simultaneously demanded corresponding holiness. Thus we can affirm that the measure of the greatness of a mission is always the yardstick of the degree of sanctity God requires of him whom He has appointed as His messenger.

Let us be frank and admit that we have not insisted enough on this fundamental principle. We can even say that sometimes in the formation of priests there has been a certain tacit approval of the idea that a minimum of spiritual formation was sufficient. We are reminded of the story of Gideon: one would say that more hope has been placed in 3,000 professional soldiers than in the grace that sustained 300 picked, hardened men.

There seems to be a fear of asking too much, when in fact it is simply a question of demanding what a priest is obliged to give in justice and out of love. On the other hand, there has not been enough fear of the thousand times more harmful plague of priestly mediocrity. Let us uphold with honor the traditions of our priesthood. Do not stay on the ground: rise high on the wings of great desires; work hard to become saints; fear one thing only: mediocrity!

Often think over these words: "Sancti estote. . . . Estote perfecti . . ." (Lev. 11:14). Keep in mind, as Dom Marmion tells us, that this command does not merely announce the law of salvation, but rather the law of holiness. If these words are not applicable to us priests, consecrated men, when and where and to whom will they be applicable? It would be incredible if they were meant for a Thérèse of Lisieux and not for an *Alter Christus!*

One final thought: everyone knows that not all forms of the sacred ministry are practical for all regions, for all parishes, or even for all priests. I know of only one form of work that is suitable to all places and to all priests, and which must everywhere and always be the foundation of all apostolic works whatever they may be, and that is *priestly holiness!*

Whether you are bowed down under the yoke of fatigue and old age at 80, or broken by sickness at 35, have one dominant ambition at all times: to present to the Master of the harvest a priestly heart burning with a desire to love Him as only the saints know how to love. Believe me, a priestly heart on fire with love will make up a thousand times over for what is lacking in your external ministry and will result in some very great surprises for you when you stand before the tribunal of God. This is the *unum necessarium*—the *only* possible thing God will demand from you.

St. Pius X was right in saying—for Rome and for the Missions—"Those who are obliged to form Jesus Christ in the souls of their brothers, must have first formed Him in their own souls, thereby becoming Christs and making the words of St. Paul a reality: '*mihi vivere Christus est.*' "

If you are obliged to become a saintly priest, then your first duty is to have an intense desire to do so. During your thanksgiving, renew the sincere, manly desires for priestly perfection: to advance each day toward the summit of holiness, even though it be but one step. Never forget that in the eyes of God, who sees everything, sincere, loyal, burning desires are already an act of genuine love. Recall the words of St. Francis de Sales: "To want to love *is* to love."

Grace will never be lacking, for by virtue of your priesthood and your Mass you receive it in abundance, and it will be superabundant to the degree that you draw it down in torrents by the greatness of your desires.

With a manly will, then, make every effort to go higher, for He who has called you to the priesthood and the apostolate has also called you to sanctity: "Put out into the deep" (Luke 5:4). He who is able to celebrate Mass and to save souls for eternity, can—and must—certainly become a real saint.

But once more, you must *will* it with a sincere, manly, and priestly will!

> *Heart of Jesus, burning with love for me,*
> *inflame my heart with love for Thee!*

I am the way (John 14:6).

2. The Simplicity of Sanctity

TO ENUNCIATE and lay down principles is not enough; it is also necessary to smooth the path for their application, to give courage, and to show how to put them into practice. That is the purpose of this conference.

The theme of the previous chapter was that the dignity of the priesthood demands of priests and future priests nothing less than *sanctity*. I know many priests who admit this principle theoretically, but in practice live lives of discouragement or indifference as far as its application to their daily lives is concerned.

I would like to confirm this fundamental principle by showing, not necessarily the *facility*, but the *perfect simplicity* of the means that God wishes us to use in sanctifying ourselves in what I like to call the *royal road of daily duty*.

I repeat, if by reason of my great dignity, and because of my lofty mission I am obliged to tend toward perfection and strive to become a saint, I certainly must be able to do this, for there is no such thing as a duty impossible of fulfillment. I have my defects and my weaknesses; but if I am a priest and can say Mass, then I have all I need to be a saint. "To think the contrary," says Dom Marmion, "would

7

be a doctrinal error and a sin of timidity inexcusable in a priest."

What road is to be followed? What providential route has been mapped out for the priest to help him to reach these spiritual heights? In other words, how may we become saints without ever leaving the place where God wills us to be? The road to sanctity is not necessarily the road to the nearest Trappist monastery! Listen to this doctrinal answer given by Cardinal Mercier, speaking with personal authority: "By living your priesthood fully." He adds: "We do not believe enough in the power of the grace of our priestly character. . . .

"The grace of the priesthood," he continues, "is in itself so powerful and so efficacious, that without anything else the truly faithful priest can become a man of God, a saint." In truth, the sacrament of holy orders which raises me to the unique dignity of Christ, should be able to realize in me what this dignity demands of me. And the very first requirement is that I be, not a mere likeness of Christ, not a watered down Christ, but a Christ whole and entire, an integral Christ.

Thus in virtue of the ex opere operato, the sacrament of holy orders confers upon me, together with the character and priestly powers, sufficient grace to enable me to live up to my lofty dignity, that is, to sanctify me. It follows that it is the ex opere operantis which has to fructify and develop in me the germ of priestly sanctity planted by the sacrament of holy orders.

Never forget that according to our Lord's plan, our sublime dignity does not consist exclusively in the priestly character, but in what this character demands as its accidental and moral complement, namely our personal and supernatural perfection, the living of our priesthood to the full! In this sense—which is the only true one—we can state and affirm that ordination is always an official and solemn *call to that sanctity* without which our priesthood remains in part inefficacious. It clearly follows that the master who calls me to holiness of life offers me in the sacrament itself the necessary grace to accomplish fully His Will. I have a right to this grace, because of the wisdom, the justice and the love of Christ, who wills that I be a one hundred per cent priest! And He who owes it to me wants this grace to be rich and superabundant, for He knows—with sorrow —that by my lack of holiness I could waste the treasures of my priesthood, and that it could even be a crushing weight for me and sterile in giving supernatural life to souls.

It was because of this doctrine that St. Ephrem could state: "The priest is a stupendous miracle, with unspeakable power; he touches heaven, mingles with the angels, and is on familiar terms with God."

May we always have an unbounded and lively faith in the marvelous grace of our priesthood!

And now, to be practical, a few encouraging and solid considerations regarding our great duty to sanctify ourselves. How best utilize the grace of our priesthood in order to reach that fullness of divine life that we call priestly holiness? In the first place, the very exercise of our sublime ministry should be, according to God's plan, a means of sanctifying the priest: *to give God is always to enrich oneself with God!*

As a matter of fact, in justice, the first grace of the apostolate is always for the apostle. Thus, whether you preach or whether you distribute Holy Communion, Jesus whom you give to your people, gives Himself to you in return a hundred, a thousand times over as a reward for having given Him to others, provided of course you give Him with the proper dispositions.

Was not this the case of Mary, who became richer with Jesus when she gave us Jesus? Yes, she was richer on the first Christmas day than she was on the 25th of March and still richer with Jesus when she gave Him to us on Calvary's heights.

The same is true for us: everything you do for your flock —administration of the sacraments, preaching, various activities, everything without exception, is a tremendous treasure of sanctifying grace for you, first of all, the docile instruments. But this is true only when an indispensable condition is fulfilled, namely that we be *priests* and always remain *priests* and never become machines or simple ecclesiastical functionaries.

There is no doubt about it; there exists a tacit contract between the Master of the vineyard and us the vinedressers, His official representatives. It is this: that the first fruits and also a high percentage of the income belong to those who are in charge of the administration of His vineyard. St. Paul expressed the same truth in another way: "They who serve the altar, have their share with the altar" (I Cor. 9:13). If this was said of a well-merited material offering, it is a thousand times more true when taken in the spiritual sense of compensations and rewards for the services rendered to our Lord through our work for souls: "You did it for me" (Matt. 25:40).

Have we not always been told that charity to the poor comes back to the benefactor a hundred times over? Then what are we to say of that other more perfect kind of charity which the priest gives to souls and often to the most neglected souls? Why is it that this beautiful and consoling doctrine is not more insisted upon? Why, when speaking of apostolic work, do we stress the dignity of the apostle and his reward in heaven as well as the benefits he confers upon souls, and so seldom the reward given here below to the apostle himself? We should often remind ourselves of the story of Christ appearing to St. Martin, clothed in the cloak given by the saint to a beggar a short time before.

If I have already told you, "Be saints to be apostles," I now wish to add, *"Be apostles to be saints."*

Now we come to one of the most consoling principles of spiritual life and of our priestly life. It is this: the realization that we can become saints—saints with a capital "S" —in the quite simple, normal path of the performance of our daily duties. On the foundation of a solid interior life, a life of faith and prayer, the second element of sanctification is our daily life lived in all the beauty, the simplicity, and the monotony of Nazareth, and this in the place assigned to us by divine Providence. Without changing or adding anything to our program of daily duties—unless it be the addition of a strong faith and an intense love—all of us must and can become genuine saints.

I agree with Dom Marmion that there are ". . . some people so narrow-minded that they are scandalized at the simplicity of this divine plan." They are the same ones who often confuse the *mission* of the saint with his *life*, and who cannot think of sanctity without the "fireworks" of miracles and the halo of charisms. They seem to forget that nothing was wanting to the sanctity of Mary at Nazareth, and yet her holiness was without ecstasies or marvels. She, the only perfect saint, was certainly the humblest and the simplest of creatures, living her life in the background and shadows, doing the will of God in an astounding way. *On the other hand, Judas probably worked miracles, but is far from being a saint!*

The will of God is sanctifying in itself, if only we knew how to accept it and fulfill it. This is true especially of the two phases of the pattern of our daily life. The first phase consists of *the duties of our priestly state.* For us they are well defined. We must not perform them like soldiers or pagans, stoically, or fatalistically; but with love, love for the Crucified.

Then there are *the thousand and one crosses,* big and small, which are an integral part of our state of life. I call these the "classical penances" of the life Jesus has willed for each one of us. Here is a type of mortification for priests a thousand times better than hair-shirts or fastings, one whose irritations and sharp points can make of us great penitents. If you perform no other kind of penances than those which our Lord sends you each day, and accept them with love, believe me, before God the mortified monks of the penitential orders will have no greater merit than you.

Have a great love for the thrice holy cross of your priestly state. Don't drag that cross. Certainly it is a heavy one, but like the heavy wings of huge planes, this weighty cross should be for you a means of getting off the ground and soaring aloft.

There can be no sanctity without penance. But in the chalice of suffering of every priest, Jesus has placed just enough providential penance to supply this need and to make of him a holy priest and a successful apostle.

It is a good idea to go back frequently and meditate on the incomparable lesson Nazareth has for all of us. Here we are taught to follow in the footsteps of Jesus, Mary, and Joseph, the earthly trinity. We do not have to invent anything new to become saints. The path is already laid out for us. It is Jesus Christ Himself who is constantly reminding us: "Come after me. . . . I have given you the example. . . . I am the way."

Keep in mind that the Incarnate Word willed to live our life to the full, to perfect ours by His, and to identify Himself with it down to its smallest details. He did this precisely in order to simplify and to make possible the realization of our own important duty of Christian and priestly holiness. Since the time of Nazareth, then, nothing is insignificant or trivial in this life. But above all, in the life of a priest, the other Christ, everything is great and everything should be divine and holy, provided that we have a lively faith and a burning love. "All is great where love is great!"

No need to seek the summit of sanctity outside of or away from the altogether simple life led at Nazareth. Here it is to be found in all its marvelous simplicity. Do not dream of finding perfection in another way, but look for it within the framework of your seemingly commonplace life. With some variations, this was the often tiring and rough life led by St. Paul and St. Francis Xavier. *Therein and only therein lies your perfection, because it is the will of God!*

Let us be frank and admit that this is something we have in great part forgotten, little understood and, in general, not sufficiently preached. How many good priests have I not met—well-trained priests in other respects—for whom the preaching of this doctrine has had the appeal of a new discovery or of a genuine novelty. Yes, a novelty, one that dates back to Nazareth, to the Gospels!

Once more I maintain that it has not been said and re-said enough that *any priest whatsoever, no matter how ordinary his assignment, who lives his priesthood to the full by giving his whole heart to the Church and to souls, can become a true saint, and in the eyes of God, a big one.* For this only one miracle is required of him, that of a holy daily Mass!

The candidates for the priesthood who come to us have not been sufficiently reminded that they can become holy without the charisms or frightening austerities of the Curé of Ars, and be as holy as he! They have not been told that they can sanctify themselves without the ecstasies during Mass of a St. Bernard or a St. Philip Neri; that they can be real men of God without the extraordinary marvels of a St. Vincent Ferrer or the altogether special way of life of a Charles de Foucauld, or the unusual gifts of a St. Francis Xavier, provided of course they have their great faith and love. The genius is born a genius but the saint is made a saint.

The paths followed by the saints can be, and often are, quite different. But what is common to them all and what makes the saint, is the doing of the will of God, accepting it lovingly whether it is a question of the great and marvelous Teresa of Avila or the no less marvelous Thérèse of Lisieux walking in her "little way" of Nazareth.

I can think of no more solid or appropriate doctrine for priests than that, if they want to steep themselves in the spirit of the Heart of Jesus, and to find in Him new strength to continue climbing the difficult hill of perfection. "*Duc in altum*" (Luke 5:4). It is because we have forgotten much of this that divine Providence, always vigilant and wise, has loudly sounded the powerful warning bell of Lisieux. It seems that heaven has let fall around the Little Flower a veritable shower of miracles, in order to remind both theologians and little souls of these important truths:

—That it is possible to become a saint in any state of life, by any method, but that the path of simplicity and humility is the surest way of becoming a *big saint*, provided you love with a great deal of love.

—That by your *generous love* you can *transform* the most insignificant events of daily life.

—*That sanctity does not consist in doing extraordinary things, but in doing the ordinary things with an extraordinary love.*

We have the authoritative words of Pius XI on this subject: "St. Thérèse of Lisieux is truly the *Vox Dei*, that will lead consecrated souls, especially priests, her brothers, and missionaries, her privileged friends, to the heights of sanctity by the path of her 'little way,' which is that of Nazareth. Here is a method of sanctifying yourself that is within the reach of every one of you. It is the best, because it is the one followed by Mary and Joseph. It is also the surest, for it does away with illusions and self deception."

The Master is calling you: "Come after me . . . I have given you the example . . . I am the way . . . Be perfect!"

Get rid of anything that might be the cause of illusion or discouragement, resolving to sanctify yourself in the perfect fulfillment of your duties. You will find our Lord waiting to accompany you on this road and to give you His graces in abundance.

Sanctify yourself, then, by your daily meditation, regular and frequent confession, and by the devout recitation of your Divine Office.

Sanctify yourself in the exercise of your ministry, often tiring and monotonous, but the one assigned to you by the Church and your superiors.

Sanctify yourself in the joys and sorrows, in the consolations and deceptions that come to every zealous priest.

Sanctify yourself wherever you are, whether healthy or sick, in abundance or in need, encouraged or criticized, always trying to see, to fulfill, and to praise the Will of God.

Sanctify yourself in the thousand and one seemingly insignificant events of daily life, which are a hidden treasure for us priests.

Above all, become a saint through the fervent and careful celebration of the Holy Sacrifice of the Mass, and sanctify yourself to offer it less unworthily.

Have courage! Keep climbing higher and higher, following in the footsteps of Jesus, Mary and Joseph, remembering that all is great where faith is great, but especially that *all is great and divine where love is great and where love is burning!*

He chose for Himself a priest
to offer to Him a sacrifice of praise.

3. Holy Mass, the Means of Priestly Holiness

I CONSIDER the subject of the Holy Sacrifice of the Mass so important that before beginning I should like to offer a prayer in union with the Queen of the clergy, that my heart and my pen will be less unworthy to write on such a great mystery of faith and love.

"Glory to the Father, in thanksgiving for the wonderful gift of the Word, His Son, in the mystery of the Incarnation!

"Glory to the Son of God, the Lamb, in thanksgiving for the mystery of the Redemption through the shedding of His blood on the cross.

"Glory to the Paraclete, the Spirit of Truth and substantial Love, in thanksgiving for the incomparable gift of the priesthood, by virtue of which we go to the altar and offer the Father the spotless Victim.

"Glory, praise, and love to the three adorable Persons of the Blessed Trinity, *per Christum Dominum Nostrum,* the Mediator and Victim in the Holy Sacrifice of the Mass."

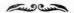

According to God's plan, Holy Mass should daily accomplish two miracles, that of transubstantiation, and that of the sanctification of the celebrant, which are, or ought to be, the corollaries and the first fruits of his Mass. The first of these two marvels is always and infallibly brought about in every Mass; the second, sad to say, suffers many exceptions.

If the host and the chalice could speak, how often would they not say to the celebrant: "At your priestly word the substance of bread and wine have disappeared; we retain only their accidents, their appearances; we have become 'The Christ, the Son of the living God.' And you, priest-consecrator, when will you work this miracle of love in yourself? When will you have at the altar and in your ministry by the virtue and grace of the Mass, only the appearance of a man, having become in reality an *Alter Christus?*"

In giving Himself up to us under the appearances of bread, our Lord wished to consume us while allowing us to consume Him. To consume Him is easy, for that is why He gives Himself to us. But to allow ourselves to be consumed by Him and with Him in the fire of the divine sacrifice, that is, to be transformed into Jesus, supposes on the part of the celebrant a generous and total oblation that the Heart of Jesus unfortunately does not always find.

We shall give ourselves up to His Love when instead of merely pronouncing through routine the sacred words which sum up all the power and dignity of the Holy Sacrifice, *"Per Ipsum, et cum Ipso, et in Ipso est tibi, Deo Patri omnipotenti, omnis honor et gloria,"* we say them from the bottom of our hearts and really try to live them. When each one of us has become a "celebrant and victim" together with Jesus Christ, only then will our Mass be in reality the all-powerful source of sanctifying grace for us priests, of redemption for our people, and the best possible hymn of praise and glory to the Blessed Trinity.

A priest may have many outstanding qualities, but if he has not grasped the tremendous meaning of His Mass in relation to his priesthood and to his spiritual life, he is far from the ideal willed by God. In this regard I like to recall the story related to me by the great Dom Chautard, former Cistercian abbot and author of *The Soul of the Apostolate.* He and two companions were returning from an Eucharistic Congress. As they were taking a short cut to their monastery they approached the home of a peasant, before which a small boy was playing. When the boy saw the three monks approaching, he ran toward his house shouting, "Come quickly mother, *three Masses* are coming down the road!"

The learned Dom Chautard turned to the two priests and remarked: "Fathers, of all the discourses on the priesthood we heard at the Congress, that is the best of all!"

As Cardinal Mercier tells us, "Any priest who has understood the sublimity of his Mass, and who seriously tries to make it the center and the divine source of his priestly life, such a one at death will be capable of being canonized!"

How many priests there are who waste the rich treasures of their priesthood, simply because they consider their Mass as just one of a number of priestly functions, instead of making it the most important of their priestly duties so that their entire priesthood gravitates around the altar! *We are priests to celebrate the Holy Sacrifice.*

In this connection, listen to this excerpt from a conference given by a Bishop at Lourdes during a Priests' Congress: "Sometimes you think the priest is above all the man of the Gospels and of apostolic activities, and that the best priest is the one who devotes himself entirely to various apostolic movements. Some there are who think the very essence of the priesthood is the care of souls. No! The priest is before and above all the quasi-divine man of the Mass, the one who offers sacrifice. The Mass is his specialty, he is the Mass, and he is fully a priest only at the altar. As it is the happiness of Jesus the adorable Victim to find His priest at the altar, so it should be the joy of the priest to find Jesus the divine Victim in the Mass."

It is a truly divine vocation that places us almost on the same level as Jesus Christ as mediators and victims when we celebrate the "great action," as the Mass was once called.

And now I ask our Lady to enlighten me and bless me, for I should like to present her as the ideal of the priest offering sacrifice and deeply penetrated with the meaning of the action he performs.

There are three mysteries in the life of Mary in which she is represented as fulfilling a sort of priestly function, of which our Mass seems to be a mystical reproduction.

"*Et verbum caro factum est de Spiritu Sancto ex Maria Virgine.*" When Mary became the mother of the Incarnate Word, was not her first act to offer to the Father the One He had confided to her? And is not this precisely what every priest does each morning, on the paten of the Heart of Mary, as he renews Mary's offering made the very day of the Incarnation? The divine oblation and its ends were the same on that 25th of March at Nazareth as they are every morning on our altar. Would that Mary would share with us the splendor of her purity, the beauty of her humility, the intensity of her love, in order that we might celebrate Holy Mass with these dispositions of priestly holiness!

But this first oblation was made in secret, in the privacy

of her soul, and so it had to be made outwardly, sacramentally, if I may use the expression. Thus it was that "according to the law of Moses, they took him up to Jerusalem to present him to the Lord" (Luke 2:22). There Mary Immaculate offered the spotless Lamb in the Temple to the Father, for the glory and salvation of His people. Our Lady is mother of the Messias only that she might cooperate in His redemptive mission and offer Him for the glory of Him who had sent Him. Through Mary's intercession may our daily Mass please the Father as did the oblation of the Child Jesus in the Temple, when he was presented to the Father through the hands of His most Holy Mother.

Finally we come to Calvary. "He was offered because it was his own will" (Isa. 53:7). At the side of the Victim "stood the mother," renewing the offering she made on the day of the Incarnation and of the Presentation in the Temple. For if Jesus delivers Himself up through love, so also Mary, with the full right of her divine motherhood, delivers Him up to the Father through love, mingling her bitter tears with His Most Precious Blood.

As you well know, our chalice of the New Covenant renews this mystery of blood in an unbloody manner. As on Calvary, so also at the solemn moment of our Mass, we need Mary to strenghten us and above all to inflame our hearts!

Ask the "Mother of priests" for the supreme grace of being delivered once and for all from the terrible evil of the sin of routine in the celebration of the mystery of the Holy Sacrifice of the Mass.

At this point I should like to stress certain dispositions or prerequisites necessary for priests who wish to draw abundant fruit from the fervent celebration of the Holy Sacrifice.

Above all else make a careful preparation for Mass. Despite your overload of work and despite the unforeseen tasks added to your daily program, make an effort to prepare your Mass well. If you habitually neglect this preparation, you run the risk of wasting in part at least the extraordinary grace of your Mass. Get up early enough to prepare your Mass. To do this, go to bed as early as you can; this is the meaning of the expression, "Go to bed early and save your soul!" Never go from your bed to the altar. If through no fault of your own you have five minutes to pray before Mass, use four of them as preparation. I recommend the prayerful reading of the Canon of the Mass or the entire Mass of the day as one of the best and most priestly preparations for Holy Mass.

Ask our Blessed Mother to help you in this preparation, by communicating to you her spirit of prayer and the dispositions of her Heart on Good Friday, while a few feet away, under her very eyes, they nailed to the cross her child and her God.

Next, celebrate your Mass with great piety, having no other thought or preoccupation than that of glorifying the Blessed Trinity, who at this moment receive through Jesus Christ the most perfect homage possible, the only one worthy of the divine Majesty. When I say "with great piety," I mean to accentuate the great simplicity and the intensity of faith and love which this "great action" demands of the celebrant, at this sacred moment more than ever a Christ. We should be penetrated with the greatness of this mystery, as though for an instant the veil were lifted and we saw what John saw on Mount Thabor and on Calvary: the majesty of the glorified Christ and the crucified Christ, the two mysteries that are combined at the altar.

Sometimes our Lord does "lift the veil" to strengthen our faith, and allows us to see that the Mass is indeed

Calvary surrounded by the glory of Mt. Thabor. During one of my Masses in Europe, a man who had been out of the Church since he was a boy claimed he saw Christ "all in glory but with His wounds, and with His lips moving as though speaking to someone," standing in my place at the altar. In the sacristy after Mass he excitedly told me this vision lasted from the Consecration to my Communion. A fervent confession and complete amendment of life convinced me that he had seen with his bodily eyes what we priests should see daily with the eyes of faith.

If St. Francis of Assisi had been a priest, imagine how he would have offered Mass after the miracle of Mt. Alverno! Yet it depends upon you to have the stigmata in your heart in order to celebrate as fervently as would the Seraphim of Assisi.

Ask our Lady to give you the grace of graces: that of a daily increase in a spirit of lively faith, and of a daily advance in love as you offer the Holy Sacrifice. Even though it be for only one half-hour, try to have some of the fervor of the Curé of Ars. Afterwards you certainly will have the apostolic and missionary powers of St. Francis Xavier, even though you do not have his gift of miracles.

Note well, however, that I am not speaking of sensible devotion, nor feeling. Not at all. I am speaking of the fervor that is based on a lively faith, that is fed by meditating on this great mystery, and that is increased by having great desires.

Unfortunately, we become too accustomed to the sublimity of our Mass. I dare say with feelings of adoration and gratitude that it is partly the fault of our Lord Himself, for He has given us too much. It is in this above all that He has loved us, His friends, to excess. If Mass were a rare privilege, for instance, an extraordinary recompense for a high degree of generosity we have shown in our ministry or for some miraculous conversions brought about through our heroic sacrifices, it would be different. But no, Mass is an every-day affair, for the saintly as well as for those large numbers of priests who never think of becoming saints, but who have, at the same time, no intention of giving up such a great privilege.

"If thou didst know the gift of God" (John 4:10). If you were enlightened by a more assiduous spirit of prayer, and by a more ardent faith; if above all your life were deeper and more intense, how you would appreciate the gift of gifts of your priesthood, the most sublime function of your ministry, which daily makes of you at the altar a true Christ! I am convinced that even the greatest saints have had overwhelming surprises in heaven when they understood in the light of glory what it means to celebrate the Holy Sacrifice of the Mass.

I remember witnessing at Naples the miracle of St. Januarius. After having had the privilege of holding in my hands the vial containing the congealed blood that was shed a thousand years ago, a few minutes later, before my very eyes, I saw this same blood ruddy, seething as it was the day the saint was martyred. I was affected but only momentarily. A minute later I remembered my chalice, the mystery of the transubstantiation of my Mass, and I lost my emotion. There is no doubt about it, I had seen a great miracle. But the miracle of my Mass is even greater. In fact between the two there is an infinite distance.

I am waiting for my last hour lovingly to challenge my guardian angel. I am going to tell him: "Through the mercy of Jesus, soon I hope to be your companion for all eternity. But despite my great misery, I will forever be more beautiful than you, for I will bear in my soul a likeness you do not have, a likeness to the Lamb of God stamped upon me by the blood of the Lamb.

"And still more: for all eternity I will be more noble than you—not by nature but through mercy—for the Lord is of my race and of my blood, and through condescendence His Father is my Father and His mother, my mother. And so is He my eldest Brother, a title you do not possess.

"Dearly beloved Angel, listen to this, the height of glory: even as I adore with you the All-High, in truth I can glory in having commanded my God at the altar where He always obeyed me. Thus in virtue of my priesthood, I have been the master of my King and Master, a power and privilege you never had."

My guardian angel will answer: "So be it, sing forever the greatness and the mercy of the Lord, who has raised you above the Princes and the Thrones of Heaven."

Even if our Lord, to test my faith, offered to take me up each morning to the third heaven like St. Paul, or to allow me here below to enjoy the treasures of paradise, and all this in exchange for my Mass, I would fall on my knees and beg Him to allow me to keep until death my sacred right to stand at the altar. For this privilege I would freely renounce the charisms of St. Paul and all the saints. For they are pale rays from the sun of glory and of love, the Holy Sacrifice of the Mass!

It is not enough to be convinced of the beauty and the grandeur of your Mass. You must *want* to live it and know *how* to live it. This means that once you leave the altar you should as far as possible live as did the Blessed Virgin after the Annunciation, for like her you bear within you the God-Emmanuel.

Listen to what St. John Eudes has to say on this subject:

The Holy Sacrifice of the Mass is so sublime that we would need three eternities to honor it worthily. The first would be by way of preparation; the second to celebrate the divine mysteries in an ecstasy of love; the third would be to bless and thank the Lord for this incomparable gift.

Yet we will have only the third eternity to return adequate thanks, and for many of us this eternity will be spent making reparation for our tepidity and our shortcomings at the altar.

Earnestly ask our Lady for the grace of knowing how to make your daily Mass the heart and center of your interior life and of your active ministry. Your entire life should gravitate around the Holy Sacrifice, which through your deep faith and life will then become more than ever a well-spring of divine life for those around you and for many others near and far. This means: *Live your Mass, live for your Mass, live from your Mass.*

To help you to do this, here is a practical suggestion: make your favorite prayer and practice the saying of the Offertory prayers (the *Suscipe* and the *Offerimus*), the formula of the consecration of the bread and wine, and the prayers immediately before Communion beginning with "*Domine non sum dignus.*" I call this practice the "Mass of St. John," because it is a short form of the Mass containing its true essential elements. Learn these prayers by heart or carry a leaflet in your Breviary. Say them in spare moments or when visiting the Blessed Sacrament. This priestly practice will help you to *live* your Mass. (cf. Appendix.)

Prepare and celebrate your Mass each morning as though it were the first and last Mass of your life. If you have truly mastered this science, you know everything: "and all these things shall be given you besides" (Matt. 6:33).

One final word concerning the efficacy of your Mass in relation to the conversion of souls. I repeat: any priest who tries to be a true Christ at the altar is by that very fact a true apostle. How few are those whom the priest reaches through his preaching and his ministry! But through his Mass he can influence souls all over the world. The reason is obvious: It is Jesus Christ Himself who, renewing His redemptive sacrifice through our hands, offers to His Father this triumphant prayer: "Father forgive them . . . hallowed be Thy name . . . Thy kingdom come . . . Thy will be done. . . ."

In this regard let me quote another striking thought from the late Bishop Tissier of France:

Sometimes I hear discouraged priests complaining of the sterility of their ministry and that the only thing they can do is to celebrate Mass in an empty church.

The only thing they can do? But they are saving sinners, they are the ransom for the guilty nations and they are bringing salvation to a world which certainly would burst asunder were it not for those redemptive Masses.

How explain those otherwise unexplainable conversions except by the Holy Sacrifice of the Mass? How account for the veritable Pentecost of grace we sometimes receive all out of proportion to the efforts and time we spend in our active apostolate, except through our Mass? Believe me, it is your chalice which cries to heaven for mercy, for it overflows with the Precious Blood: "Behold the Lamb of God, behold Him who taketh away the sins of the world."

How much more effective and fruitful would be the marvelous apostolate of your Mass, if you added to the ex opere operato of the sacrifice itself the faith of St. Francis Xavier, the fervor of the Curé of Ars or of St. Vincent de Paul. Be sure of one thing: before God your mission has both its starting point and its crowning grace in your daily Mass. Offer your Mass with such fervor that the sublime prayer of Jesus at the Last Supper will be realized at the altar: "Holy Father, . . . that they may be one even as we are" (John 17:11).

Make your Mass an anticipated heaven and the perfect ransom for the souls entrusted to your care. And make the Mediator and the Victim of your Mass the "Deus meus et omnia" of your entire life. This is the way to become each morning at the altar the "disciple whom Jesus loved." (John 13:23). But at the same time, by your intense love, your faith, and your fervor, as you go to the altar, be also the "disciple who loved Jesus."

Whatever you give to Mass in the way of purity, spirit of faith, fervent prayer, is certainly benefiting your own soul as well as the souls of others. What a powerful means of sanctification and salvation is the chalice!

Never forget that the Holy Sacrifice of the Mass must be your greatest sermon as well as the most perfect priestly homage you can give to God. Make every effort to be a Christ at the altar, especially by careful preparation for Mass. Your Mass will be what your preparation has been. What your Mass is, that you are in the eyes of God. *Qualis Missa, talis sacerdos et talis apostulus.* One day you will be judged according to the amount of purity of faith and love you have put into the offering of the Holy Sacrifice.

Avoid one thing at all costs, and that is saying Mass out of routine.

At the Memento for the dead pray especially for the souls of deceased confreres. If you help them today, one day you will be helped a hundred times over.

May you hear these words of the Father every morning when celebrating Mass: "This is my beloved Son in whom I am well pleased. . . ." and these other words of Jesus, "This day Thou shalt be with me in paradise . . . and on Calvary."

Yes, it is really paradise and Calvary, the altar of our daily Mass!

He hath regarded the humility
of his handmaid. Because I was
little I pleased the Most High
(Luke 1:48; Liturgy).

4. Mary and Humility

THIS entire conference will be offered as a filial homage to the Immaculate Heart of Mary, mother and Queen of Apostles. In her school we will meditate on three great priestly virtues, beginning with the one that is at the base of all holiness: *humility.*

For every height there is a corresponding depth. In the divine plan, Mary occupies the highest place among creatures. Mary is the highest summit of the earth, touching God, bordering, as it were, on the Blessed Trinity.

By means of her unique, incomparable eminence, we can measure the depth of the abyss of the humility of Mary. She is the greatest, the holiest of creatures, because she was the smallest, the most humble.

The Gospels confirm and elevate certain virtues known to the pagan world, such as the Chinese family traditions of filial respect and obedience. In this case Christianity merely had to build on the solid ground of natural goodness.

On the other hand, Christ revealed to us the beauty of, and has imposed on us the practice of, certain virtues completely unknown before His time; for instance, the forgiveness of injuries, the love of one's enemies, virginity and chastity, but above all, it is safe to say, the eminently Christian virtue, humility of spirit and of heart. And perhaps, I might add, the one most difficult to practice. Why? Because it is diametrically opposed to the most firmly rooted tendency of our fallen nature, disordinate self-love.

The Word became flesh and capable of dying in order to prove to us His infinite love; "For God so loved the world . . ." (John 3:16). But it seems quite evident to me that He also chose the path of suffering to give us a serious and much-needed lesson, saying to us, as it were, "If you really want to belong to Me and come after Me, choose this infallible path: follow Me by humbling yourself, and you will find Me."

This is so true, that the touchstone of true Christianity is and always will be the virtue of humility. Strictly speaking, it is possible to be chaste in heart and in body, and yet be a demon in pride. Remember the frightening case of the convent of nuns at Port-Royal near Paris, whose superior was the renowned Mother Angélique. Infected with Jansenism, they proudly refused to submit when Rome condemned the heresy. They were called "angels of purity but demons of pride." More fundamental than purity, important and delicate though this be, is the virtue of humility.

Humility consists on the one hand of a feeling of deep reverence before the majesty of God, and on the other hand, of a sincere and frank acknowledgement of our great weakness. But it is not sufficient merely to acknowledge our misery, for at the sight of it we could be provoked and even angry. Such is the case of a girl angrily breaking the mirror that reveals a physical defect.

Hand-in-hand with the recognition of our weakness must go peace, and even more, *love of our weakness*. When St. Teresa asked our Lord why He so loved humility, He replied, "Because I love the truth." Therefore, humility and truth are convertible terms. I love my weakness, my spiritual poverty, my helplessness, because I love the truth more than I love myself. Without this peace and love, humility is impossible.

This is an attitude that was never found among pagans. The non-Christian might acknowledge his weakness because it humbled and shamed him: "It is good for me that thou hast humbled me" (Ps. 118:71). But this is precisely the reason that this virtue is so rarely found even among the good. As a matter of fact, it is easier to find a mortified man than one whose humility is as great as his austerity. An example of the latter would be the quite recent and wonderful case of Charles de Foucauld, the humble penitent and apostle of the Sahara desert.

Because humility is such an extraordinarily difficult and delicate virtue, however, it is the outstanding characteristic of great souls. A Russian Orthodox diplomat said of St. Pius X, as he stood before his coffin, "He was more the pope, more the representative of Christ, because of his humility than because of the tiara!" If you want your people to praise you sincerely, live so that they may say the same of you.

Yes, let them praise you for your zeal; let them admire you for your charity toward the poor and the sick, but let them also be able to say of you what a skeptical curiosity-seeker said of the Curé of Ars: "They talk a great deal of the miracles of the Curé of Ars. Well, as far as I'm concerned, the greatest miracle of all is his humility."

Let us now consider the three foundations of our humility. The first, and most evident, is our natural helplessness in the physical order. For instance, a man in the pink of health can be laid low by the bite of an insect, a draft of air, or an invisible microbe. And yet we are proud of ourselves!

Here is an interesting case: a monk had consecrated the best years of his life to the study of manuscripts, and as a result, his health broke. Nevertheless, he had reached his goal; he had found what he was looking for and the results of his long years of research were contained in carefully written notes. He had a magnificent file, a monument of erudition . . . now people would take notice of him!

But what happened? One night a spark set fire to his manuscripts and in a few minutes the fruits of his years of unwearying toil were a pile of ashes. So upset was the poor monk that he went out of his mind.

This reveals what we really are: tiny ants, upset by a mere trifle. And when we find ourselves face to face with the unleashed powers of nature—a hurricane, a storm at sea, an earthquake or an erupting volcano—our helplessness is even more evident. Yet we remain full of ourselves, proud of what we call our powerful minds.

All this is very striking. But it is nothing when we consider another embarrassing weakness: our powerlessness to do good. We have the explicit words of our Lord on this point: "Without me you can do nothing" (John 15:5). Note well that He uses the word *nothing*. He did not say, "You can do something," but "NOTHING, without me." Not even an ejaculation can be said with merit without Him—nothing!

Yet there is something worse than this. Worse than nothing? Yes, indeed! For there is in each one of us a frightening tendency toward evil. Have no illusions on this score: *any one of us is capable of committing the worst of crimes!*

"Lord," said St. Philip Neri, "place both of Your hands on my head, for if You withdrew one of them I could betray you this very night, even worse than Judas did." And he was telling the truth, for we carry within us, as it were, a nest of vipers, lying in wait for a moment of inadvertence on our part, a moment of weakness, to do their deadly work. This explains the fall of the "cedars of Lebanon," the stars of Heaven. As I write this I have to remind myself, if I am not humble and prudent, tomorrow I could be what St. Paul called a "castaway." And note well that when a giant cedar falls in punishment for pride (I am speaking now of the fall of a consecrated soul, a priest, for example), the fall from such a height is a frightening thing, "*corruptio optimi pessima!*"

Tell me, what do we have to be proud about? In reality we possess only two things: our good qualities and talents —a treasure that belongs to God alone and is merely loaned to us—and our terrible misery, concealed in every one of us and belonging exclusively to us. Can we possibly be proud of our misery without being considered a fool?

That you may never be guilty of this culpable foolishness, have a strong hatred—stronger than you have for impurity—for the most impure of all impure loves, that of self-love and pride! Fear it as the capital vice of all vices. Friends of our Lord, who one day became traitors, fell for the most part because of pride, the root of a thousand other dreadful weaknesses. Remember the case of de Lamennais of Tyrell and Loisy?

If you knew with what severity our Lord often punishes here below the revolt of the proud! I have seen the case of Nebuchadnezzar in the person of a rector of a university, horribly humiliated because of his terrible pride and his blasphemies. He was struck down, not by a mental affliction, but by a strange disease, which without causing the loss of his use of reason, forced him to live for two years like an animal, degraded in a way that cannot be described. Be on your guard; have a healthy and holy fear of succumbing one day to this disease of pride, cause of all scandals and of all failures.

～⦿～

What is the best way to defend oneself against this enemy? The answer is simple and practical. There are two ways to attack pride at its very roots and to become, little by little, humble in spirit and of heart.

The first means to use is one I do not hesitate to call infallible: that of *obedience to one's bishop or superiors* —but *perfect* obedience. Obey, bend your character to the yoke of submission without reservations, love to be directed, prefer the opinions and likes of your superiors to your own, follow their directives, and you will have a granite base on which to build the edifice of your priestly life.

Never forget that your success in the eyes of God (and this is the only success that matters) is closely tied in with your spirit of obedience. Yes, God will always give you graces in abundance if you come to Him by the path of obedience. When you make a mistake, the virtue of obedience will correct the error and double your merit. Leave the responsibility to those in authority, and remain in the peace that comes to those who obey. In a certain sense they enjoy a sort of moral infallibility: they will always be right, even when, objectively, they are wrong, for obedience is the surest guarantee of being right before God.

Learn to act in this supernatural way. Acquire these divine convictions. Make use of this criterion, so different from the wisdom of this world. This is the way the saints reasoned and acted. Basically this is nothing else than the "foolishness of the cross" of which St. Paul speaks, but which should be the one and only wisdom for you. We are living in a difficult period, one that is quite opposed to this doctrine. We breathe in everywhere the stifling, deadly, poisonous gas of revolt. That is why it is of the utmost importance for us to lean heavily on this eminently evangelical and supernatural principle of obedience.

Be on your guard against a certain spirit of arrogance and disordinate independence which is raging all around us. In this regard we are passing through a terrible crisis. But the Church will always be the guardian of fundamental principles. However, it is up to us priests to be living examples of these principles and not merely to speculate on them and preach them to others.

What a sublime example the Master has given us on this point! At Nazareth He was "subject to them" (Luke 2:51)! During His Passion, He was "obedient unto death" (Phil. 2:8). Imitate this incomparable model. Put your whole heart resolutely into this task, for it will pay rich dividends in the future.

Now for another practical piece of advice. What is the second means of blocking the flood of pride and of learning the lesson of humility? I reply by asking you a question. What is the best way to learn a language? By practicing it and sometimes even by murdering it, so as to speak it fluently. When I was in Korea, missionaries told me the story of one of their number who had a hard time mastering the language. Once when preaching to men on heaven, he used the wrong inflection and, instead of saying, as he intended, "Heaven will one day be your reward," he solemnly told them, "One day your reward will be a lady's hat!" This is learning the hard way.

In your dealings with those in authority and among yourselves, you have plenty of occasions. You will find them in your daily life, if you cooperate with grace. Remain silent when you are blamed for something which could easily be explained. "But Jesus kept silence" (Matt. 26:63). Swallow that bitter pill. And if a confrere, for example, has hurt you in a moment of excitement or through carelessness, go and shake hands with him, do something for him in a friendly way, to master your nerves and to place a restraint on your heart, vibrating with feelings of indignation and desires to assert its rights.

Through this practice do violence to yourself, and you will acquire that meekness and humility of heart so indispensable to your priestly ministry. We know the beautiful theories by heart. It is even possible to write magnificent dissertations on the grandeur of humility and at the same time be burning up with pride. Learn this divine language by *practicing* it daily.

The third and final basis for humility is our helplessness in our ministry. I refer to our absolute powerlessness to touch and convert souls, despite our eloquence, our knowledge, and our hard work. Once more, without Him who "gives the increase," we can do nothing. Even though you have labored throughout the night, casting your nets right and left like the apostles, Jesus has kept to Himself the secret of catching souls, and He reveals this secret only to those humble souls whom He knows will not attempt to rob Him of His glory.

How mortifying it is, after so much tiring labor, to have nothing but empty hands, when in our vanity we promised ourselves a tremendous harvest! Have no doubt about it, you can do a great deal of good, but only on the condition that you possess a great store of humility.

After many exorcisms, a priest commanded the evil spirit to leave the possessed person. Much to his embarrassment, the devil answered, in a tone of irony and triumph, "I refuse to leave." "And why?" demanded the priest. "Because," answered the devil banteringly, "You and I are cousins, we are both proud!"

This answer explains the sterility of our ministry. The devil resists our efforts in the pulpit, in the confessional, and in our ministry, because we are lacking in humility. The proud priest has no power over the angel who fell through pride.

On the other hand, see how divine Providence always uses little people, "nothings," to accomplish great things in the Church. Often when God wants to renew Pentecost, to stir up souls by an extraordinary and miraculous event, His instrument in general is a straw, a child. Isn't this the case of St. Margaret Mary at Paray-le-Monial? of Bernadette at Lourdes? of Thérèse at Lisieux? With these grains of sand, our Lord overturns the world. With straws from Bethlehem, he sets fire to the stars. Fortunate then, a thousand times fortunate are the humble, the little ones. "The weak things of the world has God chosen to put to shame the strong!" (I Cor. 1:28).

Do you really want to become the intimate friend of your King and Saviour? Do you truly want to glorify Him in the work to which He has certainly called you? Do you sincerely wish to become docile instruments to carry out His plans? Then be humble, very humble, and you will win His Heart. Then in this Heart you will find the secret of saving, of converting, of sanctifying souls, His treasures and your heritage. Say often with your lips, but more often with your deeds, this beautiful prayer: "Jesus, meek and humble of heart, make my heart like unto Thine!"

Every morning during your thanksgiving, promise the Heart of Jesus to accept generously the *humiliations of the coming day.* Offer them to Him in exchange for certain conversions you have in mind, whose greatest obstacle is often too much reasoning, a great lack of humility. Un-

bend yourself, humble yourself, that they in turn may un-
bend, docile to the action of grace. Acquire humility by
humbling yourself and by perfect obedience of spirit and
heart!

At the cross her station keeping, stood
the mournful mother weeping.

5. Mary and Sacrifice

WHEN the Word of God decreed that He would save us through the shameful death of the cross, one thing was lacking for the carrying out of this divine plan: the capacity to die. Because of His divine nature He was immortal life itself.

Then it was that He had recourse to Mary, asking of her not only His human nature, but also her free cooperation in the work of salvation, which was to begin with the Incarnation and to end on Calvary. Mary's *Fiat* was decisive in the mystery of the Redemption. Thirty-three years later, at the side of the crucified God, she obtained the marvelous title of Co-redemptrix.

It is quite evident, then, that the Saviour willed to associate Mary with every phase of His work. This is so true that, even though He could have saved His mother from every sort of bitterness, Jesus did not spare her one tear. In fact, on Good Friday, He crowned her Queen of Martyrs and Sorrowful Mother.

"Well-beloved Mother of Apostles, Queen of the Cenacle, appointed to continue the work of your crucified Jesus, which is also your own, by the martydrom of your sorrowful Heart, teach us the great lesson of Calvary, and help us generously to practice it for the glory of your Son and for the glory of you, His Mother!"

❧

Priests—truly apostolic priests—are no strangers to the subject of sacrifice. In fact, self-denial—sometimes to the point of heroism—is the daily bread of the priest. Nevertheless, permit me, unworthy though I am, to speak about the spirit of immolation, the very essence of your priestly calling.

If, like St. Paul, you had to draw up a list of your daily crosses, it would certainly be a long one. Briefly, let me sum them up for you. They fall under two headings: physical crosses, and the ones we call moral or spiritual.

Physical crosses are usually of a personal kind, and are often aggravated by the very nature of the active life we lead as priests and missionaries, active beyond the limits set by human prudence. Take, for example, the cross of bodily infirmity. You have no time to pamper or even take proper care of your body, occupied as you are with priestly duties. Especially in the missions, how easily it succumbs to the attacks of various diseases, worn out as it often is by incessant travelling and intemperate climate.

Then, because He knows it is good for you, our Lord completes your immolation, impressing on your body the likeness of His own wounds, allowing you to share in His sufferings. Generous priests are not afraid of what St. Francis called "Sister Sickness." Not only does it not frighten them, it does not even stop them. They bank on this priceless treasure to help them pay the ransom for their flock, to purchase their conversion. At this time they say with St. Paul: "For when I am weak, then I am strong" (II Cor. 12:10).

A greater source of suffering for many a priest is the isolated life he is forced to lead. Even the fact that he has

God of the tabernacle as his faithful companion and friend
does not make him indifferent to his loneliness, and consequently does not take away the merit of this particular
kind of suffering—for some, great suffering. There is no
question about it, this type of cross is, in general, a hard
one to bear, for, with the exception of a special vocation, it
is difficult for a priest to accustom himself to living separated from his confreres, often with the feeling that he is
forgotten and abandoned. This was one of Father Damien's greatest sacrifices.

But I do not hesitate to say that if this first category of
crosses were the only one the generous priest was called
upon to bear, he would seriously begin to wonder if the
good Lord had lost confidence in him or was unwilling to
accept his total offering. Happily, this is not the case, for
physical crosses are but the first step in his ascent to Calvary. *Moral and spiritual* crosses are to be found in the life
of every priest—keen sufferings that sometimes border on
martyrdom. There are a few which we have all experienced
and which, like St. Lawrence, we can point to as our greatest treasure.

First of all, there is the terrible, incessant warfare unleashed by the devil to counteract the effects of your ministry. How often we priests are overwhelmed at the thought
of the dangers which we foresee for the souls of our people,
whom we love so much! Then it is that a priest is tempted
to say with Moses: "Either save them, Lord, or efface me
from the book of life" (cf. Exod. 32:32). Missionaries
exiled by the Communists from their people know what
this suffering is.

Sometimes our Lord permits a relative victory for the
enemy, allowing you to taste the bitterness of defeat. Your
voice is like that of one crying in the wilderness; the seed
you sow falls on rocky soil or among thorns; your nets
break because of the fury of the waves: not for you is the

satisfaction of a miraculous draught! How heartbreaking it is for a priest, wearied in soul and body after so much hard work, to realize the futility of his devoted efforts. He wears himself out without always seeing the results of his self-sacrificing labors: "What profit is there in my blood?" (Ps. 29:10).

And as though the chalice were not bitter enough, suddenly all sorts of difficulties arise, adding to the contradictions and troubles already experienced. Instead of help and encouragement he waited for, the priest sees nothing ahead but a dark and gloomy horizon. If it were not for his Mass and the presence of our Lord in the tabernacle, the priest would often be tempted to ask to be transferred to a more fruitful field. This is particularly true when a wave of discouragement sweeps over him as he drinks the chalice of ingratitude of certain souls, for whom he has done so much, and who repay him with cowardice or forgetfulness when he really needs their help.

How many times the priest is convinced he knows by personal experience the meaning of the taedium, the terrifying anguish of the Heart of Jesus at Gethsemani! Then his own bitterness seems to parallel to some degree the cruel and poignant suffering of the Saviour in His agony.

Add to this list the destruction caused by some natural catastrophe. After long years of hard work, of begging for funds, of worry and sleepless nights, disaster suddenly strikes and in a few hours or even minutes, the fruits of years of toil is swept away. Then it is you are tempted to ask "Why? Dear Lord, why did You permit?" But, knowing well all this was permitted by a wise and loving God, you say "Fiat," and start all over from scratch.

Isn't it true, with some variations, that this is the actual experience of each and every one of us? This is what we call the martyrdom of everyday life.

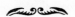

Let us now turn the page to the great, divine lesson taught by these crosses and trials. What do the wisdom of God and the love of Jesus have in view when causing you to live and work under such pressure? The answer is: Their glory in you, and Their glory through you!

Their glory in you means above all and before all your *personal sanctification*. This is an inexorable law: if you are obliged to be saintly priests in order to become successful apostles, the cross is indispensable. You preach the cross in order to save and to Christianize the souls of your brothers; but it is the cross which will make you worthy of such a lofty ministry.

You know better than I the history of the saints. And undoubtedly you have rubbed elbows with certain priests who have been models of unusual priestly virtue. Thus you know to what point suffering is the indispensable element to complete in you what is wanting in your prayer and in your Mass, in order to make of each one of you an *offerens et oblatio*.

Divine life is always preceded by death. In the degree that this principle becomes a reality, you can say, "For to me to live is Christ" (Phil. 1:21). We have to die to live God's life and consequently we have to die to become saints. But your priestly life, made up as it is of such hard daily mortifications, is in itself a slow death.

How insignificant seem many of the added penances of the saints, excellent and admirable as they are, when compared with the inherent austerities of your daily ministry! Sometimes I wonder if certain penitents we rightly admire would have had the courage to live to the full and joyfully to practice another kind of austerity, that of your daily life, the most holy, the most divine, because it is the state of life willed by Almighty God for you.

There is no lack of crosses to make penitents and saints of you. Besides, it is not the cross itself that has the power to sanctify, but rather, love for the Crucified. Therefore you must love one and the other wholeheartedly, without separating the two: Jesus Christ and His cross, or better still, Jesus Christ in all your crosses.

It is this love of self-immolation which makes you desire and rejoice in the "baptism of blood," which should reproduce in you a divine resemblance to Jesus. He willed to become a victim that in His own blood He might mold His intimate friends and especially form holy priests, heirs of His chalice and of His Calvary.

In the future, when crosses come to you, no matter under what form, this is the time to say wholeheartedly with St. Andrew: "O blessed Cross . . . receive me from men and give me back to my Master, that He who redeemed me through thee, may receive me likewise through thee." Yes, the cross will bring to you the treasures of the Heart of Jesus, His graces of predilection, the secret of intimate friendship with Him, the great secret of priestly sanctity.

But there is something else. *Actually your self-sacrifice is the most supernatural of all your apostolic efforts.* How applicable to you are the words of the Saviour: "And I, if I be lifted up from the earth, will draw all things to myself." (John 12:32).

Preaching is certainly a powerful means for conquering souls because our Lord so willed it: "Go and preach." Add to this two-edged sword—the word of God—the marvelous acts of our priestly ministry: the administration of the Sacraments and its fruits, the only treasure of which you are justly proud.

But there is still another source of blessings in your work of saving souls and one which, in my opinion, has not been sufficiently exploited: suffering and the very weakness of the priest! In one sense, suffering is a more efficacious form of preaching than words, no matter how eloquent they may be. Pain is something that must be the basis of all priestly acts, for it is a sap without which neither apostolic works nor the prayer of the priest can have the supernatural fertility which God expects of them.

Any priest who suffers, *and who knows how to utilize his sufferings*, is by that fact alone a real apostle, even though otherwise he is unable to perform his priestly duties. According to the Saviour's plan, suffering fills up what is wanting in our apostolic activity. For all apostolic undertakings are imperfect and incomplete in themselves as long as our crosses are not there to crown our work with success and make it truly fruitful.

Thus it is safe to say, that after Holy Mass, suffering is the most perfect and most powerful means of apostolic action. Furthermore, it is capable of radiating far beyond the reach of your preaching and your works of zeal. No doubt about it, your catechism classes, your schools, your preaching, have great influence, yet always within a relatively limited field. On the other hand, your crosses, your trials—bitter setbacks, painful sickness—can have repercussions that are well-nigh limitless.

<hr />

Listen to this interesting true example. A youthful deacon was obliged to bear arms during the last war. As a result of being struck by an exploding shell he was grievously wounded; the doctors found more than thirty wounds. Almost miraculously he survived, although a physical wreck. But despite it all, he was obsessed with this one thought: I must become a priest!

Finally, through friends, he obtained an audience with the Holy Father. Kneeling before the Sovereign Pontiff, he pleaded his cause: "Holy Father, grant me the great favor of allowing me to be ordained a priest so that I may save souls."

Greatly moved, the pope replied, "But how? You cannot preach, you are unable to work, you are an invalid."

"Most Holy Father," replied the sick man, "what you say is true; I could never be an active priest. But think how many souls I could save by uniting my sufferings to my chalice." And he continued to insist, "Holy Father, do not refuse me the grace of being able to suffer and offer Holy Mass so that I may be an apostle."

The favor was granted, and I can assure you that with his Mass and his wounds, with his great sufferings and with great love, this human wreck is saving many souls. Already he may have reaped a greater harvest than many of us despite our active apostolate. And who knows? Perhaps some of you here have received, through the power of God, a shower of graces coming from afar, from the crosses and altar of this wounded veteran, wounded especially in his heart! Before God this invalid is a truly great missionary.

It seems to me that we have not sufficiently penetrated into this consoling mystery of the apostolate of our sufferings, as doctrinally true as that of Calvary. Never forget that, even though the preaching of Jesus was incomparable, He preached relatively little. On the other hand, His apostolate of suffering extended throughout His entire life from the Incarnation to Golgotha.

I mentioned that this is a consoling mystery. As a matter of fact, not all priests can continue preaching and working until they drop in their tracks. But everyone who, despite his years, is privileged to remain on the battlefield, as well as those who are forced to relinquish their post and their arms to others, can and must—without exception—love while suffering and suffer with love, for the salvation of souls. In this way you can be an apostle until the moment of your death.

Once more I remind you of the lesson taught us on Calvary by Mary, Queen of Apostles and Queen of Martyrs. There is no question about it, all the preaching of the apostles never had the efficacy of those three hours of mortal agony at the foot of the cross. Mary was by no means merely giving us an example of her love for her Son. She was the incarnation of a profound doctrine. She was preaching what the Saviour was preaching and practicing as He hung there nailed to the cross, namely, that there is only one way to save souls, and that is by mixing with the Precious Blood of the chalice our own blood, that is to say, our sufferings and our love. The more we are hosts—*offerens et oblatio*—for the salvation of souls, the more our priesthood will be exercised for the glory of God.

Always consider the sufferings and trials of your daily life—the ones that are a part of your priestly state—as your number one penance and as the great secret, after Holy Mass, of all apostolic success.

As a practical consequence, *love your crosses:* contradictions, criticisms, sickness; yes, love these providential penances, all the more so because you did not look for them.

Without this fundamental mortification, there can be no supernatural success, no divine harvest, for, "Without the shedding of blood there is no forgiveness" (Hebr. 9:22).

6. Mary and the Apostolate

OFFICIALLY it was Peter who presided over the Cenacle. But Mary was there in her capacity as Queen of Apostles, and consequently as queen of Peter himself. Mary is the queen of the Cenacle because she is the mother of Christ the Saviour. But more than this, she took part in and was the sole witness of some of the most sublime events of Christianity.

She is the sacred ark of the mysteries of the Incarnation, the infancy of Jesus, and His thirty years of hidden life at Nazareth. Who other than Mary could possibly have known of the miraculous generation of the Infant-God, and so of her virginal maternity?

It seems probable enough that Mary discreetly revealed these depths of grace and of redemption to the apostles, eager as they were after Pentecost to be instructed in these historical facts, whose key remained exclusively in her hands. I like to think we still preserve one of the most beautiful—and perhaps the most intimate—examples of these confidences in the daily recitation of the Angelus.

Let us then gather around the mother of the apostles, the gentle queen of the Cenacle. May our filial piety obtain from that Heart, which guarded the secrets and the words of the great King, the light and fire needed to help us carry out perfectly the mission that has been entrusted to us. "Queen of Apostles, make each one of us a truly docile instrument for the accomplishment of the merciful designs of the Saviour, your Son!"

"Come, follow me," the Saviour has said to you. "Leave all things, for I will make you fishers of men . . . Go, preach the Gospel to all creatures . . . go and teach . . ." (cf. Matt. 4:19; 28:19).

This is your mandate, a divine mandate if ever there was one. In it is to be found the fundamental reason for your apostolic calling. You do not find yourself on this path of complete loyalty to Christ because of your own choice. "I have chosen you" (John 15:16), were His words to you. You are His messengers, and every one of you can say in all humility and truth with St. Paul, "I am an apostle of Jesus Christ," a title that is backed up by the God-given priestly character, and strengthened by all its powers.

Just what do we mean by the apostolate? Substantially it means: *with Mary and like Mary to give Jesus to souls; with Mary and like Mary to give souls to Jesus.* This definition seems to me to be both complete and substantial, for in reality you have no other end in view, no other obligation, than the complete realization of this ideal. Your goal is all the more glorious because it involves lifting souls out of the depths of paganism and this means the renewal of the apostolic marvels wrought by the first twelve messengers of the Good News. You are their legitimate successors; you walk in their footsteps, other Pauls and Francis Xaviers.

This being so, what is zeal? Zeal is "divine heat radiating from a divine fire." Here is another definition: Zeal is the anguish we feel at the sight of a God so little known and so much insulted; of so many souls in danger of perdition.

Both definitions presuppose the same foundation: a heart on fire, an all-consuming love, the heart of an apostle. For how can we warm others if we ourselves are not on fire? How can we feel anguish of heart at the sight of God so little known, if we do not love Him with a more than ordinary love? How love souls in danger of damnation and how devote ourselves to their salvation, if we are not burning with love for Him who first of all gave His life to save them and us? Thus zeal, true zeal, is nothing else but the logical and spontaneous expanding of a heart being consumed with divine love. Yes, he who loves, and only he who loves, can repeat the words of the apostle: "For the love of Christ impels us" (II Cor. 5:14).

Only those who have given their hearts entirely to the adorable Master can make their own and sincerely repeat the words He Himself addressed to St. Margaret Mary: "Being no longer able to restrain the flames that consume Me, I must spread them through you."

I think you have understood. When love consumes you interiorly you feel the need of obtaining relief by letting it overflow on others, by letting the fire within you enkindle the souls of those around you. Love and zeal, then, are actually the same thing. When we speak of an internal fire, we mean love: when we speak of flames radiating from a heart all on fire and feeling the need to spread fire far and wide, we are talking of zeal.

Listen to these words of St. Francis Xavier, which seem to spring from the depths of his heart: "Would, my God, that I could multiply myself and my work; would that I could give a thousand lives and die a thousand deaths to make You known by all creatures!" This is what we mean by zeal. Keep in mind that this doctrine of love turned into all-consuming zeal is all the more solid, inasmuch as the first commandment is always fulfilled and perfected by the second. A good example is that of Father Damien, whom I like to call a "martyr of the *First* Commandment —total love."

When we love God, and because we love Him, and solely in the measure that we truly love Him, do we love our neighbor, not only as ourselves, but more and to such a degree that we are ready to give up our time, our health, our rest and our very life. This is the case of every generous priest! He is the living confirmation of the definition of zeal given by William of Paris: "A flame from the furnace of the Holy Spirit."

And now what is the definition of a true apostle? "*A chalice filled to the brim with Jesus and overflowing on souls.*"

Note well that I said, "filled to the brim with Jesus." This means that an apostle is not necessarily one who works a great deal, but with a mere spark in his heart. We could call such a one a good worker, but not a great apostle. All the apostles were wonderful workers, but, sad to say, not all hard workers are apostles.

An apostle, above all and before everything else, is one who radiates a divine fire, working when God wants him to, but likewise wearing himself out in the silence of the hidden life, without working, when this is God's will, and with astonishing success in the winning of souls. From among thousands of examples we cite that of the Star of Lisieux, St. Thérèse.

What was St. Francis Xavier? What was St. Thérèse of Lisieux? With two burning hearts, marvelous in their redemptive power, following two completely different paths, but equally great in their radiating, fruitful apostolic action, both were "overflowing chalices."

This is the reason I am so obsessed with the idea of

preaching love for the Heart of Jesus to choice souls, especially to priests, as the foundation of all apostolic work. If the heart is not full of divine energy and blood is not beating strongly, how can we ask the hands to work, how can we hope to form apostles?

For too many, there is no fire, no motivation. Their love is weak. This is the reason why they bargain with God. This too explains their lack of success despite hard work, for again, it is not so much work that constitutes the essence of the apostolate, but rather the love that animates the worker.

How often we find priests by nature very active—perhaps too active—and who according to all appearances seem successful in their efforts. And yet it is easy to see that the lasting and genuine result of so much hard work is often lacking. Why? Because in all this activity there is more feverishness than love and true zeal. Only life can beget life, and only divine love is truly fertile. The best proof of this is the example of each one of the saints. There are no exceptions.

In the course of these conferences I will have occasion to remind you again of the necessity of a solid formation of the heart of the priest, of the need of teaching him how to love our Lord with a great love, in order to make of him, no matter what his field of work, a real apostle, a successful missionary.

But for the moment I beg of you, ask the Sacred Heart of Jesus and the Queen of Apostles for the gift which is the source of all fruitful apostolic activity, the very soul of your priestly ministry, the "knowledge of the love of Christ!" I am sure I am not wrong in saying that this is the secret of the success that has for long years accompanied the work of priests everywhere.

Blessed be the seminary which has formed priests "that

you should go and bear fruit, and that your fruit should remain."

∼∽∾∽∼

Allow me now, respectfully but with conviction, to give you some advice concerning your apostolate. Never aim at what is called "success," behind which is often hidden refined self-love. Rather seek the glory of our Lord, as He understands it; work for the salvation of souls, but according to God's will. That is sufficient. "For my thoughts are not your thoughts; nor your ways my ways."

Success and the glory of God, success and the salvation of souls, are not always synonymous terms. There are even certain brilliant successes that are failures in disguise, just as there are setbacks which are blessings and hidden victories. And speaking of failures, do not fear them too much, for they do not always correspond to the reality which God alone knows.

Remember the failure of Calvary, humanly speaking the greatest in history. Yet see how it was all part of the plan of divine Providence, and how in reality it was the victory of victories: "O death, where is thy victory?" (I Cor. 15:55)

Do your duty conscientiously and supernaturally, and allow our Lord as He knows best to draw His glory from your success, your setbacks, your failures: "For those who love God all things work together unto good" (Rom. 8:28).

And now I ask the Heart of Jesus to make you realize that it is truly He who is the inspiration of this doctrine. Let His Heart speak to you! When you are teaching catechism and preaching His Law, above all preach, I beg of you, "in season and out of season," the *adorable Legislator!* As the foundation of all your preaching, no matter what the subject, bring out forcefully the adorable person of our divine Lord, so little known, sad to say, by Christians, and even by those who call themselves His friends.

In your ministry, make a living reality of these words spoken by the angels to the shepherd on that blessed Christmas night: "For behold, I bring you good news of great joy which shall be to all the people; for today . . . a Saviour has been born to you, who is Christ the Lord" (Luke 2:10–11).

Yes, before and after having explained the Law, be sure to stress the person of the Saviour whose very name possesses unique power.

There is something seriously lacking in certain preachers and catechists who stress so strongly the positive law and the penal law but hardly touch upon the divine figure of Jesus Christ. It is quite possible to be a master jurist and to be familiar with the entire Napoleonic code without knowing the history of Napoleon. But you cannot be a true Christian, perfectly faithful to the divine Law, without knowing and intensely loving the Legislator, Jesus Christ. In the case of the Jews it was all right for Moses to remain in the background, provided they knew the Law. But as for you, bring out into the open the Sun who is the very soul of the Christian Law. "That they may know thee, the only true God, and him whom thou hast sent, Jesus Christ" (John 17:3).

My long experience has taught me that everywhere there are numerous Catholics, especially among the graduates of Catholic schools, who know the entire Law by heart, but who are poor Catholics because they are both ignorant of and have no love for the divine Legislator.

Here is another important remark. As you preach the adorable person of Jesus Christ, be sure to insist with great conviction on His doctrine of charity; that is, preach His love, His Heart. "I have come to cast fire upon the earth, and what will I but that it be kindled? . . . Come to me, all you . . ." (Luke 12:49 and Matt. 11:28).

Never forget that, fundamentally, the great and divine novelty of the Gospel is that of a God *who loves* and who, to prove this love and to get us to love Him in return, did what St. Paul calls the "foolishness of the cross" which presupposes the "folly" of the Incarnation. Always remember that the First Commandment, *"diliges,"* is and always will be the first and the greatest, in every latitude and for every race, in Rome as well as in the Orient. The Second Commandment and all the others are founded on the first and flow from it.

Say and repeat in every language and in every dialect with a holy tenacity, that God *is love* and that His first right is to be loved *"ex toto corde et ex tota anima et ex tota mente,"* thus with our entire being.

With St. Paul, teach that "he who loves his neighbor has fulfilled the Law," and likewise "he who does not love abides in death" (Rom. 13:8 and I John 3:14). If you build on this doctrinal rock neither the winds nor the floods of temptation or persecution will overthrow the house of the Lord.

Do not lay any other foundation, for this was the one laid as the cornerstone by all the apostles for the very first preaching of the Gospel. I am profoundly convinced that the theology which proved to be the opening wedge in a completely pagan world, and the Pentecost which brought about the astonishing expansion of Christianity in the first centuries of the Church, was the good news, the overwhelmingly good news from on high, that God *is love* and that He came to earth to beg our love at the price of His blood!

I am sure you also have noticed, as I have, that this doctrine, which sums up the entire catechism, is the most catholic, the most universal of all our dogmas. For it is a dogma that everyone—children, youth and the aged, the simple and the learned—understand with astonishing clearness. It is the key, the only supernatural and adequate explanation of all the mysteries of our faith, without exception.

When your prospective converts ask you the "how" and the "why" of the facts of the Incarnation, the cross, the Eucharist, the Church and the sacraments, what other answer can you give save the one that shines forth like the sun from every page of the Gospels and in all St. Paul's epistles, "For God so loved the world that he gave his only-begotten Son"; "He has first loved us"; "Jesus . . . loved them to the end" (John 3:16; I John 4:10; John 13:1)?

From this affirmation the conclusion follows logically: "Who would not love in return the One who has loved us so much? My child, give Me your heart."

If St. Thomas himself, like St. Paul, had been called upon to dispute before pagan intellectuals honestly and sincerely seeking to grasp the mystery of Christianity, he would not have found an answer more enlightening or more doctrinal. This must be the foundation of every Christian edifice, whether it be that of the Catholic University of Louvain, of Milan or of Washington, or that of the much simpler but no less important Christian edifices in mission lands.

"But we . . . preach a crucified Christ" (I Cor. 1:23). This is the Christ who is the way and the truth. But He, infinite Love, is also the revelation of His Father's love, He is our way, our redemption, our life; and tomorrow He will be our reward in heaven only because He is merciful Love.

Once more, base all your evangelical work on this, the most sublime, the most easy of access, and the most eternal of all truths: "Deus caritas est." Preach and teach that, in giving Himself to us through love, He asks only one thing in return: the gift of ourselves, our love. "Love therefore is the fulfillment of the Law" (Rom. 13:10).

Each day before your Mass, ask the Mother of Fair Love to teach you the science of sciences, to obtain for you the gift of gifts, that of a truly all-consuming love for her Son, so that in her school you can become genuine apostles. Fervently ask that this love become a blazing fire, the motivating force and the divine obsession of your preaching and all your priestly work.

Any priest or missionary who is deeply in love with our Lord, and who, like St. John, knows how to pray, fight, and suffer in the Heart of His Master, will necessarily be a great harvester of souls, for the same love that makes a man a saint, likewise makes of him a true apostle.

For with thee is the fountain
of life (Ps. 35:10).

7. "Overflowing Chalices"

NO DOUBT each one of you has a great love for the Blessed Virgin. Try to love her more and more, but be sure your love is proved by reproducing in your soul Mary's virtues so fitting for holy priests and genuine missionaries. From her motherly Heart we must learn the secret of divine success in our apostolate, for she is the queen and model of apostles. "All her glory . . . is within," and I might add, "all her power is from within" (Cf. Ps. 44:14).

She exercised her silent but powerful apostolate from the 25th of March until Christmas; from Christmas until Calvary, and from Calvary until her glorious Assumption. From a Heart filled with God she was able to pour out God; because she was the most perfect reservoir containing substantial grace Himself, Jesus, her God and her Son, she was able to give Him to others. Besides, as universal mediatrix, she has at her disposal all the graces won by the Redeemer.

She never preached, but no one has ever been so much a missionary of the Father, and the apostle of the Son, *"from within."* This is one of the greatest lessons Mary can give to priests and to missionaries.

Despite the fact that evil is to be found everywhere, I am still an optimist. Why? Because I believe in this divine statement, "I am the resurrection and the life" (John 11:25). But let me say at once that in recalling these words I am not referring principally to our Lord's presence in the Blessed Sacrament in our tabernacles. The tabernacle, despite its divine treasure, in itself is not enough. Look at all the evil surrounding our tabernacles, despite their number and despite the real Presence!

It is evident therefore, that the eucharistic tabernacle alone is not sufficient. According to the divine plan, to complete this tabernacle there must be next to it another one, the heart of a holy priest! Without this the eucharistic tabernacle can become the silent prison of the Lord Jesus. On the contrary, wherever a *saintly* priest ministers at the altar, the eucharistic tabernacle becomes an inexhaustible fountain of life. This is the explanation of the great success of priests like John Vianney, Vincent de Paul, Francis Xavier, and Don Bosco.

Let us put it in another way: if He had so willed, God could have surpassed the bridge and the canal we call Mary, something He has not done nor ever will do. God expressly willed that Mary should be the indispensable mediatrix of the Incarnation, and thereafter the mediatrix of all graces, even though He could have distributed them Himself. What is true of Mary is also true of the priest.

The priest is, by the will of God, a necessary mediator with Christ the Mediator. We also have been appointed as dispensers of grace, as a bridge between the crucified Mediator and souls. But we exercise this mediation not only by working for souls and distributing the Church's treasures, but also by becoming, like Mary—a mediatrix, a radiating power, "from within." The great secret of priestly success is to be found in a priestly heart modeled on the

Heart of the Co-redemptrix. As of Mary, so of the priest, "all his glory, all his power, is from within."

What then is supernatural fruitfulness? Divine life radiating from a heart made divine, whether in silence like that of Jesus in Nazareth or in full activity, as when Jesus preached to the multitudes.

And what is an apostle? A chalice filled to the brim with God, with Jesus Christ, giving its overflow to souls, like a St. Francis or a Little Flower.

Activity is merely the ordinary form of the apostolate, but in activity, excellent and necessary though it be, is not to be found its substance, its soul. The secret of every form of apostolate is to be found in a soul of great faith and in a heart on fire, in a profound interior life, in a breathing of the Holy Spirit "from within." Supernatural success is always far more the ripe fruit of this spirit of prayer than the result of our labors, our preaching, our organizations. These latter always presuppose the former.

A heart on fire, the heart of a saint—even though there be no external activity—of itself constitutes an apostolic power of the highest value. Again look at Mary and, following her example, the thousands of other silent "missionaries" preaching through love and suffering. Without this interior motivating power, intense activity is fever, not zeal; it is a voice crying in the wilderness. In fact, it can become a positive danger.

～～～

Here I would like to hand on to you two important lessons our Lord taught me during my long apostolic career.

The first of these lessons was a complete disillusionment for me, but at the same time a great grace. In the early days of my priesthood, I believed for a short time in the efficacy of learning, of eloquence, of apostolic works in themselves. This illusion did not last very long, for, with-

out looking for them, I came across great masters in learning, in eloquence, and in activity, the three mirages which
at that time fascinated me most. But our Lord wished to
prove clearly to me that when these men were not masters
and doctors of the interior life, of charity, of priestly holiness, they were nothing but the "tinkling cymbals," spoken
of by St. Paul. Around them there was emptiness, a desert,
nothing—and worse than nothing! Not only was there a
frightening lack of fruit, but often ruins and corruption.

What would I not give to help you get rid of your illusions on this subject, and to replace them with quite another conviction: souls are saved above all by the holiness
of the priest!

We all have our dreams, which often last a long time.
Sometimes they turn into nightmares. Here is an example:
a young priest came to me one day and told me, "Father,
I need your advice. I am really discouraged. I am an assist-
ant in a parish where the faith is at a low ebb, and am
working with the pastor and other assistants, trying to help
these people. For five years I've done everything possible
to try to win them over, but the results are nil. I can assure
you I've tried everything and it breaks my heart to have to
admit there has been a complete failure."

Once again he repeated, "I've tried everything. Please
give me some advice and encouragement, for I really want
to be a good priest and to save souls. Please tell me, what
do I have to do to save souls?"

Expressly I made him tell me again that he had tried
everything, without results. Then I asked him, "Have you
ever tried becoming a saintly priest?" And when, surprised,
he answered "no," I told him, "Well then you haven't
tried anything! You don't begin with secondary things,
like organizations, music, and processions, you begin with
fundamentals, with the altar! On the altar is the tabernacle,
and in it you know there is a ciborium, and in the ciborium

a divine victim. You must be that living altar, that sacred tabernacle, that ciborium—an *Alter Christus*—a saintly priest. First try this apostolate, and then one day, be it only in heaven, you will learn how God is faithful!"

Listen to what a priest who was a famous orator, writer, and savant told me after a conference I gave on this subject. Profoundly affected by what he had just heard, he said to a group of astonished young priests, "Yes, I can assure you that what Father has just told you is the truth, pure and simple. It is now more than thirty years since I began to write. I have to write well, for there is a market for my books, and through them I've made a fortune. Yet despite all this, I'm ashamed to admit that during these thirty years I've never known what it is to give absolution to one person affected by one of my conferences or converted by one of my books."

What a sad admission! And how many others there would be if priests were honest enough to reveal the truth about their ministry as it is seen by God and as known by themselves.

~~~

We come now to the second lesson which reads like a page from the Gospels. Wherever I have found what I call a "straw of Bethlehem"—a humble hidden soul on fire with love for our Lord—I have always found the explanation of great conversions, sometimes bordering on the miraculous. Let me give you a striking example which is better than a whole volume of brilliant dissertations.

Years ago I was brought to the room of a sick man who had been excommunicated because of his violent attacks against the Church. What a surprise for him to see a priest at his bedside!

"Get out of here!" he yelled at me angrily. "Get out of here at once!"

I answered, "I won't leave without having given you absolution in the name of the Sacred Heart of Jesus."

"Don't talk to me about Him," he cried even more loudly. "Get out of here fast, you don't know who you are talking to."

"I know, sir, you've been His enemy, and that you've wounded His Heart. But this Heart is open to receive you, and is ready to forgive you. He has sent me to beg you to accept His forgiveness."

"Never!" he burst out. "Get out of here!"

But I was determined to win him over through the power of divine mercy and so I began pleading with him:

"Sir, you hate Him and He loves you. Repeat after me, 'I love You Jesus, because You are Jesus.' "

Every time he came back with an answer filled with hatred, I would insist, "Say with me, 'I love You Jesus, because You are Jesus.' " Ten, twenty, fifty times I repeated this powerful phrase, and I was becoming convinced that despite himself it was hitting home, that he was deeply moved.

After perhaps a half hour, during which time he had stopped his tirades, I suddenly noticed tears in his eyes! Taking advantage of the opening made by grace I again urged him to repeat, "I love You Jesus because You are Jesus."

A moment of silence, of deep interior struggle and then he burst out sobbingly, "Oh yes, I love Him, because He loves me!"

Knowing that he had been conquered by the Heart of Jesus I put my arm around his shoulders. Then like Saul he said, "What do I have to do?"

"Make a good confession. I'll help you."

An hour or so later, his face radiating joy, he called his non-Catholic wife and their three unbaptized boys, told them what had just happened, and invited them to follow his example.

And now the epilogue of this story. In it you are going to find a striking confirmation of what I have been saying: wherever you find a "straw"—a little soul but a fervent soul—you find conversions, even miraculous ones.

Would you like to know who resurrected this "whole cemetery," as the pastor put it? A month later, with the archbishop's permission, I offered Mass in the room of this resurrected Lazarus. Surrounding him were the four newly baptized: his wife and their three sons. After Mass, they sang in thanksgiving the hymn "Christ Conquers." It was really beautiful, and true. Then came the ceremony of the Enthronement of the Sacred Heart as King of this newly won home.

Suddenly from the corner, where she had been kneeling and crying softly, the old cook came over to the sick man and said to him with great feeling, "Dear sir, at this happy moment would you allow me to embrace you?" Deeply moved, the convert held out his arms. Then the elderly domestic went on to say, "For more than twenty-five years I have been working for you and during that time you thought I was only a poor servant, your cook. Oh no! I'm going to reveal a secret to you. For more than twenty-five years I've been an apostle of the Sacred Heart of Jesus, offering up my prayers, my sufferings, my daily Communions and my Night Adoration, asking one great favor of the Sacred Heart: not to allow me to die, nor to see heaven, until I had first seen heaven in this home. Now it is done, I see it, the Heart of Jesus has conquered. Now I can die, my mission is finished."

Is not this sublime and overwhelming?

And do you dare to tell me that by your preaching and your Mass, that with the grace of your priesthood, you cannot work wonders like this? Certainly you can, but only on condition that you possess the same power of that hidden apostle—sanctity!

It will always be true that when the Kingdom of God is established within the heart of a priest, he will radiate holiness, for divine life always works of itself in the heart of a man of God. This is why St. Teresa of Avila made the striking statement, "A fervent monastery has walls made of crystal." She meant that the monastery would radiate life and the fire of charity far and wide by the very fact that its members were fervent. Even if this monastery is in an isolated spot, its cloistered silence makes it all the more eloquent.

How consoling is this solid doctrine! God in His wisdom cannot ask all to have the knowledge or eloquence of a St. Vincent Ferrer, nor the charisms of a St. Francis Xavier or of a Curé of Ars. But one thing He does expect of all of us is the faith and love of these saints, especially when celebrating Mass, when praying, and in our interior life.

Once more I say to all of you: try out this powerful apostolate, the only one within range of young and old, of the healthy and the sick; the only one that is always fruitful, for this is the very soul of every successful apostolate.

We talk a great deal—too much perhaps—about the strength of the Left. For my part, I prefer to speak of "the weakness of the Right"—of God's friends. *The Left is strong because the Right is weak!* If only we priests, the extreme Right, were men of faith and love as were Francis Xavier and John Vianney!

How many times these words of our Lord to St. Margaret Mary have been abused because misunderstood: "I will reign through My Heart despite Satan and his agents." There are some who, basing their conviction on this statement, believe that as a reward for some kind of a badly understood devotion, the Heart of Jesus will crush our enemies and will reign in spite of them. But I dare to say, "No! This is not what Jesus had in mind." Humbly but categorically, allow me to correct the false assumption in this interpretation. It is true, our Lord did state that He would reign despite Satan and his agents. But listen carefully: *He never promised that He would reign despite us, His friends and apostles.*

When we priests are not His true friends and apostles, when we are not fervent, when our life is one of mediocrity, when our ambition is to be just "good" priests, then we stop Him short on His road to victory. He will not reign if John, James, and Peter are not the saints they ought to be. Certainly He will reign despite Satan and his agents, either by converting them or crushing them, but only on condition that His friends are faithful; that close to the eucharistic tabernacle there is another tabernacle, the heart of a holy priest!

It is not beautiful churches or splendid organizations that are lacking. What is missing is what Father Chevrier used to call "spiritual basilicas." "Help me," he would say, "help me to build the only basilica truly capable of saving the world."

When someone, prompted by curiosity, would ask him what he meant, he would reply, "At any cost I want to build a basilica whose foundations will be holy priests, whose pillars will be holy priests; a basilica whose sanctuary lamp will be a priest burning with love, whose pulpit will be the preaching of a holy priest, a basilica whose altar will be a holy priest saying Mass. This is the basilica we need everywhere, and the only one. What good are those marvels of art, bronze and marble, if they are staffed by ecclesiastical functionaries—good perhaps—but mere sacerdotal machines? Give me my spiritual basilica with a holy priest and I will resurrect a parish and an entire city!"

Yes, Father Chevrier was right. It seems to me we have not insisted enough on the "ex opere operantis" of the priest-apostle, of the missionary. There are too many priests who are falling back on the "ex opere operato" and who are satisfied with being honest administrators, irreproachable functionaries.

The standards of justice of honest men in the world are not sufficient for those who by vocation must implant life and who must implant it from the superabundance of their hearts. A good official may only be a good worker. But again I remind you that "worker" and "apostle" are not always synonymous terms. Christ selected you to be apostles, for he wants to make of you "fishers of men." Only the fervent priest and saintly missionary is truly an apostle and one whose work is blessed by heaven with an abundant harvest!

Take courage as you listen to these statements, for holiness is the only apostolate that depends upon yourself, and the only one that is always possible, whether at the age of thirty or eighty, in times of peace or trouble or persecution.

If a priest is truly a man of God, if he has a heart full of God, and if he offers his fatigue, his worries and his cares, his countless other sacrifices as a prayer and an oblation for souls, "Amen, amen, dico vobis," if this simple offering is united to the chalice of his Mass, it will work miracles which God may hide from him but which he will joyfully behold one day in heaven.

We have forgotten this. In the hustle and bustle of worries and work which have absorbed the attention of even the best of us, these truths have often been forgotten. But as I mentioned before, divine Providence is bringing us back to the fundamental truths with the help of striking miracles. The voice that preaches to us is simple, clear, eloquent. It is the voice of God. It comes from Lisieux, from Carmel.

Yes, Thérèse of the Child Jesus is a "vox Dei." Look at this insignificant child who became a veritable hurricane of graces and miracles which has swept through all parts of the world, but especially the missions, where she has showered down her choicest roses! This is her privilege and duty, for since 1927 she is, by decree of the Holy See, the patroness of the Missions as St. Francis Xavier is the patron.

And what does she tell us, this "vox Dei"? Exactly what Mary had already said at Nazareth and on Calvary, in fact what our Saviour taught us in the silence and obscurity of Nazareth, where He was already as much our Saviour as on the cross: that the apostolate is much more than eloquent preaching. *It is the divine life in the soul.* It is a soul filled with God, radiating.

If we need preaching—and we certainly do—we need a thousand times more to preach with our hearts, whether in the pulpit or out of it, for a saintly soul has the power to save the world through a life of immolation and prayer, even though he never utters a word.

This is the lesson of Mary at Nazareth. This is the wonderful and encouraging lesson of the Star of Lisieux: *You give God in the measure that you possess Him and love Him.* I repeat, St. Francis Xavier saved more souls by prayer and sacrifice than by his labors and his miracles. You will rarely find anyone who can speak and work as he did, but who among us cannot believe and love, and sanctify himself as did this saint?

You are priests ". . . that they may have life, and have it more abundantly" (John 10:10). But always remember that Jesus is athirst above all for the souls of His priests, His shepherds and missionaries. First He wants to reign deeply in the hearts of each one of you, in order to sanctify you. Then and only then, and in the degree that He is Life of your life, will He reign around you and through you!

Let me sum up this chapter by citing parts of two inspired texts that, taken together, bring home its fundamental idea: "Be saints . . . that you may bear fruit and that your fruit may remain."

Holiness and fruitfulness are equivalent and synonymous terms.

Be very faithful in making a good monthly day of recollection. Promise not to miss it, if you can help it, for it will be a great source of grace for you.

Above all, resolve to make your annual retreat *in a real spirit of faith*. I stress these words, *in a real spirit of faith*. By this I mean, be truly recollected and keep the silence between the various exercises. We can never talk too much about the importance of a good retreat. To make a half-hearted, so-so retreat, means without doubt the loss of the greatest grace of the year.

Make it in silence and pray fervently. After a serious examination of conscience make a good confession with the best disposition possible. And make your retreat in common whenever you can, under a retreat master, for no one is a judge in his own case. From time to time we need the words of a stranger to wake us up and to remind us of our serious obligations. Take advantage of the extraordinary grace of a retreat and in silence and recollection listen to the voice of the Lord.

Try your best to say your Divine Office, "attente ac devote." Love your Breviary and it will no longer be a burden but a source of grace, of light and supernatural strength.

Heart of Jesus, burning with love for me,
inflame my heart with love of Thee!

I will be thy reward exceeding great.

8. Holiness, the Source of Happiness

WHEN Jesus Christ restored all things by His cross and by His blood the world was not changed suddenly into an earthly paradise. Divine peace, the peace which Christ alone can give, was left to His friends and followers as the source of true Christian happiness. Our Lord was so anxious to have us believe in the great value of this peace that He speaks of it again and again after His Resurrection: "Pax vobis . . . pacem do vobis. . . ."

Christ affirms the possibility of happiness even more clearly in the Beatitudes, enumerating at length those who, despite the thorns of life and the trials of exile, are to be considered "blessed" or happy here below. What Christian in the name of some so-called philosophy would dare to correct the Master's words on this subject?

The strong, clear statements of the Gospel are sufficient to make us believe that happiness can and ought to be the portion of those who bear the sweet yoke of Christ with great faith and love. But in addition to the words of the Gospel we have another argument in support of this thesis:

the Gospel as it is lived in the lives of the saints, the happiest and the only truly happy people on earth.

The saints are happy—extremely happy—obviously with a relative happiness, but one that is very real and effective. From Our Lady singing her Magnificat down to St. Thérèse of Lisieux and Bernadette of Lourdes, all the saints can say with St. Paul: "In all my tribulations I am overflowing with happiness." All have served the Lord in joy and all have lived in unshakable peace in the midst of the storms of life.

Who worthy of the name of Christian would dare to doubt the supernatural happiness of the apostles as they came forth from the tribunal "rejoicing because they were judged worthy to suffer for the name of Jesus"? Like them and after them, there is the army of "quadraginta quatuor millia signati" of the Apocalypse, the innumerable legions of saints who lived in God and enjoyed God when on earth and whose happiness far surpassed that of all the Kings and Princes of this world despite their powers and pleasures.

It is interesting to remark, that in this deep supernatural happiness of the saints, in this peace which "surpasses all understanding," and which nothing and no one can take from them, the cross plays a most important part. Not only is it no obstacle, no negation of happiness, but according to the divine philosophy of the Gospel, according to the adorable Preacher of the Beatitudes, it is the fuel that feeds the flame of peace, a stimulant that every single one of the saints has sought after lovingly that it might intensify their own happiness.

According to worldlings, suffering and happiness, tears and peace, are mutually exclusive. According to Jesus Christ they complement each other. The saint loves and even seeks the cross, he embraces it and looks upon it as a treasure because with the Crucified it brings him a peace and joy with which no pleasure of earth is comparable.

To understand this doctrine well, think over these simple words of St. Thérèse of Lisieux: "For a long time, suffering has been my heaven here below and I can hardly imagine how I shall ever get used to living where joy reigns without any trace of sadness. Jesus will have to transform my soul, otherwise I shall not be able to bear the delights of eternity."

Judge by the following example whether happiness can be a reality in the midst of suffering, when someone lives up to the Gospel ideal.

One day after finishing a sermon I was asked to visit a dying workman who wanted to see me before he died. The room was poor and bare. Lying on the bed was a young man suffering from consumption, the signs of death already apparent.

"Are you Father Mateo?" he said, trying to raise himself up.

"Yes I am, and I am happy to come in answer to your request. What can I do for you?"

"Father, look at this picture of the Sacred Heart of Jesus, which you signed. It seems that you go about preaching that where this picture is received with faith and love, there Jesus enters as our King, and if we love Him greatly He stays in our home as a Friend who helps and consoles us. Father, I know this by experience. I have tried to love Him so much! And He has loved me. With Him I have always been so happy. I am only a poor working man. I have suffered and struggled but I have always been very happy with Him. I know I am going to die soon and I wanted to thank you and to tell you how true it is that one is always happy with the Heart of Jesus. But especially I wanted to see you so that you might sing a hymn of thanksgiving with me. I know the Magnificat. If you will begin it, my wife and children will join us in saying it."

I was so overcome that tears filled my eyes. The man

seeing this said: "I see you are unable to speak; help me up and I will begin it."

Then, leaning against me for support, he made a great effort to sing on earth what he was going to sing in heaven: the peace and happiness he had found in the love and service of Jesus Christ. He died the next morning and re-intoned his Magnificat in heaven.

Notice these words: "I have suffered and struggled. . . . I am only a poor working man. . . . I have been so happy with Him."

To return to the beautiful thought of St. Thérèse which I just quoted, all the saints could have spoken as she did of the "folly of the cross," and with a like sincerity. All the saints were human as we are; all dreaded suffering; all, humanly speaking, trembled before the cross. But the love of Jesus and His all-powerful grace have transformed their lives and turned depths of suffering into well-springs of joy—a mystery that worldlings will never understand.

Who better than the priest is in a position to live by and to realize in his own life this marvelous doctrine? Who, better than we, can and should be really happy in our vocation? Has not the priest, by the fact he is a priest, withdrawn himself from the three things that are for many others sources of sin and unhappiness? He has voluntarily renounced purely natural pleasures, and the exaggerated searching after comforts, ambition and the pride of life, together with worldly interests and the seeking after money, all of which are opposed to the life of sacrifice of the priest. But these privations, however meritorious they may be, are only a negative element—important certainly, but not sufficient of themselves to make you happy. In fact, God wishes these earthly goods, legitimate for others, but which you have sacrificed for Him, to be adequately compensated for in your divine vocation.

Much more important in this question of priestly happiness is the positive element. Once you have broken the chains that bind you to this earth, our Lord gives you a twofold treasure which can be for you, as it has been for the saints, a source of the most pure happiness.

1. *Tradidit semetipsum.* . . . Jesus Christ delivers Himself entirely into our hands; He gives us His Heart: *Tu es pars hereditatis meae et calicis mei.* . . . *Tu es qui restitues hereditatem meam mihi.* . . . *A te quid volui in coelis et super terram?* How often can it be said of some priests who have not sufficiently appreciated the grace of graces, the gift of gifts—their priesthood and all the benefits it brings them—those grave, kind words spoken by Jesus to the Samaritan woman: *Si scires donum Dei!* If you only knew what peace and joy could be yours in the exercise of your priesthood, especially in offering daily Mass! Angels looking down upon priests who are unhappy and sometimes very unhappy must ask themselves what extraordinary thing a priest must do to be happy since he possesses the very source of happiness—well nigh infinite happiness—in his daily Mass.

Recall what has been said about the Holy Sacrifice of the Mass and you will have to admit that the angels are right in being astonished at those who say Mass daily and are not perfectly happy in spite of all the trials of life. If we could only understand this truth: Jesus is the priest's source of strength and joy; His Heart at the altar is the life of his life, to such a degree that all his difficulties, all his sorrows become sweet when mingled with the Precious Blood in the chalice. This truth is the underlying thought of St. Bernard's *Jesu dulcis memoria:*

> Jesus, the very thought of Thee
> With sweetness fills the breast!

Yet sweeter far Thy face to see
And in Thy presence rest. . . .

To those who fall, how kind Thou art!
How good to those who seek!

But what to those who find? Ah! this
Nor tongue nor pen can show—
The love of Jesus, what it is,
None but His loved ones know.

Jesus! our only hope be Thou,
As Thou our prize shalt be. . . .[1]

This hymn has a solid theological foundation. Once a priest appreciates the priceless treasure of his vocation, of his daily Mass, then he will experience a foretaste of Heaven, especially when crosses complete what is lacking to his morning Mass.

Were not Mary and Joseph perfectly happy at Nazareth in the possession of Jesus? Both lived by faith, but they knew how to appreciate the gift of God—the Child Jesus —and so in spite of their many and continual troubles they were perfectly happy. So it should be with the priest who has understood the sublimity of his vocation and of the treasure entrusted to him by God and the Church. Ask priests like St. Alphonsus Liguori, St. Philip Neri, St. Vincent de Paul, St. Francis Xavier, the Curé of Ars and Father Damien, and without exception they will tell you that the spiritual joys of the priesthood far surpass all earthly happiness.

2. If all that Holy Mass gives you—Jesus Himself and His Sacred Heart—does not satisfy you, there is still another source of happiness for the priest: the souls he has baptized and the very exercise of his priestly functions.

Les Buissonnets, the home of St. Thérèse, presents a beautiful picture. Louis Martin and his family formed but

[1] From the Raccolta, No. 115.

one heart and soul in enjoying the beauties of nature, the joys of family life and especially the joys of the supernatural life, because of their fervent piety. But still more beautiful is the picture of a priest in a parish or mission, invested with spiritual paternity and surrounded by the members of his flock. After Holy Mass, nothing can compare with the power of the priest baptizing, making people Christians and children of God. Nothing can be more consoling than to train these souls, nourishing them with the bread of the Church's teachings and forming Jesus Christ in them. No earthly joy, no matter how noble it may be, is comparable to that of a priest giving Jesus, the Bread of Life, to a group of adult or child communicants for the first time.

What joy is greater than that of a priest in the confessional, who, by the power of his priesthood, breaks the chains of a sinner, restoring to him the rights acquired at baptism and the friendship of the merciful Saviour?

Is not the joy you experience on a great feast—Christmas or Easter, the Feast of the Sacred Heart, or a feast of Our Lady—when you see your people coming to the Communion rails in great numbers, not better than any earthly joy? There are times when the priest begins to enjoy the hundredfold promised to those who give up all for God and souls. No wonder a holy old priest once said, "What will Heaven be like, Jesus, if already here below I am experiencing so much of its joy?"

Even where others find nothing but sadness, the zealous priest finds reasons for rejoicing. When you are administering holy Viaticum to a dying person, all those around you are weeping. And even though you yourself may share their grief, still your heart sings with joy at the thought of Christ's triumph in this soul and of the Heaven which awaits him.

Then what about the miracles of mercy often wrought through your priestly ministry—remarkable conversions of which we are often the instruments, and which repay us in one short hour for long and painful sacrifices? Here is a personal example of the many you yourselves have experienced:

I was saying good-by to a bishop in whose diocese I had been preaching. A car was at the door to take me to the boat, for I was to sail that evening. Suddenly a man came running up to me and said excitedly, "Father, please come with me at once! My father is dying and refuses to go to confession."

I replied, "But there are a number of priests who will be glad to go with you—I have to catch a boat."

"Father," he answered, "I have already called three priests and he has sent them away. Please come with me at once! The dying cannot wait and the Sacred Heart will repay you."

Hearing this, the bishop said, "He is right, Father, the dying cannot wait. Sacrifice everything and go."

Without further ado I knelt for the Bishop's blessing and got into the car. Arriving at the house, a spacious mansion, I entered the hall and met the wife and children, all excellent Catholics and crying bitterly. I said to them, "Do not cry as though you had no trust in God. Please kneel down and pray."

Then I asked them, "Do you really love the Sacred Heart? Do you believe in His love?" In the midst of their sobs they all answered, "Yes, we do."

"Will you promise to be more than ever a family of the Sacred Heart, a really fervent family, an eucharistic family?" Again they said they would.

"Will you promise to be apostles of the Sacred Heart, to make Him known and loved in exchange for the conversion of your father?"

"Yes, Father, we promise."

"Then, trusting in your promise, and in the name of

the Heart of Jesus, I will go to the dying man while you stay here and pray."

Without knocking I entered the sickroom and walked straight to the invalid who stared at me in astonishment. Immediately, I said to him, "I have come in the name of the Heart of Jesus to offer you His mercy. You will accept it, won't you, and go to confession?"

He answered, "Yes, I want to go to confession right away!"

After the confession was over, I called in the family. What a scene of joy as amid their tears they renewed their promise to be truly devoted to the Sacred Heart. As I left the house, I can assure you I felt as if I were going to die of joy.

It will always be true, "to serve God is to reign." That is to say, the faithful priest does not have to wait for eternity to be rewarded by the Heart of Jesus. Here below he begins to receive the "hundredfold" and with it the peace and joy which more than compensate for his daily martyrdom. And this is but a foretaste of what God has in store for you —things eye has not seen, nor ear heard, nor the mind of man conceived.

Meditate often on these consoling words spoken especially for the priest who tries to be loyal to his divine Master and his calling:

Ego ero merces tua magna nimis!

*As my Father has sent me, so
also I send you.*

9. The True Missionary Spirit

THE essence of holiness consists in divine love; consequently perfection is one and the same for all the saints. But if we consider holiness in the lives of individual saints—that is to say, according to their personal vocation and the circumstances of their lives—it is evident that all do not walk in the same path, nor do all have the same characteristics. *Stella a stella differt.* What a marvelous variety there is among the saints in heaven and among those still struggling for sanctity here below!

God is admirable in His saints, for with infinite richness of shadings and variety, He reproduces in them His own beauty, which is ever ancient and ever new. This principle once established, it is evident that in the army of Christ's priests the highly privileged vocation of missionary has a spirit with clearly marked characteristics quite proper to this calling. Here then, among others, are five characteristics of the missionary vocation. And what is said of missionaries in the strict sense of the word is also applicable to all priests, for all are, in a certain sense, genuine missionaries.

A. SIMPLICITY

There must be a spirit of perfect simplicity: in a word, of evangelical holiness. There must be a great simplicity in your personal conversations with our Lord, that is to say, in your method or kind of prayer. We pray as we love. Prayer and love are two supernatural elements attainable by children as well as by learned priests.

Be very simple in your life and your rule of life: avoid all complications and formulas which will only embarrass you without being of the least advantage to your soul.

Be very, very simple in everything that concerns your spiritual life; it will be all the more solid and deep if it is exempt from "mathematical problems," as Cardinal Bourne so aptly said when speaking of the spirituality of St. Thérèse of Lisieux.

Do not overburden yourself with many devotions. Those which are obligatory are quite sufficient to sanctify you, and you cannot undertake the others in a life such as yours, so full of work and of unexpected demands on your time.

Simplicity, order and practical common sense usually go together, and this is what you need both for your own interior life and for the lessons of virtue and piety which you must give to others.

It seems to me that the common sense and simplicity of St. Vincent de Paul joined to the simplicity and learning of St. Francis de Sales, and the ardent apostolic soul of St. Francis Xavier, would make the ideal missionary. These three giants of sanctity are quite according to your spirit and your calling, and all three are a model for all by their incomparable simplicity and depth of learning and of form. If all priests are soldiers, missionaries are far more so. Many priests envy your vocation, but this is because they consider its magnificent ideal, rather than the daily monotony of a battlefield; they forget the reality of its self-sacrifice. Therefore, many of those who envy you from a distance would not dare to share your apostolate by working with you.

B. ENDURANCE

The second characteristic of a missionary's life is endurance. Yes! If it is a question of your own soul or the souls of others, you need great endurance to overcome interior trials and exterior difficulties successfully. Fortunately, you have a special call, and with it a special grace without which even the best wills would soon succumb. Is not this true? How I wish I could preach to you as if I had fought beside you in your hard battles.

Missionaries, and future missionaries, develop within you this great virtue of endurance so that you may triumph victoriously in the perilous hours when your heart is assailed. Develop this strength by increasing your personal love for the Heart of Jesus. It is only this divine fire which can give you the secret of resistance which is greater than any natural reserve of strength. Francis Xavier was the hero of a struggle which lasted ten years without intermission; Charles de Foucauld emulated him in another path of perfect self-immolation. Both of them were upheld by a love which rendered them invincible.

Notice especially that, however wonderful the endurance of the Curé of Ars, surrounded as he was by an admiring multitude, it is completely different from that of St. Francis Xavier. He was obliged to stand alone against difficulties which not only threatened to stop his work completely, but which tended to overthrow his own interior life by casting him into the depths of discouragement. Your case is that of St. Francis Xavier. Such is God's will, and therefore through love of Him and only through love of Him you must be ready to meet the difficulties and overcome them; for God's glory is at stake.

C. LOVE FOR SOULS

If it is true that people often admire your life, it is also true that they often pity you for having no home of your own, for being deprived of the affection of your relatives and for having to live far from your own people. Those who think this way have not looked into the heart of a missionary and therefore have no idea of one of the most beautiful and noble traits of your life. This trait is the intense, holy love that you have for the souls entrusted to your care, a love which attaches you to them by chains which only Divine Love can forge. You take root among your flock, and you feel so at home among them that it is a real sacrifice to have to leave them and go elsewhere, even if, from a natural point of view, the change would be an advantage and an honor.

It is an extraordinary grace not merely to be resigned but to give your heart to a people not your own according to nature, but who in the cross and for the sake of the adorable Crucified have become the object of your solicitude, of your devotedness even unto death. This is true even when, for long periods, you taste none of the consolations and rewards that you might expect and even lawfully seek. This is because you love your vocation without being deluded either by its poetry or its prose!

Whoever you are, whether missionaries of the East or West, North or South, may you be blessed a thousand times in thus consecrating all that is best in you—your heart and your strength—to the land that you water and render fruitful by the sweat of your brow, to the people of your adoption who have become your heritage of flowers and thorns, of bitterness and of joy. I know how you love this portion of the earth which is your parish, your district, which is for you a little portion of the promised Holy Land

that you hope one day to sanctify by the supreme sacrifice
—your death. May you indeed be blessed!

Love with an ever greater love this field which you have
to clear and cultivate that it may bring forth blossom and
fruit for our Lord; love this ground that is sometimes so
barren, so ungrateful, so rebellious even against all your
efforts; love it with a holy love which, like Jesus', will cause
you to shed tears over it. The Precious Blood, and your
tears and labors, will one day yield fruit a hundredfold for
God's glory and yours.

D. JOY

All those who have been privileged to see you at your
work, to surprise you in the midst of your greatest moral
or material difficulties, have been struck with the pure and
overflowing joy which springs spontaneously from the heart
of the missionary. This characteristic is so great and remarkable that, at first sight, it is apt to deceive. In seeing
you always so happy and content, people are led to believe
that you are exempt from all difficulty and care, that the
work of spreading the Gospel is done, as it were, by magic,
without great effort and always with astonishing success.

You know by experience that such is not the life of a
true missionary. Yet in spite of frequent heavy crosses, your
heart is full of incomparable peace and joy. It is rather like
the perfect joy of St. Francis of Assisi which comes from
the stripping of oneself, from the voluntary privation of
many, even necessary things; a joy which comes from following our Lord closely, from seeking nothing but His
love and His glory; a joy in fact which fills your heart in
exchange for the weariness and trouble which you never
count too great a price to pay for souls.

This intimate joy which belongs to all good missionaries
is a divine caress and encouragement from the Lord who

thus tells you how greatly He is pleased with you even in the midst of your inevitable failures, in which you suffer in greater measure than He loses.

Cultivate in yourselves and among yourselves this holy joy which so lightens your burdens and replenishes your strength. Cherish and increase it for it is the exquisite flower of a great spirit of faithful and perfect abandonment to the divine Will. Sing a joyful hymn of thanksgiving because you are the pioneers of Christ's Gospel, the precursors of His Kingdom. Rejoice in advance at the glory which throughout eternity will be for you a heaven within your heaven. Each morning when standing at the altar, fill your heart with this living water, this pure and heavenly joy which is to spring up unto life eternal. Be the happy ones of this world, you who have willingly separated yourselves from so many things that you might enrich yourselves with the Heart of Jesus, and who for His sake enrich with truth and love those who sit in the darkness and shadow of death.

In this way you will prove the truth of words which might have been written especially for you: "Superabundo gaudio in tribulationibus meis."

E. ABANDONMENT

Lastly, I find the secret of your endurance and your joy especially in a virtue which best sums up all priestly and missionary virtues: a perfect abandonment to Divine Providence. It seems to me that you have become like sailors who are so used to the ocean, which is dangerous even when calm, that your peace never leaves you and you are always able to sleep. This is not because you are so used to danger and combat that you cease to feel them or are blinded by them. Far from it. Very often your horizon is dark and the waves threaten; but you have been formed in a splendid school of valiant courage—you have learned to confide always and in everything in a Providence that watches especially over missionaries, and therefore your peace never leaves you.

As a matter of fact, how many times in hours of peril, when humanly speaking all seemed lost, have you not strengthened and comforted each other with these simple words of supreme wisdom: "We abandon ourselves into the hands of a loving God"? Shipwreck—that is to say, the ruin of the dearest work of your life—seemed imminent, and suddenly an unlooked-for solution saved both the mission and the missionaries. And when the storm passed, how often a period of peace followed, during which a quite unexpected harvest of rich conversions was gathered in, so that you truly reaped in joy what you sowed in tears.

Steady your boat, which has to navigate such perilous waters, with the divine ballast of this complete abandonment to God. At all times, but especially during hours of anguish, it will fill you with a deep peace, and will keep perfect poise in the heart of every good missionary.

If the word "missionary," means "one sent," you must have a very great faith in Him who has sent you, and who, having sent you, knows what is necessary to accomplish His divine plan according to His Will, through the instrumentality of men and circumstances.

Therefore, you have a thousand reasons for remaining calm in the midst of storm. Do your duty. Do it, if necessary, even unto heroism. Never bargain with God. Live up to your glorious traditions, sparing neither strength nor weariness and sealing all by your blood if God so wills. But once your duty is accomplished, rest in complete abandonment to divine Providence; do not be too anxious; do not have any unreasonable fear of the wickedness of your enemies.

Peace and abandonment to God, for Divine Wisdom

guides you! Peace and abandonment, for it is God Almighty who traces out your way! Peace and abandonment, for the love of God surrounds both you and all that you love in Him and for Him—your work and the souls of which you have care! "Si Deus pro nobis quis contra nos?"

Have unbounded peace, peace in a perfect abandonment to God. When the hour of supreme justice strikes "you will see the Son of Man at the right hand of the power of God." Calling you to receive the crown of eternal life, He will say to you: "Hodie mecum eris in paradiso."

10. Doctrine of the Sacred Heart of Jesus

NOTHING is more suited to help us attain the two ideals of the priesthood—to be holy priests and successful apostles—than the doctrine of the Sacred Heart, when it is really understood according to the spirit and teaching of the Church.

How the great saints of other ages would have rejoiced in knowing the Heart of Jesus as we do today! More fortunate than they, we who are living in the full splendor of the rays from that divine Sun—the Heart of Jesus—should know how to profit fully from the light and fire pouring forth from this adorable Heart upon the Church and upon souls.

"O Mother of fair love, Queen of the Cenacle, open to us priests the sanctuary of the Sacred Heart! Teach us to enter into this furnace of divine love in order to obtain therein the burning love we need for our own sanctification, and to enkindle the flame of love for the Sacred Heart in the souls, the families, the parishes, God has entrusted to our care."

Let us now try to fathom what St. Paul calls "the breadth and length and height and depth" of the love of God, manifested to the world by the love of Jesus Christ.

Theologically speaking, what do we understand by the expression "the Heart of Jesus"? We do not mean only or principally His heart of flesh, which is worthy of adoration as is the whole divine Person. Under the symbol of a physical heart the Church teaches us the same doctrine taught by St. John: *"Deus caritas est"*—"God is love." Further, the fact that our Lord Jesus Christ is the God-Man is the revelation of that infinite love which is God the Father: "I have loved you with an everlasting love" (cf. John 31:3).

Again, even as all the relations of God with His creatures begin and end in love and by love, so also, as creatures, all our relations with our Creator must, "through Jesus Christ," have their starting point and their completion in and by love.

Notice how this *Deus-Caritas* in giving Himself to us gives us only love, and likewise in exercising His rights over us, asks in return only for the love of His creatures. This led St. Paul to say "Love therefore is the fulfillment of the Law" (Rom. 13:10). To confirm and to accentuate this law of love, which embraces the entire economy of the reciprocal relations between heaven and earth, the apostle breaks forth into the most astonishing and sublime passage in all his famous epistles: "If I should speak with the tongues of men and of angels, but do not have charity, I have become as sounding brass or a tinkling cymbal. And if I have prophecy and know all mysteries and all knowledge, and if I have all faith so as to remove mountains, yet do not have charity, I am nothing. And if I distribute all my goods to feed the poor, and if I deliver my body to be burned, yet do not have charity, it profits me nothing" (I Cor. 1–3).

In this sense—and it is the only doctrinal one—"Cor

Jesu" is not a mere devotion in the ordinary and popular sense of the word but a wonderful synthesis of Catholic dogma and morals. This was the way a former archbishop of Poitiers explained to a young priest how he understood the theology of the Sacred Heart: "My dogma—*dilexit me.* My morals—*diliges*—this is what I mean by *Cor Jesu.*"

The doctrine of the Sacred Heart can be summed up in what I call "the Gospel of the Heart of Jesus" in three chapters.

The first chapter: because of His infinite, incomprehensible love, God willed to redeem the guilty world. He might have done this in one of a thousand ways, each one worthy of His divine Majesty. But He chose the lowliest way of all, that of humiliation: "*Et verbum caro factum est.*"

If a simple child or a learned theologian asks the why and the wherefore of this mystery there is but one answer —the only one that is enlightening, the only doctrinal one —the answer given by God Himself: "*Sic Deus dilexit mundum*"—love!

Let us now turn the page to *the second chapter.* The Incarnation was more than enough to save a thousand worlds, and yet God willed to do more. He did not have to become incarnate, yet He was made man. Having accomplished this stupendous miracle, being God, He did not have to die, yet He willed to become a corpse: "*Crucifixus, mortuus et sepultus.*" The astonished angels ask the "why" and "wherefore." For them as well as for us, the answer is the same: "*Sic Deus dilexit mundum.*" The "folly of the cross" can be explained only by the excess and folly of a divine love.

The third chapter: before dying and returning to His Father, Christ determined not to leave us orphans. And so, on Holy Thursday, the Man-God of the Incarnation and of the cross gave Himself to us until the end of time in the Holy Sacrifice of the Mass and in the Blessed Sacrament.

Before you ask the "why" and the "wherefore," I forestall you and repeat the words which give us the key to this mystery: "Having loved His own who were in the world, He loved them unto the end." . . . "Sic Deus dilexit mundum." The infinite charity of God; the love—and nothing but the infinite love—of Jesus Christ, is the only adequate explanation of this supreme gift of God.

Now, which one of these three chapters contains the true doctrine of the Sacred Heart? Is it the first, the Incarnation? Is it the second, the cross? Or is it the third, the Holy Eucharist? Obviously, we may prefer to meditate on or preach about one or another of these three marvelous mysteries, according to our personal devotion and attraction: "The spirit breathes where He wills."

Thus in the annals of the Church we have a great number of saints who have been attracted especially by the Incarnation. An example would be St. Thérèse of Lisieux. Many others have been fascinated by the beauty of the cross; for instance, St. Francis of Assisi and St. John of the Cross. Still others have devoted their lives to loving the Blessed Sacrament, towards which they felt a special attraction. Among these we might mention St. Paschal Baylon, Father Eymard, or St. Juliana of Falconieri. In each instance these saints followed the inspiration of the Holy Spirit according to their special vocation.

But from the moment we speak of the *doctrine* of the Sacred Heart, and not of personal attraction and devotion, there will be no longer a question of one or another of the three chapters, but of *all three. Together* they form the integral Gospel of the love of God manifested by the Incarnation of the Word, by His Passion and death and by the incomparable gift of Himself in the Holy Eucharist. Thus the Summa Theologica contained in these words of

St. John, "Deus caritas est," is not to be found in one chapter more than in another, but in the three fused into one.

⁓⦿⦿⁓

If I were called upon to reproduce this doctrine in the form of a picture, I would present it as a triptych. In the center I would place St. Thomas Aquinas kneeling in adoration before the Blessed Sacrament, singing his marvelous Tantum Ergo. On the right would be St. Thérèse of the Child Jesus with arms outstretched towards the divine Babe of Bethlehem; on the left, Murillo's painting of Jesus crucified, embracing St. Francis of Assisi. In the center, also kneeling before the Blessed Sacrament, we see St. Margaret Mary. Suddenly these three saints raise their eyes as though called by a mysterious voice. There above the altar they see our Lord as He appeared at Paray-le-Monial, His transpierced Heart all on fire in the wound of His sacred side.

Then St. Margaret Mary bids the three of them to notice how they find in "this Heart which has so loved men," the mysteries each of them symbolizes: the humiliation of the Incarnation, the folly of the cross, and the annihilation of the Eucharist, "Behold," she repeats, "this Love which has so loved men." Joining my voice to hers I add: "Who would not love in return One who has loved us so much? In exchange for His love, our love; in exchange for His Heart, our hearts. 'My son, give Me thy heart.'"

As far as sublime and abstract ideas can be painted on canvas, I think this triptych sums up the doctrine of the Sacred Heart very clearly and exactly.

⁓⦿⦿⁓

According to this reasoning, which combines doctrine and love, theory and life, I find the Heart of Jesus—that is to say, His love—in His entire adorable Person:

In His head crowned with thorns through love;

In His eyes which shed tears of love;

In His mouth which thirsted and spoke only words of love;

In His hands pierced through love;

In His feet transfixed through love;

In His side opened through love;

In His whole body which became a living wound of love.

Therefore with a saintly cardinal I repeat: "Jesus Christ whole and entire is nothing else but an infinite heart."

And just as His divine Person is love, so do all His works proclaim His love and claim ours in return: the Creation, the Redemption, the priesthood, the Holy Sacrifice, the tabernacle, grace, the communion of saints, and our Lady. Furthermore, Jesus tells us the entire law is comprised in two commandments, the love of God and neighbor; but the second is absolutely dependent upon and presupposes the first.

The Heart of Jesus, then, is the center from which emanate as from a furnace of love all the divine actions and toward which all things in the divine plan converge. It is logical therefore to conclude that *Cor Jesu* is not a mere chapter, or tract, but a complete *summa* of the most sublime doctrine. In this sense heaven will be an everlasting feast of the Sacred Heart.

It is evident then that there is nothing new as far as the *doctrine* of the Sacred Heart is concerned—it is found in the revelations of the Gospel. But as regards the *form*, the external liturgical cult of the Sacred Heart, this is new, dating from the revelations of Paray-le-Monial.

Here is one example of what I call "new" in worship and form: the solemn feast of the Sacred Heart, raised by Pope Pius XI to a feast of the first class and celebrated on the

Friday following the octave (now suppressed) of the Feast of Corpus Christi, according to the explicit request of our Lord to St. Margaret Mary.

Yes, we must never forget that the essential doctrine of the Heart of Jesus is the very substance of dogma itself. This is so true that we can affirm that in order to preach the doctrine of the Sacred Heart we have no need of St. Margaret Mary. The Gospel and our theology suffice. If, with the Church, I love and admire the great events of Paray it is because I find them to be in perfect harmony with the Gospel, as regards their requests, their spirit and their promises.

Notice for example how the adorable Master returns to Paray with identically the same aim and plan as when He came to Bethlehem, to Calvary and to our altars: to give love and to receive love; to conquer and draw hearts to His Heart. In Palestine and in Paray He suffers from the same thirst, the thirst for love. He came to earth twenty centuries ago and He appeared at Paray, for the same purpose, to enkindle a fire upon earth: "I have come to cast fire upon the earth, and what will I but that it be kindled?"

Yes, agreeing wholeheartedly with the Church's verdict on the revelations at Paray-le-Monial, we can affirm that they had no other aim than to increase the knowledge and the spirit of our adoption as sons of God, stressing our relations with God through Jesus the Mediator, accentuating the principle of a love "strong as death," and reaffirming, as the foundation of the life of the soul and of its ascension to the Father and to the Blessed Trinity, the queen of all the virtues, love. This is the real meaning of those words addressed by our Lord to St. Margaret Mary, words that have now become a classic: "I will reign through My Heart!" He wishes to conquer, to triumph through charity, through love.

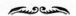

One last word on the "nova et vetera" of the doctrine
of the Sacred Heart: St. Francis de Sales says most beautifully: "If an autopsy had been performed on the body of
Jesus as is done with kings, it would have been discovered
that the wound in the Heart of Jesus did not date from
the blow of the lance on Calvary, but rather from the Incarnation—that Jesus was born with a wounded heart, a
heart wounded by love."

Paray drew attention to the opened side so that we might
enter therein and understand by meditation and prayer
what St. Francis de Sales tells us, "if the wound made by
the lance dates from yesterday, the lance only tore the
curtain that we might see the wound of eternal love."

The Son of God came to earth primarily to reveal to us
the love God has had for us from all eternity. He came to
Paray-le-Monial for the same reason: to remind us of this
everlasting love and to plead for the love of our hearts in
return.

Profit from this doctrinal devotion to the divine Heart
of Jesus to develop your interior life, for your own benefit
and for that of others. In this regard I call your attention
to two promises of the Sacred Heart, to my mind the greatest of all those made at Paray. The first concerns priestly
holiness: "Fervent souls shall rise speedily to great perfection." God is faithful, always and in all things, and especially so when it is a question of a cause above all others
so dear to His Heart, the sanctification of His priests.

The second promise has to do with your *cura animarum:*
"I will give to priests the power of touching the hardest
hearts." If you wish to possess the true secret of converting
the most obstinate sinners, if you wish to see a desert
bloom for the glory of the Lord of the harvest, then take
the triumphant standard of the Heart of Jesus, and with
it make Him the loving King of souls, of homes, of your
parish and of all your organizations; make this loving King

the center of all hearts; preach His love and His mercy; be genuine apostles of His Sacred Heart.

One day not only your faith but also your experience will prove to you how great is His fidelity in keeping and even surpassing His promises in favor of priests, who like John, are friends and apostles of His transpierced Heart. Ask the Mother of fair love to obtain for you the science of the saints *par excellence*, the one that comprises all others and without which they are useless: "The science of the love of Christ." For Jesus Himself has told us: "If anyone love me . . . my Father will love him and we will come to him and make our abode with him."

Abide in His love, for "love is the fulfillment of the Law." "Thou shalt love . . . this is the first and the greatest of the commandments . . . My son, give Me thy heart." Love with a manly love the Heart of the God who has loved you so much.

In addition to trust, the spirit of sacrifice and apostolic zeal—those three great proofs of your love—your daily Mass must be the hearth at which to enkindle the love which is so necessary for your personal sanctification and the sanctification of others.

Utilize the solid doctrine of the Sacred Heart to strengthen between your heart and His that bond of intimate friendship which He longs to see established between Himself and His priests.

It was not in vain that the Saviour explicitly promised to "raise to a high degree of perfection the faithful disciples of His adorable Heart." No priest worthy of the name would want to bypass such a marvelous blessing. Yours is the privilege of taking the place of St. John, the beloved disciple. It is yours by right, because you are priests. It was on the same Heart, whose beatings were heard by John at the Last Supper, that have been formed the saints, missionaries and martyrs. For, once again, devotion to the Sacred

Heart of Jesus, is not "a" devotion but a *life of love*: the practice of that manly virtue which is the queen of virtues and which sums up all the rest, "the science of the love of Christ."

Become a part of this movement which is a veritable breath of the Holy Spirit, flooding the Church with light and fire. Under the slogan of "Cor Jesu Sacratissimum, adveniat regnum tuum," it has become the inspiration and motivating force of all modern apostolates.

Do all in your power to make Jesus' love better known and loved, for even among the good, it is so little known. Strengthen their faith, yes, but at the same time increase their love of our Lord, give them His Heart. Otherwise you run the risk of forming lukewarm Catholics lacking love for the Eucharist, the spirit of sacrifice and zeal.

Catholics who believe are to be found everywhere, but far too many have only a spark of love, and some, none at all. It was this lack of love on the part of His friends that occasioned the bitter complaints of our Lord at Paray. As Pope Pius XI stated in his encyclical on reparation, this is the origin of the practices of reparation now widespread in the Church, such as the Holy Hour, First Friday Communions of reparation, and the great feast of the Sacred Heart.

For your part, fulfill generously all the requests made by the Sacred Heart and which have been seconded by the Church, and one day you will learn from a happy experience how royally faithful He is to His promises.

For I desired mercy
(Osee 6:6).

11. Merciful Love

MANY long years of preaching to the clergy, both diocesan and regular, have profoundly convinced me that we priests, even more than the faithful, badly need a great deal of encouragement which I call "moral oxygen" for the heart. Why? Because the struggle for priestly perfection is always rugged and rough, and the path is strewn with a thousand obstacles from within and without.

Again, even among the best of us, reserves of energy and good will are quickly used up, and we do not always see the ground gained or the progress made. On the other hand, our faults and failings stare us in the face.

If this is true of our interior life, what are we to say of that other battle in which we are engaged, the battle to do good, to save souls, to maintain the ground won so painfully, and to push on to new victories for the Master? How many combined circumstances there are that seem to be opposing our work: lack of personnel, of resources, of health, of encouragement. There are times when we seem to be overwhelmed by feelings of depression and discouragement.

Perhaps this happened to you yesterday, or maybe you are facing a similar crisis today. In any case, to strengthen and encourage you, allow me to say to you as did the angel

97

to the prophet: "Take this bread; arise and eat: for thou hast yet a long way to go."

What is this bread at once so palatable and so strengthening, and so necessary for the priest and missionary? It is the doctrine of mercy. Believe me, it is the Heart of Jesus Himself who prepared this bread for you, and He gives it to you not only during the retreat but for your entire life. "Take and eat" without limit for the adorable Master has told us: "Misericordiam volo."

⁓⁓∾∽⁓⁓

First of all, are the words mercy and love equivalent terms? Not always! For instance, the fallen angels were created through God's wisdom and love, but they never experienced His mercy. After having been masterpieces of His love they became demons.

On the other hand, man, likewise created by God's wisdom and love, was ransomed by the mercy of the same God who became man and died to save him. This is the reason the devil cried out in despair during an exorcism, "Why did you receive mercy after your sin and not I?"

Only those who have been baptized in the blood of our Saviour will be able to say in heaven, "Thou hast redeemed us for God with Thy blood" (Apoc. 5:9), while the angels will have to adore in silence.

The longer I preach, the more this doctrine becomes an obsession with me, because the older you get the more you understand that your faults are due almost always to weakness, and rarely to malice. This means that everyone needs mercy: the saints, because they know they cannot rely on the weak reed of human nature; the large army of those struggling to sanctify themselves, who therefore know their need of conversion.

I have never regretted having preached this doctrine in season and out of season and to all types of souls. Every-

where I have been overwhelmed with surprises—surprises
that would be wonderful were it not for the sad fact that
they revealed, even in the very sanctuary itself, the presence
of living corpses that divine mercy alone was capable of
resurrecting.

⁓◦⁓

What is the meaning of mercy according to the Gospel?
It signifies a divine predilection for the weak, for the sick,
for the abandoned, for the despised and the outcasts. In
order to discover Jesus it was only necessary to seek out the
sinners or the downtrodden: there He could always be
found.

Oh, the wonderful scandal of the Saviour openly seeking
the company of the publicans, even asking them for hospi-
tality and offering them, together with His friendship, the
honor of being associated with His work of salvation! In
Zaccheus and Levi we find the personification of a system
inaugurated by Jesus and which was an unheard of innova-
tion. What prophet could say as He did, "The Son of Man
came to seek and to save what was lost" (Luke 19:10)?

This special love for the lost sheep of the flock is so
outstanding that the parable of the prodigal son expressly
brings out the indignation and jealousy of the older son
who remained faithful. He had nothing to complain about,
everything belonged to him. But the Heart of God the
Saviour was reaffirming His right to celebrate a great ban-
quet in heaven in honor of the repentant sinner, rather
than for the ninety-nine just who persevered. Needless to
say, since then this familiar doctrine is always new and up-
to-date.

For instance, I have known the case of a priest who, because of his weakness, badly needed mercy, but who re-
sisted all the attempts of the Good Shepherd to bring him
back. Finally, after many long years, he was captured by

the infinite mercy of the Heart of Jesus, the only possible explanation for such a conversion. You should have seen the old priest weeping tears of joy, of sorrow and of gratitude! We cannot repeat too often that Jesus was, and always will be, above all else, a Saviour for those He has redeemed. By this I mean that here below, *in via*, en route to our heavenly home, Jesus is more a patient, kind and merciful Saviour than a terrible and severe Judge. That is why He waits ten, twenty, fifty years or more, in order to show mercy, even though it be at the eleventh hour.

Never forget, never tone down the strong and consoling doctrine of mercy found on every page of the Gospel. When we stand before the divine tribunal strict and rigorous justice will be meted out to us. In the meantime, along the way, we will find the Heart of a Saviour-God who wants us to have life, and life in abundance. "*Copiosa apud eum redemptio*" (Ps. 129:7).

There is another aspect of mercy: an offended God takes the first step towards His ungrateful sons, become His executioners. He pleads with them, He begs them to be willing to receive His forgiveness; to spare Him the sorrow of having to punish them.

Yes, the initiative for every reconciliation between the sinner and Christ, whom he crucified, has always been taken by the Victim. The unanswerable, the overwhelming argument for all this is the Incarnation. The Word "*descendit de coelis propter nostram salutem.*"

It is a remarkable fact that Sacred Scripture nowhere mentions a word about guilty Adam imploring forgiveness: on the contrary it is an offended God who offers it to him the very day of the fall. And so the Father sends His only Son in pursuit of sinners. Ever since then it is the story of the Good Shepherd looking for the lost sheep.

It is impossible to imagine peace on earth or in heaven apart from God. We cannot do without Him. And yet by sin we leave Him, we eliminate Him from our lives. He is the Supreme Being who has no need of His creatures and even less so when His subjects rebel and are knowingly guilty of sin.

But here is the unfathomable mystery: It is precisely this God of Majesty who, because of His thirst for my love and His desire for my happiness, forgets my ingratitude, comes to meet me, to conquer me with the treasures of His tenderness and His mercy. This is a wonderful and beautiful doctrine, but even greater are the miracles which confirm it.

For instance, I had enthroned the Sacred Heart of Jesus in the home of a bitter enemy of the Church. He had tolerated the ceremony out of politeness and love for his family. After a great deal of prayer and assurance from the members of his family that they would be frequent communicants and fervent apostles of the Sacred Heart, I decided on a plan which at that time seemed a foolish provocation. With no claim whatever to his friendship I wrote him a note, telling him in the name of the Sacred Heart to meet me the following Friday in order to make his confession.

It was really Jesus seeking out His enemy!

What a wonderful surprise it was for me and for his family when, at the appointed time, he arrived prepared to make a good confession. To be sure his feelings would not get the best of him, he had written down his sins, which he read with every mark of true contrition. The following day during my Mass he made his first Holy Communion at the age of seventy!

The joy in Heaven, predicted by our Lord, must have been undescribable.

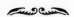

Mercy sometimes means a long and fearsome struggle for the Good Shepherd to reclaim a lost sheep fighting to escape. One would think this soul were the apple of His eye, so great is His desire to win it for heaven. Not satisfied with the miracle of his cross, He multiplies marvelous stratagems in order to conquer His prey. And the more ungrateful and guilty the sinner, the greater His efforts.

An example: I knew a clerical prodigal son who had "civilem . . . attentaverat." He had made up his mind to steel himself against grace, under the pretext of old age and a false sense of loyalty. I can still see him, fighting desperately for four days against grace. But the merciful Heart of Jesus was stronger than he, and he finally had the courage to break his bonds. He left without even getting his personal effects. He is dead now, and in heaven must be "singing the mercies of the Lord forever!"

We have cost Him so much! For this reason, and because He knows our weakness so well, Jesus forgives easily.

Another mysterious quality of divine mercy is the simplicity with which an offended God pardons His guilty creatures. Not a word was spoken by Mary Magdalene; the woman taken in adultery was dragged unwillingly to the feet of Jesus; the paralytic did not ask for pardon, but sought only a physical cure. The same was true of the blind man whose healing caused such a stir. In each of them our Lord saw the depths of their sins, but he also saw their unexpressed sorrow, and so to all of them he said the same thing: "Thy sins are forgiven thee, go in peace and sin no more." This is why He came to earth: to show forth the goodness and the mercy of His Father, of whom He is the substantial Splendor.

So great was the novelty of this doctrine of mercy, that in the early days of the Church some of the Gospel stories of His forgiveness of great sinners were suppressed.

What else is the wonderful and often forgotten dogma of the communion of saints but a marvelous proof of divine mercy? Mercy is the only explanation for the fact that you and I are permitted to pay each other's debts, thereby saving one another from the punishment of hell.

Why did God not force the guilty sinner to pay his own debts contracted by his sins? We find Him doing just the opposite. His infinite mercy, which has foreseen every detail of our lives, which is constantly hovering around us, is determined that we shall be saved at any cost. Over and over again, it is the story of the arms of the Good Shepherd pressing the prodigal son, the lost sheep, to His Heart, offering complete pardon and an eternity of happiness in heaven.

The price of these miracles of mercy and salvation is the countless sacrifices and prayers of that army of living victims whose self-immolation is the most glorious of apostolates. St. Teresa of Avila was a soul of this stamp; more recently and even more evidently, St. Thérèse of Lisieux, that wonderful missionary of love. Following their example, thousands of other hidden apostles continue to people heaven with the souls they save through their prayers and sacrifices. How often an act of pure love, a sacrifice, has won the grace of salvation for a dying sinner, about to be plunged into hell!

I knew a sister, whose brother had been leading a life of sin. For years she had been praying and sacrificing for his conversion. As time went by, he grew worse. All hope seemed to have been lost. Yet she never gave up praying nor did she falter in her trust in the mercy of the Sacred Heart. One day she received the sad news from her family that her brother had committed suicide. He jumped from a high bridge over a river and was drowned. Everyone who knew him thought he had lost his soul. All except his sister. It was impossible, she reasoned, that the years of

prayers and sacrifice would be in vain. Somehow, she believed, her brother had been saved.

God rewarded her faith in a remarkable way. One night
she was awakened and in her room saw her brother in the
flames of purgatory. He thanked her for her prayers and
her faith. Although he was suffering in purgatory, his soul
was saved. "God gave me the grace to make an act of contrition as soon as I jumped from the bridge." Between the
bridge and the river! I would not advise anyone to try
that. . . .

We priests should never forget that our own vocation is
an act of mercy shown to us by our Lord. Let it always be
a canal through which floods of mercy pour out on souls
entrusted to our care. We are proofs that the Master never
abandons the sinner, the prodigal son, the lost sheep, but
rather seeks him out wherever he may be. Priests are living
reproductions of Him whom the Father sent into the world
for the salvation of those who live in the shadow of death.
"As the Father has sent me so also I send you." We are
living proofs and perfect examples of the doctrine, "I will
have mercy. . . ." The priest preaches mercy and he shows
mercy. This being so, you can expect to receive mercy in
abundance both in life and in death. "Blessed are the
merciful, for they shall obtain mercy" (Matt. 5:7).

In your hours of difficulty, in the face of obstacles that
discourage you and cause you to lose confidence; when
Satan tries to discourage you by pointing out your weaknesses and exaggerating your deficiencies; especially when
he tries to convince you that all your efforts to sanctify
yourself and others are a waste of energy, then is the time
to hold fast to the solid doctrine of blind confidence in the
merciful love of the Heart of Jesus.

Yes, preach divine mercy to others, but above all apply
this consoling doctrine to yourself. By so doing you will
please the Heart of Jesus; He will supply for what is want-

ing in you and will preserve your soul "unto life everlasting."

For a priest who *lives* the doctrine of mercy, there is no
problem in believing in it. But we cannot stop there. We
must hand it on to others, in the confessional, in the pulpit, and whenever we come in contact with souls, with
their thousand and one problems. Explain often to them
that wonder of mercy, their baptism. Stir up their zeal for
the salvation of others by giving them a clear picture of
the meaning of the dogma of the communion of saints,
that outstanding proof of divine mercy. Let this limitless
treasure of grace be for them a stimulus to work for the
conversion of those who do not have the gift of faith or
for those who have lost it.

Most Sacred Heart of Jesus, burning with love
for me, inflame my heart with love for Thee!

I know whom I have believed
(II Tim. 1:12).

12. Confidence!

LAKE GENESARETH is still shrouded in cloudy darkness. Suddenly, as the disciples struggle against the storm, Jesus comes walking to them upon the water. They fail to recognize Him, and are seized with terror, taking Him for a phantom. Suddenly, they hear these reassuring words, "Fear not . . . it is I."

What doctrinal truths are contained in these few words of the Master! "Fear not." Why? Because, "It is I." If I were an angel, a prophet, even a saint, you would have reason to fear, for none of these could know you through and through as I do. Above all not one of them can offer you infinite mercy and forgiveness. But, because "it is I," Jesus, you have nothing to fear. Place all your trust in Me!

How badly we priests need the doctrine of confidence! "Once he finds himself in the ranks of the combatants," says Cardinal Manning, "no priest has any reason to fear."

Yet because of our terrific responsibilities, resulting from our duty of saving souls, we sometimes think we have found a pretext for giving in to discouragement. Add to this the daily realization of our weakness, and our lack of trust often does seem justified.

Certainly we have to be practical and be reminded, or remind ourselves, of the dangers we incur by neglecting our duties and otherwise trifling with grace. Some retreat masters and writers, however, seem to go too far, driving priests further down into the slough of despondency rather than giving them the encouragement they need and deserve. We must always counterbalance the dark side of the picture with the doctrine that alone is capable of imparting new supernatural energy, the doctrine of confidence. Side by side with the abyss of our miseries we must place the deeper abyss of divine mercy. If our wretchedness is great, we must likewise clearly state that the remedy—mercy—is infinite and its source close at hand.

How can a priest be a good Samaritan to others, if he himself is weighed down by his own shortcomings, is helpless to react against them, and drags himself along because of his lack of trustful love?

First of all, confide blindly in the infinite wisdom of Him who alone knows how to draw good from evil, health and strength from illness, and life from death itself. Have such a tremendous faith in the *wisdom* of God, that you let Him do with you whatever He wants. Allow Him to work out His plans as He wills, to the extent of going against your own plans, overthrowing your own projects, even though they be, as far as you can see, for His honor and glory.

Trust in His divine wisdom, which never destroys except to rebuild with eternity in view; which never sends a trial except to give peace and joy to the soul that He permits to suffer.

Trust in the divine wisdom that has mysterious plans which escape our comprehension. He Himself has said,

"For my thoughts are not your thoughts: nor your ways my ways, saith the Lord" (cf. Is. 55:8).

When I was a young priest in Valparaíso, Chile, after much begging and hard work, I succeeded in building a law school. Three months after its dedication in 1906, an earthquake leveled it to the ground. At the time I was tempted to ask, "Why? Why did You allow this to happen? This was for You and Your glory." But I did not, and today I know the reason God permitted this catastrophe. Had it not been for the earthquake I would not have had the great privilege of becoming a world-wide preacher of the merciful love of the Sacred Heart.

What marvels are being accomplished daily by God's wisdom! Only in eternity will they be unfolded before our astonished eyes. Then we shall clearly see the orderly course of events great and small, events permitted or willed, now inexplicable puzzles but in heaven seen as part of God's wonderful plan.

Eternity will be all too short to thank and praise this infinite Wisdom which, without ever consulting us, so often went against our ideas and projects, causing us suffering and sorrow only that we might be happy in heaven. Like little children we often rebelled, but there the purpose and tenderness of these seeming cruelties will be made clear. How well will we understand the wisdom and folly of the cross, and the unreasonable folly of our arguments, our calculations, our poor human wisdom! Perhaps if our Lord had permitted us to carry out our plans, we might have been lost forever.

This is what the Sacred Heart had in mind when He said to St. Margaret Mary, "Give Me a free hand . . . let Me do what I please." In these words we will find our security, our merit and our peace.

I once had to change trains going from Lourdes to Paris. By mistake I got aboard the wrong train. By the time I found out my error, my train had left. Naturally I felt annoyed, for it meant I would arrive many hours late for a retreat. But when I saw the next day's paper, I realized what a providential mistake it was. The train I should have taken never arrived in Paris; it was wrecked in a terrible accident, in which many were killed and injured.

We have all had similar experiences. They should teach us to never to get upset if things turn out different from the way we had planned. Never ask for explanations. Simply trust blindly the One who loves us and who permits many mysterious things to happen to us, because He loves us. Always take Jesus' "train" and you cannot make a mistake!

A second source of peace and confidence is the infinite *justice* of God, that justice so extraordinarily beautiful and so badly understood, so reassuring yet so calumniated, even by educated Catholics. How many there are who look upon it as synonymous with punishment and hell!

It is all too common to attribute damnation to justice and salvation to merciful love. Yet the truth is there are as many souls in heaven because of God's justice as because of His love.

Too often we forget that precisely because God is just He must be tender and bountiful. That wonderful little theologian St. Thérèse understood this when she wrote, "I trust His justice as much as I do His love."

Quite the contrary was the statement of a converted sinner, who in his happiness at being restored to the friendship of a God from whom he had expected nothing but punishment, made this classical remark to me: "Fortunately for me, God is *unjust*—otherwise I wouldn't be here!"

Yes, fortunately for us, we shall all one day be judged,

not by an unjust judge, but by a Judge of infinite justice, who knows and weighs all the evidence; who, unlike men, is able to distinguish between ignorance, weakness and malice; who, consequently, never makes a mistake. His decisions are always just because they are based on infinite wisdom.

This infinitely just Judge cannot demand of a fledgling what He expects of an eagle. That is why, to the astonishment and even scandal of certain severe, ignorant or hypocritical minds, Jesus pardons great sinners far more easily than does the most loving of mothers. He knows us far better than our own mothers know us.

What surprises await us in Heaven! Remember the three great surprises enumerated by Gregory the Great? The first, "I am in Heaven!" What a surprise for those who feared God's justice so much. The second, the fact that some soul you thought so pious, so saintly, "hasn't arrived yet!" The third, when you see someone you did not like on earth, "What are you doing here?" What a surprise!

How I love St. Paul's words on this subject, words inspired by deep conviction: "There is laid up for me a crown of justice, which the Lord, the just Judge, will give to me in that day" (II Tim. 4:8). Notice that St. Paul does not appeal to the Saviour of Mercy but to the Judge of infinite Justice, claiming the crown He has promised and which, he says, He owed him in strict justice.

Had St. Paul forgotten his violent persecution of and hatred for Christians? Had he forgotten his past sins? Not at all. Because he believed with a firm faith in the pardon promised to him ("but I obtained the mercy of God because I acted ignorantly, in unbelief" [I Tim. 1:13]), he did not hesitate to claim his reward.

How few Catholics—even priests—reason this way! Many look back over their lives and worry over past sins; by their attitude they seem to doubt God's pardon, and thus offend both the justice and the mercy of God.

This deplorable and dangerous frame of mind is due to a certain Jansenistic spirit which is still quite widespread. Jansenism, which dries up the heart and freezes the blood, is rooted in a hidden pride; it is still the worst of heresies for it has succeeded principally in deceiving many of the leaders among the elite.

Years ago, when preaching in England, a bishop said to me, "Father the nuns to whom you are going to preach have the reputation of never smiling. If you can change this Jansenistic spirit it will be the greatest thing you have ever done."

On my way to the convent I wondered what I could do to break the ice. I hit upon a scheme. As soon as the sad looking portress opened the door I told her to inform Reverend Mother I wished to speak to the entire community in the chapter room at once. Sister was to take me there immediately. Startled though she was by this unusual request, she left to carry out my instructions.

Standing in the back of the chapter room I watched the nuns file in, one by one. They were indeed a sad looking group, and the saddest of all was the Reverend Mother.

When all were assembled, I pretended to want to leave, saying I had made a mistake, that I was told by the bishop I was going to preach to a community of *sisters*. "Well, what do you think we are?" demanded the superior, rising to the bait.

Then I struck home. "You are not *sisters*, you are a community of *war widows* mourning the loss of your husbands!"

The startled sisters raised their eyes in surprise. Then someone laughed and soon the entire group burst out laughing. Seizing the opening I proceeded then and there to give them a badly needed lesson on joy and happiness, on trust and confidence in religious life.

Later the bishop told me, "That is one of the greatest miracles I have ever heard of!"

The third reason we should trust the Sacred Heart of Jesus is because of His infinite *love* for us.

Rare indeed are those who can say with St. John, "And we have come to know, and have believed, the love that God has in our behalf" (I John 4:16). Truly we can say, "He came unto His own, and His own knew Him not."

Yet God is nothing but love; Jesus is love. When He commands, when He forbids, when He rewards, when He corrects, when He punishes, it is always the Heart of Jesus manifesting itself. Even the severity which God sometimes displays here on earth is only the proof of His infinite mercy. It is His Heart chastising in time, that He may save in eternity. That is why rigorous justice in this world is in reality infinitely tender and merciful, for it often spares us a terrible purgatory and even hell itself.

Here is an example. A priest was severely punished by his bishop even though his guilt was not fully proved. Everyone agreed the punishment was too severe and friends of the priest all feared a violent reaction. But the excessive severity proved to be a boon. It opened his eyes, he acknowledged his wrong, accepted his penance, and made reparation for the harm he had done. He became a fervent priest and often thanked the divine mercy that inspired the severity of the bishop.

In our own case, is it not true that as we look back, our physical and moral trials, the bitterness we often had to suffer, the contradictions we have met with, have all been permitted by divine Providence, and have proved to be blessings in disguise, gifts of the loving Heart of Jesus?

You will never make a mistake when in your darkest and most painful hours, whether it is a question of your own interior life or your work for souls, you show a blind and unshakeable trust in the Heart of Jesus. Under the guise of virtue you can fear to excess, but you can never exaggerate the trust and confidence that go hand in hand with love and humility. In fact, it is precisely because you acknowledge your weakness and helplessness, which is true humility, that you should have such childlike trust in the Heart of Jesus. "I know whom I have believed."

The loving confidence I urge you to have is not a virtue for saints confirmed in grace, but rather for those striving to become holy, who are fully conscious of the *"fomes peccati"*—their potentiality for sinning. Trustful love, or loving confidence, is above all for the weak who want to become strong, for those who know their own sinfulness by painful experience, but who in their humility sincerely wish to react against the current of human nature that would drag them down. For your encouragement, keep in mind that eighty-five per cent of the saints were penitents!

St. Thérèse of the Child Jesus understood this doctrine. As she so admirably put it:

It is not because I have been preserved from mortal sin that I go to God with confidence and love. I feel that even if I had committed all possible crimes, I should lose nothing of my trust; but with a heart broken with sorrow and repentance I should throw myself into the arms of my Saviour. I know how He cherished the prodigal son; I have heard His words to Mary Magdalen, to the woman taken in adultery, and to the Samaritan woman. No, no one would be able to frighten me, for I know what to expect from His love and mercy.

In other words, have boundless confidence in the Sacred Heart, *not in spite of but because of* your wretchedness.

Jesus is our Saviour; He is our Physician, our Good Samaritan; He is the Good Shepherd. All these titles suppose on His part divine pity and infinite mercy; on our side, weakness and faults. He Himself has affirmed that "those that are well do not need a physician, but those that are sick."

In the course of my many long years of preaching I have had some very striking confirmations of this doctrine. One of them was the case of a nun who had the privilege of having our Lord as her director. The bishop asked me to talk to her a number of times. Apparently the case was genuine because of her humility and obedience.

One day after Communion the nun was crying. "Why are you crying?" asked our Lord. She answered, "Because this morning I saw myself for the first time as I really am." "And what are you?" asked Jesus. "I am nothing but a miserable rag!" Then came this wonderful answer: "If you are a miserable rag, take courage, place your trust in Me, for I am the divine Rag-picker!"

Yes, dear Fathers, He is just that, for were He not a divine Rag-picker, you and I would not be priests!"

If you would please Jesus, then, tell Him that you will keep your peace in the midst of the most violent storms; that you will acknowledge always and everywhere the reassuring and perfect harmony that exists between His justice, His wisdom and His infinite love.

And add with the psalmist: "In thee, O Lord, have I hoped, let me never be confounded" (Ps. 30:2).

The older I get the more convinced I become that we priests are not always the effective instruments of grace God wants us to be, because of our lack of confidence! If this is your case, remedy it by fighting the battle of your sanctification without ever retreating because of pessimism or discouragement. Be fearless in your ministry to souls, sustained by unshakeable trust. Stir it up especially in times of crisis, when overwhelmed with work, or stopped short by setbacks.

When, humanly speaking, you feel like doubting, that is the time to make an act of absolute faith in the wisdom, justice and love of our Lord. Hold your lines, advance, battle against the current, for if God is with you, and the Heart of Jesus is in your own heart, who can possibly have any success against you? That is the time to prove that these magnificent words were written for you: "*Et nos credidimus caritati!*"

> *Most Sacred Heart of Jesus, burning with love*
> *for me, inflame my heart with love for Thee!*

> *Most Sacred Heart of Jesus, I place my trust*
>   *in Thee!*

13. The Primacy of Love

SOMEONE has written: According to Christian ideals, St. Paul is greater than the philosophers of Greece, and the blood of martyrs more sacred than the ink of the learned. This does not mean that thought is not divine, but that love is even more divine than thought. Thought inaugurates—love achieves. Only when faith blossoms into charity does it become enlightened and operative.

Far more profound, though, are these words of St. Paul: *Plenitudo legis dilectio.* This means that the perfection of the law and of all virtue, the perfection and full realization of Christian and priestly holiness, is love. As in heaven, so here below: the queen of virtues, the only everlasting virtue, is love.

Never forget that it is possible to believe without loving; that, unfortunately, faith and charity can be separated and in practice very often are. One can have faith—even a very lively faith—and yet have only a faint spark of charity, if even that. St. Paul tells us that faith and all the other gifts are useless without charity.

All priests have faith but all do not love sufficiently. That is why our faith and our hope grow weak; they are not being nourished by the strengthening food of love.

Only in a saint do we find perfect harmony between

these two great virtues, for a saint loves with a boundless love what he believes, and he adores with an intense faith what he loves. That is why the "scientia caritatis Christi" has always been the secret and the science of the saints. For what is holiness save living through God and in God, and with God who is in us? But God is nothing but love.

Here is a very simple truth, but one which is rarely thought about: God created us only through love that we might love Him in time and in eternity. This is the essence of the Good Tidings of the Gospel and its novelty. Pagan philosophers had arrived at the knowledge of the existence and nature of God, but only Jesus Christ made known to an astonished world that God is a Father of incomparable goodness and tenderness; that we are really His children and that He desires to be loved. This is what St. Paul calls the "era of grace." Ever since this revelation of our adoption as sons in Jesus Christ there has been a new spirit in our attitude toward God; "divina institutione formati, audemus dicere: Pater noster."

This is the reason our Lord affirms that the first and the greatest commandment is: *diliges Dominum Deum tuum.* But the stupendous facts of the Incarnation, the Redemption and our priesthood oblige us to love this God who is all love far more than the commandment: "Sic nos amantem quis non redamaret?"

Add to this a personal motive for loving our Lord: all that is good in you, everything you are, all that you have received from the time of your baptism through your ordination to this very moment, your entire personal history, as God alone knows it, is nothing else but a miracle of merciful love. If this is true, then each of us should be a "miracle" of grateful love. That is why God's love presses you and surrounds you like a consuming flame: "*caritas Christi urget nos!*"

After all that has been said, it is evident that great attention must be paid to the formation of *priestly hearts*. I stress the phrase "priestly hearts" to bring out the necessity of teaching future priests to love God and His Son, whom He has sent.

The training of the intellect is certainly necessary and even indispensable. But this alone is not enough. Undoubtedly religion is truth and light, but it must be a truth lived through love.

Knowledge and love will be all one in Heaven, but here below they may be, and often are, separated. If it is true in general that *instruction* is not *education*, how much more true is it that a priest may receive a splendid intellectual formation and yet one which leaves his heart far from the ideal of holiness appropriate to his state of life?

There are plenty of specialists in the art of subtle speculation, theological and otherwise, but unfortunately saints are lacking because they do not live up to these fine principles. And the reason is obvious: they do not love. That is what the author of the *Imitation of Christ* had in mind when he wrote: "It is better to love the Blessed Trinity than to write learned dissertations about the Trinity." How often do we not find mediocrity in virtue, devotedness and zeal among those who are versed in the knowledge of the "scientia sine caritate!" For the total and integral formation of the priest more is needed than the cold artificial light of electric bulbs. What we need is the light and fire, the knowledge and love of the Sun!

In expressing my sincere convictions on this subject, please do not think I am alluding to mere sensible love or still less to a vague sentimentality—far from it! I have in mind, on the contrary, that love "strong as death" which does not consist of feelings and words but in knowing how and being willing to sacrifice self after the example of the Master, who "loved me and delivered Himself for me." It

is because too little importance is attached to this fundamental doctrine of love that often we build upon sand—
the foundation is weak.

For instance, in the formation of seminarians and priests,
stress is rightly laid upon mortification, humility, chastity
and zeal. This is good. But it is not enough. Too often not
enough emphasis is placed on the one and only thing that
can develop all these priestly virtues: the love of our Lord
Jesus Christ.

As a matter of fact, who will be more mortified than he
who is deeply in love with Jesus crucified, and therefore,
with His Cross?

Who will be truly humble to the point of dying to himself, of loving humiliations, except the one who is an intimate friend of the divine Heart of Jesus who said, "Learn
of me, for I am meek and humble of heart"?

Who will be chaste in mind and heart if not he who has
filled his heart and life with a divine love which shuts out
all unlawful earthly affections?

Who will be more eaten up with zeal for souls than the
priest who has exchanged his heart for the Heart of the
Saviour and who, because of his burning love, can say with
St. Paul: "I will most gladly spend and be spent myself
for your souls" (II Cor. 12:15)?

And who will really and truly love his brethren more
than he who has a strong personal love for God?

In the light of all this, I think I understand why our
Lord's sole complaint at Paray-le-Monial was that He was
not loved. He had every right to complain of want of faith,
of the spirit of sacrifice, of generosity. Still He only spoke
about the lack of love. Why? Because when this is missing,
everything else is missing. When we love but little or
wrongly, the spiritual life within us dies out: "Qui non
diligit manet in morte" (I John 3:14).

Make love the cornerstone of the foundation of your

spiritual life; let it be the soul of your apostolic zeal. In season and out of season meditate on this most divine of eternal truths: God is love and our baptism and our priesthood oblige us before all else to give Him total love in return, loving Him *ex toto corde, ex tota anima, ex tota mente.*

Love—love with a boundless love that your priestly work may be fruitful, that it may really give glory to God and be a source of grace for souls and for yourself. "It is God who gives the increase" and "God is love."

Love—love with a boundless love that self-sacrifice may become sweet and the cross of your vocation light, that your self-immolation may be a source of priestly sanctity for you and of supernatural life for others. To this end, *suffer through love and love through suffering.* Love is self-immolation!

Love—love with a boundless love in reparation for the shortcomings of your priestly life, to fill up what is wanting in you, to make up for what you have failed to give to God and souls. Remember "Charity covers a multitude of sins"! Love is reparation!

Finally, love—love with a boundless love, that the lamps of your hearts may be ready and burning when the Lord comes to render to each one according to His works. Love is heaven!

But if, on seeing Him at that hour, you are troubled and fearsome, may He Himself reassure you with His own words: "Pax tibi . . . noli timere . . . ego sum" (Luke 24:36)!

And if, in your humility, thinking always of your failures you reply with a justifiable filial fear: "Lord, what about my many shortcomings, my defects, my sins and my responsibilities? . . . Jesus, how can I help but fear in the presence of my Judge?" may Christ be able to console and calm you with a tender smile and with words that will enable you to expect a merciful judgment: "My friend, my priest, all that you recognize as imperfect in your life is true. But, My peace be with you!"

"But why, Lord?"

"*Because you have loved much!* You have loved Me much and you have been the apostle of My love . . . Pax!"

Then in your last agony, resting on the Heart of your Saviour, you will say to Him, if not in words at least with each beat of your heart: "I have found the Heart of a King, I have found the Heart of a Brother, I have found the Heart of a Friend, O most kind Jesus! O how good and how sweet it is to live and die in this Heart! It is good for me to be here forever!"

Unus est Magister vester . . . Jesus Christus.

14. Love that You May Understand

THE words applied to St. John, our Lord's precursor, *lucerna ardens et lucens*, should be true of every priest. Because of his mission, he should be a burning flame of love to enkindle love in the hearts of others and at the same time a burning light to enlighten and guide those whom God has entrusted to his care.

When love is not merely a spark—ordinary virtue—but an ardent flame, it always gives off a strong light which, rising from the heart of the priest to his mind, becomes for him a vital element of supernatural knowledge. Hence this axiom well-known to the saints: "Ama et cognosces—love and you will understand." This means simply: love God fervently and He will reward your love by manifesting Himself to you. Love your Saviour, and His Heart, touched by your love, will reveal secrets reserved for His intimate friends.

So often we are told: "To know God is to love Him." This is a necessary prerequisite in the philosophical order: *Nihil volitum nisi praecognitum.* But it is only the first step: "Know Me that you may love Me." The second *supernatural* step towards perfection is: "Love Me that you may know Me . . . intimately."

This is what our Lord said to St. Angela of Foligno: "He who loves in fire will know in charity."

Therefore I repeat: the flames of ardent love generate an extraordinary light in the order of divine and supernatural knowledge. Experience teaches that saints are always clear-sighted in spiritual matters, because they have been divinely enlightened. Two examples come to mind: St. Teresa of Avila and St. Thérèse of Lisieux. Both saints had a profound grasp of deep theological truths because both were on fire with love for our Lord.

This brings up an interesting question: what is a theologian in the strict sense of the word? Is he exclusively a learned priest, one versed in ecclesiastical sciences, a doctor of theology? In other words, are "theologian" and "doctor" convertible terms?

No, not always, for there are certain theologians with a true and extensive knowledge of divine things who are not doctors in the academic sense of the word. Nevertheless they merit the title of "theologian" because they have a knowledge of God and His mysteries which sometimes has a depth far exceeding that of certain doctors.

Let us never forget that the supreme pinnacle which is God—His nature, His workings through grace, His ways and His plans—infinitely surpasses the power of all created intelligences. Certainly our faculties are indispensable instruments and they are a necessary starting point. Moreover, study is a natural need and for the priest is a grave duty binding in conscience. But we must never forget that the knowledge of God and divine things acquired by study is always restricted and limited.

When the theologian, then, desires to reach the inaccessible and unapproachable heights of God, he requires other means than talent, other lights than those acquired by mere study. He must also possess the powerful and divine enlightenment that comes from prayer. Only when he really

knows how to pray, as well as and better than he knows
how to study, will heaven descend toward him and unfold
itself before him; then the man of God and of prayer will
ascend to heights unknown to the genius; then the saint
will see what the merely wise and learned will never see
nor understand.

He, then, who wishes to be a true theologian in the
spiritual sense of the word—and all priests should aspire to
possess this beautiful title—must necessarily aim at becoming, through humility and prayer, "one who sees," a *videns*,
like Moses on the mountain.

It can never be sufficiently emphasized or repeated too
often (especially to seminarians) that to know, to penetrate the mysteries of God, a theologian must be not only
a learned man, but in a far greater measure a man of deep
interior life, a man of God; not a mere searcher of libraries
but a man deeply in love with the tabernacle, a friend, and
an intimate friend, of the only real Master, Jesus Christ.

Who really knows our Lord as much as He can be known
here below? Only the friend to whom Christ manifests
Himself; only he to whom, in the intimacy of prayer, He
reveals secrets which He does not make known to the
learned ones of this world.

What astonishing things are known to the friends of
Jesus, even by those who have never studied! Thomas
Aquinas reached the skies by his prodigious talents; but
Saint Thomas went far beyond. This often happens to the
humble who have no opportunity to read or study like
Thomas, but who like him have prayed and meditated.
Revelasti parvulis. . . .

Here is a striking example I have often related and one
that caused the late Cardinal Billot to say when he heard
it, "This should be written in letters of gold as a lesson in

theology for seminarians and priests." Struck by the enlightened comments made by a peasant at Lourdes on one
of my sermons on the Sacred Heart of Jesus, the King and
Friend of Christian families, I invited him to come to my
hotel. My idea was to listen to him at my ease and take
notes on his simple but doctrinal commentaries. He came
punctually and at my request began to comment again on
the subject of my sermon. I was so amazed at the wisdom
and eloquence of this peasant that I forgot even to take
notes of his words, save for a few thoughts here and there.

However, I made up my mind I was not going to lose the
lesson so providentially given to me. So I begged him to
send me all he was saying in several letters, writing them
if he wished in pencil. For a while he was silent, but when
I insisted, he burst out laughing, saying, "But I do not
know how to read or write."

Taken off guard, I exclaimed, "Then who has taught you
all this?"

Here is the marvelous answer he gave me, spoken in
grave tones, but quite simply: "As a priest you say Mass
daily, as a Christian I receive Holy Communion daily.
Therefore we both have the same Master. It is He who has
taught me all I know."

I remained silent with astonishment. Thinking I had not
understood, he explained himself by a comparison of extraordinary doctrinal simplicity:

"Father, suppose this table were an altar. You are there
holding in your hands Jesus, the true Sun. Close to you
and to Him am I, about to receive Communion. Between
us, Jesus, the Sun. If I see Him and you do not, it is not
the fault of the Sun, but of your eyes!"

Is this not admirable? Many masters and doctors do not
know what this theologian—taught from the tabernacle—
knew.

Certainly we need theologians everywhere—men with

the theological knowledge willed by God and demanded by the Church, but also with souls aflame and hearts on fire like that of the peasant of Lourdes. Science without a deep interior life, book-theology without love of God and priestly holiness—*scientia sine caritate*—is a weak electric light that leaves vast spaces in total darkness.

Once more, studies are necessary both in and out of the seminary—for this is a duty binding in conscience. But to believe more in study than in the divine Master in the tabernacle is a grave and dangerous error, both for seminarian and for priest.

Never forget that all treatises of theology are merely prefaces to the living Book—Jesus Christ Himself! Try to acquire both "light and heat"; develop the light through the flame; love without measure, and the Lord will treat you as an intimate friend; He will manifest Himself to you as He promised: "He who loves Me will win My Father's love, and I too will love him, and will reveal Myself to him." Then, and only then, will He teach you the things He has heard from His Father, *Dixi vobis quaecumque audivi a Patre meo.*

"Come after Me," says our Lord. "I am the Light of the world and he who follows Me does not walk in darkness."

From what has been said already another important lesson can be drawn. There is not only the mystery of God but also that of souls. You are priests for them. This brings us face to face with a great mystery which engrossed all the saints and should be of paramount concern to us.

By the fact of our office as priests, we are directors and advisors, whose words, example and teaching will have eternal consequences. It has been well said, "Priests are the mouth of God, the spoken word of the invisible Word." This adds an overwhelming weight to our responsibility if we do not live up to it. And the responsibility is all the greater inasmuch as the faithful are obliged to consult us, to obey and let themselves be guided by us.

To direct souls inside of and outside of the confessional, to trace out their path, to show them their duty, to help them make decisions with consequences in time and eternity—all this is a great privilege, but also a great responsibility.

It is far from sufficient, then, that the priest be a good administrator, a good business man. God, the Church, souls, expect more from him than this. He is expected to be the father of the souls confided to him, the dispenser of the sacraments, the guide and counsellor of his people; the shepherd who knows his sheep by name. He is not only the motor which raises the plane, but also the pilot who directs its course.

Here we may ask: who is this priest who is a true counsellor and director of souls, full of wisdom, prudence, and zeal, with the tact of a father, the clear-sightedness of a doctor, the devotedness of a true apostle? This chosen and privileged priest is none other than the friend of Jesus who has already given him the key to His Heart as a reward for his piety. With this same key he can also unlock the tabernacle-door of the heart of man, for one and the same key fits the Heart of Jesus and souls!

This is the way that doctors of the Church, such as St. Francis de Sales, and simple priests like the Curé of Ars, learned to penetrate the depths of the human conscience. Certainly they consulted treatises on moral theology; but more often they consulted the Master. He is the only one who can enlighten the priest in the solution of certain cases which no book can foresee.

Be quite convinced that the "paternity of souls," even more than that of nature, is a mystery and also a gift which can come only from on high. The solution of this problem presupposes a priestly soul moulded by grace and by the twofold light of study and a deep interior life. Both are necessary in order to avoid mistakes and blunders, the consequences of which may be fatal and irreparable. *Haec oportet facere et illa non omittere.*

The art of guiding souls is a divine work and extremely difficult; only priests of much prayer, real men of God, can excel in it. To cooperate with Him in His plan of redemption, God in His wisdom never makes use of a merely "good, honest priest" who does his work mechanically, even though he be a great intellectual.

If you really want to be doctors in this double science of knowing God and of being able to penetrate into the secrets of souls, often meditate before the tabernacle on this wonderful assertion of St. Thomas Aquinas: "When I desire to see clearly and to sound the depths of some supernatural mystery, I plunge my mind, my head and my heart into the tabernacle."

To solve the problem of really knowing our Lord and souls, go often to the tabernacle to speak heart to heart with the Heart of the Master.

Magister adest et vocat te.

15. "Bethany of the Sacred Heart"[1]

I HAVE been requested to give a doctrinal definition of the work of the Enthronement of the Sacred Heart in the home, which I have been preaching for so many years. I acquiesce most willingly to this request. With the simplicity which for many years has been my sole apostolic eloquence, I shall write down, in the form of a fraternal heart-to-heart talk, just what I mean by the Enthronement, and exactly what is its doctrinal basis. The Breath of the Holy Spirit will do the rest! May the adorable Paraclete, who is Light and Fire, pour down upon these lines a veritable Pentecost, which will be at once a "vision" and a "love"! To see clearly and to love much—in these consist the classical gifts which make an apostle. May the loving Queen of Apostles and of the Cenacle take part in this modest work—for such is her right—so that its supernatural success may be as perfect as possible!

My exposition will be made up of three chapters: I. The Doctrine of the Sacred Heart of Jesus; II. The Revelation at Paray-le-Monial; III. The Enthronement of the Sacred Heart in the Home (as it has been approved and blessed by Rome). May the Well-Beloved be in my heart, and in

[1] This essay was composed in 1946 by Father Mateo, who at the time was a patient in St. Joseph's Hospital, Three Rivers, Canada. He believed this to be the best summary of the nature and spirit of the Enthronement he has ever written.

the hearts of those who will read these lines, *ut adveniat Regnum Regis amoris!* "That the kingdom of the King of Love may come!"

I. THE DOCTRINE OF THE SACRED HEART OF JESUS.

Let me make it clear at the outset that I am writing for all friends of the Sacred Heart, but especially for priests, to whom I address myself with mingled feelings of respect and priestly tenderness.

Necessarily we begin with some fundamental principles. For we must be on our guard against a deformation of our work, brought about by the very fact of its development. The evil of "elephantiasis" in Catholic activities is much more common than one thinks. The body—that is to say, the organism—very often over-develops to the detriment of the soul, the spirit. Yet, on the other hand, development is but a law of nature and of grace. As a matter of fact, every living thing in nature and in the Church must grow and evolve, or wither and die.

The same holds true of virtue and sanctity, of intellectual and moral qualities, and likewise of Catholic activities. Time was when these were but grains of mustard seed in the hands of the Sower, then growing plants, and finally great trees sheltering the birds of the air. But in their very growth there is always some danger.

This is exactly the case with the Enthronement. In 1908 in Valparaíso, Chile, it was but a grain of mustard seed; in 1946 it is, thanks be to God, a great tree whose branches cover the entire earth, and whose fruits delight the friends of the King of Love and the very angels in heaven. But, needless to say, if the roots and sap are always the same, the tree of 1946 has characteristics, or better, has developed a spiritual beauty and a supernatural fecundity which were present only potentially when the seedling was transplanted from the nursery of Paray-le-Monial to the garden of Valparaíso. And this is as it should be, for it is a perfectly normal phenomenon.

Let me explain. If those who listen to me today in Canada had heard me in 1908, they would easily remark that the style, or rather, the tone of the preacher has considerably changed, even though the dominant theme of his preaching is the same. Today there is less "color" and "music" in the presentation of his theme; for he lays greater stress on its doctrinal aspect, which he expounds, not with less sincerity, but with a stronger and more apostolic conviction.

No one should be surprised if I say that I have learned to preach by preaching, according to the axiom: "Fabricando fit faber." "One learns how to build by building." In the measure that I advanced, I understood more clearly that in the apostolate of the Social Reign of the Heart of Jesus it was necessary to place on the same footing, in perfect doctrinal harmony, the sublime teaching of St. Paul on charity and the revelations of the Sacred Heart at Paray-le-Monial. If *devotion* to the Sacred Heart was cradled in the chapel of St. Margaret Mary, the wonderful *doctrine* of the Sacred Heart stems from Bethlehem and Gethsemane, from Calvary and the Cenacle, from the inspired writings of St. John and St. Paul.

Yes, in our preaching we must inseparably unite St. Paul's theology of charity to devotion to the Sacred Heart, which the Church has so clearly approved and so strongly encouraged. Think of it—what a sublime and glorious hymn could be modeled on the sacred text: "The charity of Christ presseth us. . . . love is the fulfilling of the law." The celestial melody of this would be: "Behold this Heart which has loved men so much. . . . I will reign through My Heart!" Our preaching will be one hundred per cent more effective, if we unite the statements of St. Paul and St. Margaret Mary—that is to say, the Pauline thesis on love and the authentic doctrine of St. Margaret Mary, presented to us by Holy Mother Church, as she blesses the devotion to the Sacred Heart.

When one has meditated on and appreciated the sublime passage which begins: "If I speak with the tongues of men and angels, but have not charity, I am nothing," then and then only will the "sitio" and the complaints, the requests and the promises of the King of Love, speaking to the Church through St. Margaret Mary, have an irresistible power and a sovereign claim on our souls.

The triumphant eloquence of a true apostle comes from the truth of the doctrine which he expounds. We shall conquer souls if, in the apostolate of the Enthronement and in all that concerns the Sacred Heart, we begin with what I like to call "the altar stone"—namely, the Gospel and St. Paul. Only afterwards do we place on this magnificent altar the "candles and flowers" (practices of devotion) asked for by St. Margaret Mary in honor of the Sacred Heart.

Is it not true that very often our apostolate is reduced too much to the level of a simple devotion, and that we do not insist enough on the doctrinal substance underlying this incomparable devotion? If the cause of the Sacred Heart is not yet completely won, especially among the clergy, is this not due partly to an imperfect presentation of the subject, or at least to one that is not sufficiently doctrinal?

The Enthronement helps to bring out the depths of the relationship of ideal and doctrine between the great Apostle to the Gentiles and the Messenger of Paray-le-Monial—between St. Paul saying: "He loved me and delivered Himself for me. He who loves, has fulfilled the Law," and the revelations of the requests and complaints of the Heart of Jesus, but also His promises that He, the King of Love, will reign by the power of His Heart, despite Satan and his agents!

To grasp more clearly the inseparable doctrinal bond between *doctrine* and *devotion*, let us make a simple comparison. The Hail Mary, and hence the Rosary and the entire Marian cult of Lourdes and Fatima, are based on the Mystery of the Annunciation or, more properly, on the dogma of the Divine Maternity of Mary. For we must never forget that in the first place comes "Marian theology," on which is constructed, as a Catholic monument of the first rank, "Marian devotion."

Our friends and collaborators should be made to understand clearly that every devotion, in the strict sense of the word, *always presupposes a dogma*; a devotion, to be truly Catholic, must be thoroughly dogmatic.

Now, among the numerous and very beautiful devotions approved by the Church there is certainly not one more "dogmatic," more "evangelical," than devotion to the Sacred Heart of Jesus. For it embraces in an enlightening and solid manner the three great chapters which contain the "Credo" of our Catholic Faith, namely: a.) the mystery of love, the Incarnation; b.) the mystery of love which is the "folly of the cross"; and c.) the gift of love, *par excellence*, the Eucharist—sacrifice and sacrament.

Enlightened by this fundamental doctrine, we shall grasp more readily both the beauty and the significance of the requests concerning the Feast of the Sacred Heart, the celebration of the First Fridays in a spirit of eucharistic and reparative love; the Holy Hour, vigil of penance and reparation; and finally the consecration to the Sacred Heart (that is, to His Love) of all that is beautiful and vital in the Church, honoring at the same time in an explicit manner the image of this adorable Heart, the material symbol of His infinitely merciful love. The word "heart" is a symbolic, figurative term in both human and divine language. Therefore, when the Saviour says: "Behold this Heart which has loved men so much," this is equivalent to saying: "Contemplate in My Heart the love I have for you . . . and in exchange for this Heart, for My love, give Me your love, your heart."

The great Cardinal Pie expressed this idea magnificently when he said: "The whole Christ, from His Head crowned with thorns through love, to His Feet pierced through love, is nothing but an infinite Heart, who through His wounds offers naught but love, and claims nothing but love in return."

As a final comparison to clarify the foundation of this doctrinal alliance between the Gospel, St. Paul, and Paray-le-Monial, let us suppose that the thesis, *"Caritas Christi urget nos,"* were a masterpiece of sacred painting. The frame best suited to display this painting would be the revelations of Paray-le-Monial. Again, if this sublime thesis *"Dilexit me et tradidit semetipsum pro me"* were (let us say) a Mass, the practical and sacred formula for celebrating this Mass would be, again, devotion to the Sacred Heart, the external form of worship as proposed by St. Margaret Mary and approved by the Church.

What did Jesus the King say at Paray? Fundamentally, He repeated what He had already preached by His tears and His miracles, in the crib, on Calvary, and in the Cenacle. "Behold this Heart which has loved you so much, and which has performed these marvels in order to make Itself loved. I desire to conquer and possess you by the power of My love."

To close this section, I propose to make two statements, both striking and doctrinal. The first is: "Unum est credere, aliud est amare." ("It is one thing to believe, quite another to love.") An act of faith, the submission of the mind to a revealed truth or to a mystery, is not of itself an act of charity, the gift of self, which is called love. As a matter of fact, we can believe (and St. Paul even speaks of faith that can move mountains), but if we do not live our faith by love, then that faith merely makes us more responsible. Oh, yes, one can believe without loving, but one cannot love without believing! A true Christian is he who believes with a great faith, but who also loves what he believes with an even greater love. The perfection of faith, of hope, and all the virtues is charity, or love!

It follows that *to preach faith is only half of the Gospel;* therefore, let us preach love which perfects and vivifies faith. Note well that Jesus complains of a lack of love! Does that mean that the other virtues are to be found in abundance? Not at all! On the contrary, when love, the queen and source of virtues, is lacking, the rest will be lacking too.

Let us who are preaching the Heart of Jesus be apostles of love! Love is certainly not a sickly feeling, still less an effeminate sentimentality, but the *total gift of self,* the ability and the grace to give oneself to Him who out of love has delivered Himself for us! The God of Love whom we adore and preach wants to be loved absolutely!

As a second and final observation on this admirable doctrine of love, I would speak here of three ineffable gifts which the love of the Heart of Jesus has presented to His Church.

The *very first gift* is the knowledge and love of His Father. "Prompted by divine instruction, we make bold to say, *Our Father*." Here we have basically the wonderful novelty of the Gospel: "God, our Father; we, His adopted children!" It took nothing less than the Incarnate Word to reveal to us this mystery of divine love, supreme gift of a supreme love. And ever since that revelation we call the Man-God our eldest Brother; His Father is our Father, and His Mother is our Mother!

The *second gift is* Himself. He gives Himself to us forever. He is our Treasure, our Good! And this gift is irrevocable; the Eucharist fixes His abode among us in this land of exile; "Until the consummation of the world."

The *third gift*, worthy of the adorable Giver, is *Pentecost*. "It is expedient for you that I depart. For if I do not go, the Advocate will not come to you, but if I go, I will send him to you" (John 16:7). The Holy Spirit did come, and on Pentocost Sunday the Church was born in the Cenacle. Truly, since the love of Jesus bestowed these three wonderful gifts upon us, we can almost say that omnipotence has exhausted itself. And as He promised, when we love Him who is Love Incarnate, the three Divine Persons take up their abode in us, and we become living monstrances of the most august Trinity. We who preach the Enthronement should break this alabaster vase so that every home of the Sacred Heart may be thoroughly filled with the odor of the thrice-holy oil of this sublime doctrine.

Once more, let us proclaim in season and out of season that the great doctors of this divine theology of love are Paul and John the Evangelist, Bonaventure and Bernard, Thomas Aquinas and Francis de Sales. Yes, long before the beautiful devotion to the Sacred Heart was revealed through St. Margaret Mary, these spiritual giants were already the great apostles of the Heart of Jesus.

If we preach in this way, we shall transform the marvelous little Chapel of Paray-le-Monial into a truly Catholic sanctuary! This was the thought of Leo XIII when he said:

"The greatest private revelation was the one made at Paray-le-Monial. After Calvary, its altar is the most sacred, and around it gravitates the thought and love of the Church."

"I am a King," were the words of Jesus before Pilate, and St. Paul declares: "For He must reign." But before the ecstatic eyes of St. Margaret Mary, He assures us that He longs to reign and that He will reign through His Heart! It is for this reason the Church forbids the crowning of the image of the Sacred Heart: Jesus is King by nature, and also by right of conquest through the holy cross of redemption.

II. THE REVELATIONS TO ST. MARGARET MARY AT PARAY-LE-MONIAL

Let us enter, on bended knee, this new Gethsemane, which still echoes with the sad complaints and stirring requests of the King of Love. Its history is well-known; therefore, I shall merely recall briefly the statements of the Saviour to His confidante and messenger.

Jesus repeats over and over that He thirsts for love. But He complains bitterly of so-called friends, of mediocre friends who wound His Heart, because they do not truly love Him. The King of Love is indeed a beggar for love! He desires to reign, He must reign, because He is a King; but He wills to reign, not by destroying, but by converting and pardoning. But above all, consecrated souls must love Him with a perfect love! Priests and religious, the appeal and perhaps the reproach are especially for us! Note well, the greatest promise concerns us: "I will sanctify My friends by a special grace." Happy those who understand that the Good Master desires to perpetuate the succession of John, the beloved disciple. Yes, He wants intimate friends—"Johns," of whom He wants to make "Pauls," apostles of fire.

For our own sake let us stress this idea. Jesus desires and demands of us, His consecrated friends, a love unto sanctity. To His fervent and faithful friends He promises an extraordinary grace, a sort of charism, that of converting and softening the most hardened hearts. But let us never forget, the apostle most powerful in the work of salvation is always the intimate friend who, having won the Heart of Jesus, dispenses His treasures for His glory and the salvation of souls.

～⚬～

Naturally this leads us to the pleasant but important duty of reparation, characteristic of devotion to the Sacred Heart. A love which is thrust aside, forgotten, and outraged, demands from friends a kind of compensation, which, having appeased His justice, obtains an outpouring of mercy. Because He is truly a just God, He finds Himself obliged to punish and chastise: for He is as much Justice as Love. But as far as we, poor exiles, are concerned, one would say He is more a "divine pity," more a dispenser of mercy, than of rigorous and vengeful justice.

Still, in order to restore the balance upset by sin, He urges us to make reparation, to offer Him a penitent love, so that, His justice appeased, He may exercise His mercy. For this purpose, He Himself places the purchase price in our hands. Thus, He asks that the First Friday be consecrated to Him in a special way as a homage of eucharistic and reparative love. As a recompense for this offering of love, He gives special graces. Finally, He asks St. Margaret Mary to rise at night to watch with Him, to console Him even better than the angel at Gethsemane. And so He institutes the Holy Hour which from that time on has played such a great part in the extension of the reign of the Sacred Heart.

～⚬～

But, let it be well noted, just as the greatest revelation took place during the exposition of the Blessed Sacrament on December 27, the feast of St. John, so also the entire message of Paray is eminently *Eucharist*. By this I mean that, in the history of the revelations of the Heart of Jesus, everything stems from the Eucharist, and everything without exception returns to the Eucharist.

As will soon be pointed out, in this eucharistic love we must maintain the scale of doctrinal values which places before everything else the eucharistic sacrifice, Holy Mass, as the foundation and source of all eucharistic piety. After that comes the sacrament: Holy Communion, the tabernacle, and the monstrance for adoration and other practices of devotion.

The great feast of the Sacred Heart is a splendid summary of all the requests, and it should become through our efforts a striking triumph for the King of Love. Regarding this feast, let us remember that it is the Saviour Himself who selected and fixed the Friday after the octave of Corpus Christi as the day of its celebration. Let us keep to this day and not transfer this marvelous feast to a Sunday, for very special graces are attached to it. Encourage the families of the Sacred Heart to make it a true family feast so that the doctrine and the devotion of the Heart of Jesus may become a sacred tradition in the home, one to be handed down, as are family traits, from generation to generation.

Finally, Jesus is so determined to make us understand His desire to be ardently loved, that He demands a special homage for the very symbol of His love to which He designs to attach special blessings.

꧁꧂

I would like to make an interesting observation regarding the so-called Garcia Moreno picture of the Sacred Heart, which is, after all, the magnificent Labarum (or standard) of our crusade, even though its use is not obligatory for the Enthronement. It came to us from the great

Christian hero, the former president of Ecuador, Gabriel Garcia Moreno, "who fell beneath the steel of the enemies of the Church," as Pius IX and Leo XIII have solemnly said. The symbolism of this picture is perfect, for it depicts in truth the King of Love.

I inaugurated the work of the Enthronement by raising this glorious standard, and for more than fifty years I have been its happy guardian. Some few years ago the Reverend Carlos Monge, the Chilean provincial of the Fathers of the Sacred Hearts, felt it his duty to hand over this treasure to the Episcopacy of Ecuador at their urgent request.[2]

The golden key to this chapter on Paray is a moving parallel between Margaret Mary and Thérèse of Lisieux— two great saints, truly twins because of their intimate vocation, although quite different in their style and their mission, yet two conquering, triumphant messengers of the King of Love, who begs for love. The two would seem to be born in the wound of the Sacred Heart. Indeed, a flame has been enkindled wherever the message of St. Margaret Mary has penetrated, and the same is true of Thérèse, wherever her autobiography has made her known.

What a supernatural affinity, despite some very great differences, between the victim of Paray and that of Lisieux, both of them holocausts of love, both apostles of love and mercy! Two statements sum up the ideal of the two providential missionaries of love.

"My vocation is to love," says St. Thérèse. "No, I cannot take any rest until the end of the world . . . then I shall be able to rejoice because the number of the elect will be complete!"

---

[2] It is now preserved in a national shrine in Quito, Ecuador. An exact copy was made at the request of Father Mateo, and enthroned in the Catholic University of Washington, D.C., in 1952.

"To love Him unto folly," says St. Margaret Mary, "and to make Him greatly loved, that is enough for me."

May they be our guiding stars!

III. THE ENTHRONEMENT OF THE SACRED HEART IN THE HOME

As founder of this work, I have been asked to give a definition which corresponds exactly to its ideal and spirit. *In nomine Domini*, I shall do my best.

Is the Enthronement nothing more than the image installed in the place of honor? No; there is more to it than that! Is it perhaps but a beautiful and simple consecration of the family to the Sacred Heart? The consecration is included indeed, but there is much more than that!

What then? There is a marvelous statement made by Jesus to St. Margaret Mary which I give as a synthesis of our crusade, at least as far as its supreme ideal is concerned: *"I will reign through My Heart and I promise to reign!"* The Enthronement is the apostolate which is trying to make this divine affirmation something lived in the home, the social cell. That is why the idea of *royalty* expressed by the term "Enthronement" is not just an arbitrary title given to our work, and that is also the reason that I have continued to use it, despite criticisms of all kinds, for in itself it constitutes an entire program of action.

Here is another definition, more technical in content: the Enthronement is the homage of adoration, of social reparation, and of fervent love, which the family, as the social cell, offers to the Heart of Jesus considered as King of Society. In this sense, which is strictly doctrinal, the Enthronement is not merely a beautiful but simple consecration; it is an homage of *latria*, made in a spirit of love and reparation for the *modern social apostasy*. In other words, it is the *Ave Rex*, (Hail, King) the "We want this Man to rule over us," of the miniature nation of the entire nation.

Now, how bring about in daily family life the practical application of this doctrine of the divine rule of Jesus? By carrying out in the home, not one or another of the requests made at Paray, but indeed *every one of them*. One of these requests refers to the honor to be given to the image of the Sacred Heart. This image is only a symbol, a reminder, of the presence in the home of a living King, recognized as such in everyday life. But since it is the King of Love who is enthroned, it goes without saying that it is the entire doctrine of St. Paul on love which is presented to the family as an ideal, as it is likewise the integral devotion of Paray-le-Monial that we propose to the family as its very heart and soul. Thus the family becomes the living throne of a King whose sovereign dominion is accepted with as much faith as love.

The well-beloved King of Love is at the same time the great Friend of His friends of Bethany: "You are my friends." And He is even more a King among His own, precisely because He is a true Friend, loved wholeheartedly. Thus, a great intimacy should be established between this King and His friends, an intimacy which is the outpouring of hearts filled with confidence like those of Lazarus, Martha, and Mary, into the ever-faithful loving Heart of their Divine Friend. And this friendship must result in an intimate sharing of the daily life of the family with Jesus, and consequently of Jesus with the family: "Remain with us, O Lord."

The family of the Sacred Heart must never take its pleasures or sorrows alone; Jesus, the Friend, always has His part, and the very first, at that, in the sorrowful and joyous happenings of parents and children. For His Heart is the very center of this happy family. Naturally, this means that on certain outstanding family celebrations and cherished anniversaries, on First Fridays, the family should gather at the feet of the royal Friend, and renew its offering of total love to the Heart of Jesus. There you have Jesus Christ become a God-Emmanuel in the Christian home.

But all of this necessarily presupposes a great eucharistic fervor. Consequently, the home must become, little by little, a veritable *tabernacle*. Therefore, *daily Mass* and *Communion* must become for the family a law of love, a pressing necessity, in truth its *daily Bread!*

This is the proper place to emphasize a principle which is not always understood or practiced in pious circles: namely, that in eucharistic love the Holy Sacrifice of the Mass must always occupy the first place. Alas, for many good Christians the Eucharist consists merely of Holy Communion. They do not come to Mass for the purpose of adoring, praising and blessing the Most Holy Trinity, "per Ipsum, et cum Ipso, et in Ipso," but only in order to receive Holy Communion. For too many Holy Mass is, after all, but the liturgical key which opens the tabernacle door. The official praise given to God by the Church through the Holy Sacrifice of the Mass is very often entirely overlooked.

Let us do our best to re-establish the scale of spiritual values in a manner of such transcendent importance. Sacrifice and sacrament must remain inseparable, but the Sacred Fountain, without which there is neither Communion rail, nor tabernacle, nor monstrance, is the Holy Sacrifice: "Inexhaustable fountain of life." A great theologian has well said: "He who does not appreciate Holy Mass will never be an eucharistic soul; daily Communion itself will be a matter of routine and without fruit if the chalice is not recognized as the fountain." Yes, families of the Sacred Heart should love Holy Mass with their whole heart and soul.

In order to increase the flame of charity, let us light that lamp of penitent and reparative love, *nocturnal adoration in the home*. This means that we should try to organize, even though it be with groups of elite families, an eucharistic vigil, a perpetual Holy Hour. Here again we have a Bethany turned into a sanctuary, a tabernacle.

Nocturnal adoration has had a success which has surprised even the most optimistic, including myself. But its success in the supernatural order has been everywhere a spiritual renovation, a rebirth of eucharistic fervor—and I might add, a source of remarkable conversions! It is in itself a remarkable powerhouse of grace, for it comprises the three vital elements of Christian life, prayer, expiation, and love. Therefore you, who are apostles, hold fast to this apostolate with all your hearts, but see to it that *you yourselves are the very first adorers in spirit and in truth!* With this supernatural method of apostolate, then, make the Enthronement a work of social salvation! In it find the means of the sanctification of friends, and for the conversion of so many who are lukewarm and for sinners, found in great numbers even in the best families.

Our work has always had its special characteristic; indeed, it has been "canonized" by heaven. It has harvested for the granaries of the Father a great number of publicans who have been mortally ill. It possesses the secret of conversion and spiritual resurrection. But since I am speaking to apostles, I allow myself an observation: if the marvel of grace which is the Holy Mass does not succeed in sanctifying all who offer it (and this because of our own fault), the Enthronement, *ex opere operato*, cannot be expected to do more! Thus, it is absolutely necessary that we, the apostles, make up our minds to live to the full the law of charity and the spirit of love, which we preach to families. This is what I call the *sincerity* of our preaching.

The King will give in superabundance whatever He has

promised, but only on condition that we be, like Margaret Mary, extremely docile instruments, ready to live and to preach His love.

At this point, I must not omit certain counsels of extreme importance for the progress of our work. I mean to say that, not satisfied with contributing to the divine victory with all the fire of our faith and our enthusiasm, we must also multiply around us apostles of the social reign of the Heart of Jesus.

Religious communities, be they devoted to prayer and penance or consecrated to the work of education, will become an incomparable army if they are truly won to this cause.

Wonderful conquests have been made, due to the zeal of our junior apostles, members of the League of St. Tarcisius. Wherever Sisters have wholeheartedly tried to stimulate their students by enkindling the flame of zeal, they have witnessed the power which the childlike hearts wield over the Heart of Jesus. Piety without zeal is nothing but a flash without an aftermath; but piety with zeal is a God-given blessed fire, a fire which radiates, and which endures. There is no doubt that the greatest profit from this apostolate comes to the communities, for they bring down upon themselves the blessings promised by the Heart of Jesus. But we must not forget that there is also a great blessing for the spiritual welfare and the perseverance of the student-apostles. Let us train them as early as possible in the duty of the apostolate, a duty which is one of solid piety of true love.

Let us also utilize the communities engaged in charitable works, and ask them to contribute their sacrifices and their sufferings to the extension of the reign of the Sacred Heart. I make a suggestion here which already has had excellent results: that the Sisters and nurses in hospitals should continue to be enrolled in nocturnal adoration. How powerful it is to have thousands of nurses making their nocturnal adoration beside the bed of the sick and dying, and thus proving their solicitude for the agonizing and crucified King, as well as for their suffering charges! For this great army of charitable workers, and their unfortunate charges, the apostolate of suffering will become a marvelous supernatural solace, and at the same time will contribute most efficaciously to the success of our apostolate. For to suffer with love as an apostle means that one is already preaching with an eloquence which is always fruitful.

And now to terminate in a serious vein, the present situation of society and of the world is extremely grave. Yet, we must have confidence in Him who has conquered the world! I myself heard the great Pius XI solemnly declare *"Humanity is living in its darkest hour since the deluge. But the Church has a great hope of salvation, for we are living to the full the hour of the Sacred Heart."* "I will reign despite Satan and his agents," was the explicit statement of the King, but He added that He would reign through His Heart! And the rock on which we must construct the Christian fortress is, and will always remain, the home, under attack today with a diabolical hatred. It is true that the tempest of hate, which is concentrating on the family, is fear-inspiring. Nevertheless, we have cause to rejoice, for we have His marvelous promises. "Help will fail you," said the King to St. Margaret Mary, "only when I shall be lacking in power." Thus, if the King of Love is with us, who shall stand against Him, and against us?

In conclusion, I wish to stress very strongly the importance and timeliness of the Enthronement. We have placed it in the ranks of a true crusade, and indeed it merits this title in the strict meaning of the word. For what could be greater as an enterprise of social salvation than the work of saving the Christian fortress—the home, where the Sacred Heart reigns as King, and where He is loved as an adorable Friend? What is more powerful than a home which is a tabernacle of prayer, a tabernacle of eucharistic fervor, and a sanctuary of Christian penance? There you have in spirit and in truth the authentic Bethany of the Heart of Jesus.

When the Enthronement merited the blessing and even the praise of St. Pius X, Benedict XV, Pius XI, and Pius XII, it was precisely because they considered it as a work of Christian restoration, and an apostolic organism of the highest value. If, in this great struggle, the Church protects us, and encourages us in such a maternal and wholehearted way, certainly we may be permitted to say that God is with us. "Let us also go, that we may die with Him! For He must reign!"

16. To the King of Love Through the Queen of Hearts

THIS allocution was delivered by Father Mateo on September 10, 1921, during a Marian Congress at Brussels. The occasion was a gathering of the Association of Priests of Mary. His Eminence Cardinal Mercier presided at the meeting which was attended by well-known ecclesiastics including the Superior General of the Company of Mary and of the Congregation of Wisdom. Later, this discourse was published with an introduction by Cardinal Mercier. In it the great Cardinal said in part:

"In this allocution the fervent apostle of the Sacred Heart seems to wish to synthesize these great devotions: *to live a life of union with Jesus* in order to enter more profoundly into the secrets of love contained in the Immaculate and Sorrowful Heart of Mary; *to live a life of union with Mary* in order to go through her to Jesus; to become a slave of the Queen of Love as 'the King-Jesus despoiled Himself in her womb, becoming her own, her child and her captive nine months before Bethlehem and for thirty years at Nazareth;' and to do this 'not out of fear of Jesus but because I am certain that by going to Him through Mary I love and please Him more; I correspond with His providential designs thereby increasing a hundred times over the value of my gift.'

"Worthy of our meditations are these words of the servant of Mary, St. Louis Marie de Montfort: 'Many do not reach the fullness of the age of Christ because Mary is not sufficiently formed in them.'

"My dear brother priests, all of us long to reach the fullness of the age of Christ; let us then allow Mary to perfect in us her work as our Mother. Listen to the voice of her dying Jesus: *Fili, ecce Mater tua.*"

At the end of the Appendix will be found the "Message of the Heart of Jesus to the heart of the priest" cited by Father Mateo in several places.

~~~

Dignare me laudare te, Virgo sacrata (Liturgy).

The most beautiful homage that can be offered to Mary is a diadem, the jewels of which are priests of Mary.

Although this crown is in itself a precious gift—*Sacerdos alter Christus*—still its value can and should be enhanced by sacerdotal sanctity and to such a degree that every priest may dare to say in all truth, *Ego Ipse Jesus.*

Let me explain. On Easter morning, Jesus, glorious and transfigured, presented Himself to Mary. Her ecstasy of sorrow was suddenly transformed into one of jubilant happiness. Jesus, dead to the life of the body, had found in the tomb a new and glorious life.

Now He stands before Mary and tells her: "Mother, change your mourning and your tears into joy: *Ego Ipse Jesus.* I am your son. Do you not recognize Me? Once more you have found your Jesus."

That the Queen of Mercy may recognize *her Jesus* in each of us, more and more she must find in our priestly souls the elements which constitute the well-formed priest:

God acting through us, tremendous power! *Alter Christus.*

God acting in us; element of priestly holiness: *"Ego Ipse Jesus."*[1]

Power and holiness—a sublime dignity together with superhuman powers grafted onto a nature of average supernatural life, of ordinary virtue. A lack of balance here could be dangerous. Who is going to re-establish the proper equilibrium? Mary!

Sacerdotal powers are inherent in the Sacrament of Holy Orders, *ex opere operato.* Holiness depends upon us in union with Mary, *ex opere operantis.* Thus it is up to us to establish a perfect balance in our priestly life by our fidelity to grace.

We need saintly priests and we need them urgently, for all signs point to the coming of a terrible crisis. Yet this crisis could result in another Pentecost, provided God receives the cooperation of *holy* priests. But why are there not enough of them? St. Louis Marie de Montfort answers: "Many do not reach the fullness of the age of Christ because Mary is not sufficiently formed in them. . . . He who wishes to have the fruit of life, Jesus Christ, must have the tree of life, which is Mary." She is the safest, the shortest and the most beautiful way: *excellentiorem viam demonstro.*

Once again, see how the Holy Spirit, with the cooperation of Mary, creates this new Jesus, the priest. The Holy Spirit in union with Mary bestows upon him his external powers through the Sacrament of Orders, making him, as it were, the arm of God; the virginal and maternal fecundity of Mary, under the influence of the Holy Spirit, causes his interior virtues to bear fruit, forms in him the heart of

[1] "Ego Ipse Jesus." A variation of St. Paul's well-known words which sum up all Christian priestly perfection: "It is now no longer I that live but Christ lives in me" (Gal. 2:20).

God and produces the *saint!* "Know that this Mother of Divine Love possesses the secret of this wondrous union that My Heart now offers to every priest as a new grace of sanctification."[2] Creatures—even good ones—can sometimes hinder our progress toward Christ. But Mary—never! Mary is the divine path that leads inevitably into the abyss of the Heart of Christ.

Inasmuch as she is *gratia plena,* Mary exercises a privileged mission with regard to priests. Ever since Calvary she is their Mother and Queen: *ecce filius tuus.* The priest is not "another son," but in a certain sense the same Jesus! It is to this mission of Mary in our regard that we can apply the beautiful and original commentary on her *Magnificat* of St. John Eudes, who interprets our Lady's words thus: "My soul develops the Lord," meaning that she causes Him to grow in glory, grace, and productivity in the person of His "other self" the saintly priest!

This is why Father Olier states, "we make more progress in sanctity in union with Mary than by all other means together." For this reason also I affirm: supposing Christ offered me one ordinary grace through Mary Mediatrix and a thousand others without her mediation; and supposing the King of Love left me free to choose, I would go to Mary, knowing that in her and in her alone I should find everything I need: *Qui me invenerit inveniet vitam* (Prov. 8:35).

Without further ado let us turn our attention to the dominant idea of this conference. In substance, all Christian perfection is based on the affirmation of this transcendent task: "to know and to love Jesus Christ." We are led by the Son, who is the way, to know the Father and to become cenacles of the Paraclete the Sanctifier, tabernacles in which the august Trinity are pleased to take up Their abode. "Now this is everlasting life, that they may know

---

[2] *Message of the Sacred Heart to the Heart of the Priest.*

thee, the only true God, and him whom thou hast sent, Jesus Christ" (John 17:3). "No one comes to the Father but through me" (John 14:6). "If anyone love me, he will keep my word, and my Father will love him, and we will come to him and make our abode with him" (John 14:23).

Since we are now concerned expressly with Jesus and Mary let us consider for a few moments the Son and His Mother.

❦

To know Jesus in the School of Mary
To know Mary in the School of Jesus

A fundamental preparation for becoming a priest of Mary is to know Jesus with the knowledge that comes to us through His Mother. Just as our Lord said, "No one knows the Son except the Father," so, though in a different degree, we may add, "Who after the Father has ever known Jesus as His mother knows Him?"

1. In the School of Mary

Let us follow the example of the apostles, especially that of St. John, the beloved disciple, and have recourse to the lessons taught by the mother of Jesus.

It was for them and for us that Mary "kept all these words in her heart," and it is to the peaceful and enlightening sanctuary of her Immaculate Heart that the Beloved invites those to whom He wishes to impart the secrets of His Heart (cf. Cant. 8:2).

To the priests of her Heart especially Mary wishes to make known two great and precious secrets of the King:

a.) The mystery of the hidden life of Jesus, which no one knew and understood as did His mother. Jesus showed Himself to her as to no one else. The interior life of a priest should be one of recollection, prayer, and a deep spirit of faith. And its indispensable basis must be this mystery of

Nazareth—the interior life and action of Jesus known, pondered, and revealed by Mary.

b.) The mystery of the hidden Passion of the Heart of Jesus, His secret Gethsemane both before and after the agony in the Garden. The knowledge of this mystery is absolutely necessary for the life of immolation and sacrifice a priest of Mary must lead, for like Jesus and Mary he is both *offerens et oblatio*.

Priestly holiness presupposes a profound knowledge resulting from frequent meditation on these mysteries. And who holds the keys to them, except the Queen of Nazareth, the Mother of the Heart of Jesus?

The *Message of the Sacred Heart* to priests contains these words: "Many priests know the theory of union with Me, but how few there are, even among the most devoted of My friends, who know that I am there in the depths of their souls yearning to make them *one* with Me. . . . If only they would tear themselves away from material things and in solitude seek Me in the depths of their souls where I am, they would soon find Me, and what a life of union, light and love would be theirs! But let them go full of confidence to My mother who is also their mother. How she loves My priests! It is My sweet mother who urges Me to open the treasures of My Heart to them all . . . but especially to My good priests."

And *during* this exile show unto us the blessed fruit of thy womb, Jesus!

2. In the School of Jesus

St. Louis Marie de Montfort says that ignorance of Jesus comes especially from not knowing His mother. To remedy this, Mary's school and Mary the Teacher and Queen of Doctors must be more widely and better known. "Show us the Father," said the apostle; and we add "Show us also Thy mother. Reveal her to us, she who is Thy own glory!"

We know Mary more through Lourdes, Fatima and La Salette than through the personal teaching of her Son: that is why so often she is known so superficially.

All Mary's glory is within. Therefore only the King who has entered and lived in this sanctuary can teach us truly to know and love this unique virgin-mother who is all fair: *tota pulchra es Maria.*

Those who have studied in this school of prayer and personal friendship with the divine King have been without exception ardent lovers of Mary. Bernard, Bonaventure, Bernadine of Sienna, Dominic, Alphonsus Liguori, Francis de Sales, John Eudes, Louis Marie de Montfort and other lovers of Mary have learned more about her while kneeling before the tabernacle than by reading books. In fact, one would say that an ardent love for Mary and an understanding of her Heart are gifts reserved for those who are loved by her Jesus as was St. John.

Do you not think that after Calvary, when the apostles gathered around Mary in the Cenacle, they must have begged her to share with them the treasures of her understanding and knowledge of our Lord? And Mary spoke to them, explaining many things not to be found in Scripture but which have been engraved in the heart of the Church. Likewise, before His Ascension, Jesus must have spoken about Mary to St. John and to His other disciples, as He gave them His last instructions. His words on Calvary were the official words of the Pontiff-King. Now He allowed His divine Heart to overflow into theirs.

This explains perhaps, at least in part, despite the mysterious silence of the evangelists, why theologians for twenty centuries have been able to draw unceasingly from the treasures of the Church the marvelous and inexhaustible riches of Marian doctrine.

From my own humble experience I have always found that eucharistic souls have a special facility for grasping in a most profound way the perfections of Mary and for entering intimately into the secrets of love of her Immaculate Heart. This proves that the way *par excellence* to know Mary thoroughly is friendship with her divine Son.

To love Jesus through Mary and as Mary with a pure, maternal, and personal love.

To love Mary as Jesus, even to the slavery of love.

The revelation of the Father through His son, Jesus Christ, is perfected in charity. "Love therefore is the fulfillment of the Law" (Rom. 13:10). Let us love Jesus Christ who first loved us and who loved us *usque in finem*. Love Him as far as possible with the only love worthy of Him; love Jesus with the Heart and with the sentiments of Mary: *I am the Mother of Fair Love.* "I am cold, hungry, thirsty! Tell My priests to warm Me with their love. This is what I ask of My priests whom I love dearly. Tell them how greatly I love them!" (*Message of the Sacred Heart to the Heart of the Priest.*)

You are familiar with these burning words of the *Message.* And the King adds, "It is My dear mother who urges Me to open the treasures of My Heart especially to My priests. It is this Mother of Divine Love who guards this secret."

Priestly love learned in and through the Heart of Mary should have three characteristics:

a.) It should be *virginal*—that is to say, strong, intense, burning, unique, as Father Olier puts it. Jesus demands a *flame* of love, not a mere spark.

This virginal love must be also total and entire, concentrated exclusively on His divine person; a love ardent in prayer, generous when sacrifice is demanded.

In the *Message* our Lord tells us that to love with a virginal love means to gather together and to concentrate all one's affection on Him.

b.) It should be *maternal*. Yes, maternal, especially at the altar. For at each Mass *Puer natus est nobis*. I would willingly renounce, O Mary, the ecstasy of Bethlehem and all the glory of an apostolic life in exchange for one flame of your love, that I might celebrate a single Mass in a manner worthy of you, my Queen and Mother!

Sacerdotal maternity consists in the total gift of self in exchange for the total gift the Father makes of His Son in the Holy Eucharist. "For God so loved the world that he gave his only-begotten Son" (John 3:16). The priest in His turn must love the Father and the Son by giving himself to them as Mary gave herself to the Father and to the Son when the Heart of Jesus first throbbed in the manger.

O, the Mass, mystery of love and grandeur! This is the time to prove ourselves true priests of Mary. A priest who understands the meaning of sacerdotal maternity, who knows how to give himself to Jesus through Mary, as Jesus gave Himself to the Father through Mary, is very close to being a saint.

In these critical times, why is there a lack of holy priests in pulpits, in confessionals and in Catholic Action? Because there are not enough holy priests at the altar. We who offer sacrifice must maternalize our love and celebrate Mass with the sentiments and tenderness of the Heart of Mary.

c.) Priestly love must be warm and *personal*. This is the kind of love that draws us to the Heart of Jesus, guided, led, and encouraged by the Heart of Mary.

"If My priests only knew with what intense desire I long to unite Myself intimately to each one of them! But rare are those who attain the degree of union that My Heart has prepared for them on earth" (*Message*). Why? What is lacking? Faith—a strong faith in the love of Jesus—an intense confidence in the love of His Heart.

And it is here precisely that I desire the intercession of the *authentic* mother of Jesus, who so often is presented to us as a shield of mercy against the just vengeance of a fear-inspiring Saviour who actually is all love and mercy! How well the delicate shades of Mary's love were understood by the incomparable Louis Marie de Montfort! He writes: "We can and we should have recourse to the Mediatrix, to the mediation of Mary, not out of fear for Jesus, but because of the humility so fitting even in those who have a great love for the God of Love. *Apparuit benignitas et humanitas Salvatoris erudiens nos. . . .*"

Jesus, all loving, all merciful, calls to us, draws us to Himself; more than ever, in this age of His Sacred Heart He repeats His consoling words, *Noli timere*. And if, to justify our fear we allege our unworthiness to approach Him, He insists, *Nolite timere. Ego sum*—I am the God of Love, the son of Mary, the Saviour Jesus.

If Mary is kind, if Mary is tender, if Mary is merciful, it is because she shares in the kindness, the tenderness, the mercy of her divine Son.

Supposing I found one reason to fear to go through Mary, I would go directly to Jesus, for I must not and I will not fear Him, precisely because He is Jesus, the Saviour. He satisfies divine justice as regards His Father, and He waits for me with the gift of His Heart to perfect not only the work of my salvation but also of my sanctification through love.

Yet, following the example of my Redeemer, the God-Man who created Mary—Mediatrix for Himself and for us —I do not wish to go directly to Jesus. I prefer to go to Him through Mary. This I do, not out of fear of Jesus but to express a *twofold love* for Him, for I am certain that by going to Him through Mary I love and please Him more; and I correspond with His providential designs, thereby increasing and enhancing the mediation of Mary. In this sense I can say more freely and more joyously, "I love You,

Jesus, because You are Jesus!" and in an accommodated sense, "I love you, Mary, because you are Mary!"

Thus the total offering of myself to the Queen of Love, the sweet Virgin Mary, is an expression of a deeper love, a much more filial love, a more selfless love: I give myself to her because she is the mother of Jesus and my mother.

If to all these motives which are more than sufficient, I add, with St. Louis Marie de Montfort, that of humility, I increase the value of my sacrifice offered without reserve on the altar of the Immaculate Heart of Mary, my Queen, my Mediatrix and my Mother!

I adore God the Father with a peaceful, humble, and salutary fear, but I go to Him full of confidence, carried in the blood-stained arms of my Saviour. Overcome by confusion and love, I adore my Jesus and go trustingly to meet Him, my Saviour, in the arms of Mary. For through her, *inveni Cor Regis, Cor Fratris, Cor Amici benignissimi Jesu* (St. Bernard) . . . *tenui eum, nec dimittam* (Cant. 3:4).

If the phrase *De Maria nunquam satis* is true of the external Marian apostolate exercised for her glory, how much more true it should be of the interior filial love we owe her! This means that to love Mary as God wishes us to love her and as she merits to be loved, we must love her with the fervent love of the Heart of Jesus Himself.

It is precisely here that the beautiful and sublime practice of the total consecration to Mary finds its rightful place of honor. Out of love for souls and through His love for Mary, the eldest daughter of the Father, the King Jesus stripped Himself of His majesty in her womb, becoming her own child, her captive, for nine months before Bethlehem and for thirty years at Nazareth. Therein lies the measure of our love for Mary: total dependence through complete and loving surrender of our entire being to her maternal Heart.

To exchange our life for hers means to live dependent

upon her as the Infant-God was nourished by her; in so doing we surrender all our personal interests and good, present and future, provided that the Reign of Mary be the certain dawn of the Reign of the Heart of Jesus. In this sense, *tuus sum ego, Virgo Maria!*

One final thought. What have I not received from Jesus? Yet everything has been given to me through the mediation of Mary!

Well, by offering myself to the Queen of Love, it is my wish, in union with Jesus, to pay my great debt of gratitude to Mary. Jesus loves Mary with a grateful love, for she it was who gave Him the power of suffering, of agonizing and of dying, of becoming our Saviour by the shedding of His blood on the cross, of being our priest and victim, of being our own very brother. This capacity of lowliness and of mortality was assumed by the Word in the womb of the Virgin Mary. And there it was that through Him and in Him she prepared that most excellent gift, the royal unction of our priesthood.

Adequately to repay this munificence of the Queen, I want, as St. John Eudes said, "to make the Lord grow" in my soul unto the fullness of the age of Christ, sanctifying myself and thus becoming more and more a son and a priest of Mary. Next I want Him to "grow" in the souls He has committed to my care and whom in turn I entrust to the Queen of Apostles. Lastly, I wish to glorify Mary in order to repay in union with Jesus my eldest Brother the incomparable, the unique glory with which the Queen has crowned for eternity both Jesus Christ, her firstborn,[3] and —in Him and with Him—us, the "younger brothers," priests of Mary, Queen of our priestly hearts.

Sacris Cordibus Jesu et Mariae, honor, amor et gloria!

[3] A few lines above Father Mateo explained in what sense Mary has crowned Jesus. The Son of God owes to His mother His humanity and His power of suffering and dying, of being a *priest* and *victim*. In this sense Jesus is indebted to her for His Priesthood.

Appendix

1. ENCYCLICAL LETTER OF POPE PIUS XII

2. INDULGENCED PRAYERS
    A form of consecrating priests to the Most Sacred
    Heart of Jesus
    Prayer to stir up the grace of the priesthood
    Prayer for the grace of preaching holily and fruit-
    fully
    Prayers for holiness of life

3. ACTS OF CONSECRATION BY FATHER MATEO
    Act of consecration to the justice of Christ, the
    adorable Judge
    Act of consecration to the three Persons of the Blessed
    Trinity
    Consecration of priests to the Sacred Heart of Jesus

4. DOCTRINAL PRACTICES PROPOSED BY FATHER MATEO
    Little chaplet of the Paraclete
    Mass of St. John

5. CEREMONY FOR THE ENTHRONEMENT OF THE SACRED
    HEART IN THE HOME

6. MESSAGE OF THE SACRED HEART TO THE HEART OF THE
    PRIEST

1. *Encyclical Letter of Pope Pius* XII

Haurietis Aquas

on devotion to the Sacred Heart of Jesus[1]

[1] The present translation was made in Rome and was published by the Vatican Polyglot Press as "an unofficial translation." It was revised by the translator of FATHER MATEO SPEAKS TO PRIESTS and has been approved by the proper ecclesiastical authority. The outline and paragraph numbers have been added.

POPE PIUS XII

Venerable Brethren:

Health and Apostolic Benediction!

Introduction: *The Marvelous Development of Devotion to the Sacred Heart in Modern Times*

THE CENTENARY YEAR

1. "You shall draw waters with joy out of the saviour's fountain."[1] These words, by which the prophet Isaias, using highly significant imagery, foretold the manifold and abundant gifts of God which the Christian era was to bring forth, come naturally to Our mind when We reflect on the centenary of that year when Our predecessor of immortal memory, Pius IX, gladly yielding to the prayers from the whole Catholic world, ordered the celebration of the feast of the Most Sacred Heart of Jesus in the universal Church.

A PRICELESS GIFT TO THE CHURCH

2. It is altogether impossible to enumerate the heavenly gifts which devotion to the Sacred Heart of Jesus has poured out on the souls of the faithful, purifying them, offering them heavenly strength, rousing them to the attainment of all virtues. Therefore, recalling those wise words of the apostle St. James, "Every good gift and every perfect gift is from above, coming down from the Father of Lights,"[2] We are perfectly justified in seeing in this same devotion, which flourishes with increasing fervor throughout the world, a

165

gift without price which our divine Saviour, the Incarnate Word, as the one Mediator of grace and truth between the heavenly Father and the human race, imparted to the Church, His mystical Spouse, in recent centuries when she had to endure such trials and surmount so many difficulties.

3. The Church, rejoicing in this inestimable gift, can show forth a more ardent love of her divine Founder, and can, in a more generous and effective manner, respond to that invitation which St. John the Evangelist relates as having come from Christ Himself: "On the last, the great day of the feast, Jesus stood and cried out, saying, 'If anyone thirst, let him come to me and drink, he who believes in me. As the Scripture says, "From within him there shall flow rivers of living water."' He said this, however, of the Spirit whom they who believed in him were to receive."[3]

4. For those who were listening to Jesus speaking, it certainly was not difficult to relate to these words, by which He promised the fountain of "living water" destined to spring from His own side, the sacred, prophetic words of Isaias, Ezechiel, and Zacharias, foretelling the Messianic Kingdom. These words likewise brought to mind the symbolic rock from which, when struck by Moses, water flowed forth in a miraculous manner.[4]

THE TRUE NATURE OF THIS DEVOTION

5. Divine Love first takes its origin from the Holy Spirit, who is the Love in Person of the Father and the Son, in the bosom of the most Holy Trinity. Most aptly then does the Apostle of the Gentiles echo, as it were, the words of Jesus Christ, when he ascribes the pouring forth of love in the hearts of believers to this Spirit of Love: "The charity of God is poured forth in our hearts by the Holy Spirit who has been given to us."[5]

6. Holy Writ declares that between divine charity, which

must burn in the souls of Christians, and the Holy Spirit, who is certainly Love itself, there exists the closest bond, which clearly shows all of us, venerable brethren, the intimate nature of that worship which must be paid to the Most Sacred Heart of Jesus Christ. If we consider its special nature, it is beyond question that this devotion is an act of religion of high order; it demands of us a complete and unreserved determination to devote and consecrate ourselves to the love of the divine Redeemer, whose wounded Heart is its living token and symbol. It is equally clear, but at a higher level, that this same devotion provides us with a most powerful means of repaying the divine Love by our own.

7. Indeed it follows that it is only under the impulse of love that the minds of men obey fully and perfectly the rule of the Supreme Being, since the influence of our love draws us so close to the divine Will that it becomes, as it were, completely one with it, according to the saying, "He who cleaves to the Lord, is one spirit with him."[6]

PART I: *The Foundations and Foreshadowings of the Devotion to the Sacred Heart in the Old Testament*

A. ERRONEOUS OPINIONS CONCERNING THIS DEVOTION

1. *The Church Is the Guardian of this Devotion*

8. The Church has always valued, and still does value, the devotion to the Most Sacred Heart of Jesus so highly that she provides for the spread of it among Christian peoples everywhere and by every means. At the same time she uses every effort to protect it against the charges of so-called "naturalism" and "sentimentalism." In spite of this it is much to be regretted that, both in the past and in our own times, this most noble devotion does not find a place of honor and esteem among certain Christians and even occa-

sionally not among those who profess themselves moved by zeal for the Catholic religion and the attainment of holiness.

2. Modern Errors on the Part of Catholics

9. "If thou didst know the gift of God."[7] With these words, venerable brethren, We who in the secret designs of God have been elected as the guardians and stewards of the sacred treasure of faith and piety which the divine Redeemer has entrusted to His Church, prompted by Our own sense of duty, admonish them all.

10. For even though the devotion to the Sacred Heart of Jesus has triumphed, so to speak, over the errors and the neglect of men, and has penetrated entirely His mystical body; still there are some of Our children who, led astray by prejudices, sometimes go so far as to consider this devotion ill-adapted, not to say detrimental, to the more pressing spiritual needs of the Church and humanity in this present age. There are some who, confusing and confounding the primary nature of this devotion with various individual forms of piety which the Church approves and encourages but does not command, regard this as a kind of additional practice which each one may take up or not according to his own inclination.

11. There are others who reckon this same devotion burdensome and of little or no use to men who are fighting in the army of the divine King, and who are inspired mainly by the thought of laboring with their own strength, their own resources, and the expenditure of their own time, to defend Catholic truth, to teach and spread it, to instill Christian social teachings, to promote those acts of religion and those undertakings which they consider much more necessary today.

12. Again, there are those who, so far from considering this devotion a strong support for the right ordering and renewal of Christian morals both in the individual's private

life and in the home circle, see in it rather a type of piety nourished not by the soul and mind but by the senses, and consequently more suited to the use of women, since it seems to them something not quite suitable for educated men.

13. Moreover, there are those who consider a devotion of this kind as primarily demanding penance, expiation and the other virtues which they call "passive," meaning thereby that they produce no external results. Hence they do not think it suitable as a means of reenkindling the spirit of piety in modern times. Rather, this devotion should encourage open, vigorous action directed at the triumph of the Catholic faith, and a strong defence of Christian morals. Christian morality today, as everyone knows, is easily contaminated by the sophistries of those who are indifferent to any form of religion and who, discarding all distinction between truth and falsehood, whether in thought or in practice, accept even the most ignoble corruptions of materialistic atheism, or, as they call it, secularism.

B. THE ESTEEM OF THE SOVEREIGN PONTIFFS FOR THIS DEVOTION

1. *The Foregoing Opinions Disagree with the Teachings of Leo XIII, Pius XI, and Pius XII*

14. Who does not see, venerable brethren, that opinions of this kind are in complete disagreement with the teachings which Our predecessors officially proclaimed from this seat of truth when approving the devotion to the Sacred Heart of Jesus? Who would be so bold as to call that devotion useless and inappropriate to our age which Our predecessor of immortal memory, Leo XIII, declared to be "the most acceptable form of piety"? He had no doubt

that in it there was a powerful remedy for the healing of those very evils which today also, and beyond question in a wider and more serious way, bring distress and disquiet to individuals and to the whole human race. "This devotion," he said, "which We recommend to all, will be profitable to all." He added this counsel and encouragement with reference to the devotion to the Sacred Heart of Jesus: ". . . hence those forces of evil which have now for so long a time been taking root fiercely compel us to seek help from Him by whose strength alone they can be driven away. Who can He be but Jesus Christ, the only-begotten Son of God? 'For there is no other name under heaven given to men by which we must be saved.'[8] We must have recourse to Him who is the Way, the Truth, and the Life."[9]

15. No less to be approved, no less suitable for the fostering of Christian piety was this devotion declared to be by Our predecessor of happy memory, Pius XI. In an encyclical letter he wrote: "Is not a summary of all our religion and, moreover, a guide to a more perfect life contained in this one devotion? Indeed, it more easily leads our minds to know Christ the Lord intimately, and more effectively turns our hearts to love Him more ardently and to imitate Him more perfectly."[10]

2. Salutary Results of the Devotion in Our Times

16. To Us, no less than to Our predecessors, these capital truths are clear and certain. When We took up Our office of Supreme Pontiff and saw, in full accord with Our prayers and desires, that the devotion to the Sacred Heart of Jesus had increased and was actually, so to speak, making triumphal progress among Christian peoples, We rejoiced that from it were flowing through the whole Church innumerable and salutary results. This We were pleased to point out in Our first encyclical letter.[11]

17. Through the years of Our pontificate—years filled not only with bitter hardships but also with ineffable consolations—these effects have not diminished in number or power or beauty, but on the contrary have increased. Indeed, a variety of projects has happily begun which are conducive to a rekindling of this devotion. We refer to the formation of cultural associations for the advancement of religion and of charitable works; publications setting forth the true historical, ascetical and mystical doctrine concerning this entire subject; pious works of atonement; and in particular those manifestations of most ardent piety which the Apostleship of Prayer has brought about, under whose auspices and direction local gatherings, families, colleges, institutions, and sometimes nations, have been consecrated to the Sacred Heart of Jesus. To all these We have offered paternal congratulations on many occasions, whether in letters written on the subject, in personal addresses, or even in messages delivered over the radio.[12]

18. Therefore when We perceive so fruitful an abundance of healing waters—that is, heavenly gifts of divine love—issuing from the Sacred Heart of our Redeemer, spreading among countless children of the Catholic Church by the inspiration and action of the divine Spirit, We can only exhort you with fatherly affection, venerable brethren, to join Us in giving tribute of praise and heartfelt thanks to God, the Giver of all good gifts. We make Our own these words of the Apostle of the Gentiles: "Now, to him who is able to accomplish all things in a measure far beyond what we ask or conceive, in keeping with the power that is at work in us—to him be glory in the Church and in Christ Jesus down through all the ages of time without end. Amen."[13]

3. The Faithful Are Urged to Study the Sources of the Devotion

19. But after We have paid Our debt of thanks to the

Eternal God, We wish to urge on you and on all Our beloved children of the Church a more earnest consideration
of those principles which take their origin from Scripture
and the teachings of the fathers and theologians and on
which, as on solid foundations, the worship of the Sacred
Heart of Jesus rests. We are absolutely convinced that not
until we have made a profound study of the primary and
loftier nature of this devotion with the aid of the light of
divinely revealed truth, can we rightly and fully appreciate
its incomparable excellence and the inexhaustible abundance of its heavenly favors. Likewise, by devout meditation upon and contemplation of the innumerable benefits
produced from it, we will be able to celebrate worthily the
completion of the first hundred years since the observance
of the feast of the Sacred Heart of Jesus was extended to
the Universal Church.

c. god's love, the principal object of this devotion, as revealed in the old testament

1. *The Importance of Devotion to the Sacred Heart Can Be Shown from Scripture and Tradition*

20. Moved therefore by this consideration, to the end
that the minds of the faithful may have from Our hands
salutary food, and, after such nourishment, be able more
easily to arrive at a deeper understanding of the true nature
of this devotion and possess its rich fruits, We will undertake to explain those pages of the Old and New Testament
in which the infinite love of God for the human race
(which we shall never be able adequately to contemplate)
is revealed and set before us. Then, as occasion offers, We
shall touch upon the main lines of the commentaries
which the fathers and doctors of the Church have handed
down to us. And finally, We shall strive to set in its true
light the very close connection which exists between the

form of devotion paid to the Heart of the divine Redeemer and the worship which we owe to His love and to the love of the Most Holy Trinity for all men. For We think if only the main elements on which that most excellent form of devotion rests are clarified in the light of Sacred Scripture and the teachings of tradition, Christians can more easily "draw waters with joy out of the Saviour's fountain."[14] By this We mean they can appreciate more thoroughly the full weight of the special importance which devotion to the Sacred Heart of Jesus enjoys in the liturgy of the Church and in its internal and external life and action, and can also gather those fruits of salvation by which each one can bring about a healthy reform in his own conduct, as the bishops of the Christian flock desire.

21. That all may understand more exactly the teachings which the selected texts of the Old and New Testament furnish concerning this devotion, they must clearly understand the reason why the Church gives the highest form of worship to the Heart of the divine Redeemer. As you well know, venerable brethren, the reasons are two in number. The first, which applies also to the other sacred members of the body of Jesus Christ, rests on that principle whereby we recognize that His Heart, the noblest part of human nature, is hypostatically united to the Person of the divine Word. Consequently there must be paid to it that worship of adoration with which the Church honors the Person of the Incarnate Son of God Himself. We are dealing here with an article of faith, for it has been solemnly defined in the general Council of Ephesus and the second Council of Constantinople.[15]

2. Reasons for the Worship of the Sacred Heart

22. The other reason which refers in a particular manner to the Heart of the divine Redeemer, and likewise demands in a special way that the highest form of worship be paid

to it, arises from the fact that His Heart, more than all the other members of His body, is the natural sign and symbol of His boundless love for the human race. "There is in the Sacred Heart," as Our predecessor of immortal memory, Leo XIII, pointed out, "the symbol and express image of the infinite love of Jesus Christ which moves us to love in return."[16]

3. There Is No Express Mention of the Sacred Heart in the Old Testament

23. It is of course beyond doubt that the Sacred Books never make express mention of a special worship of veneration and love made to the physical Heart of the Incarnate Word as the symbol of His burning love. But if this must certainly be admitted, it cannot cause us surprise nor in any way lead us to doubt the divine love for us which is the principal object of this devotion; since that love is proclaimed and insisted upon both in the Old and in the New Testament by the kind of images which strongly arouse our emotions. Since these images were presented in the Sacred Writings foretelling the coming of the Son of God made man, they can be considered as a token of the noblest symbol and witness of that divine love, that is, of the most sacred and adorable Heart of the divine Redeemer.

4. The Covenant Between God and the Jews Was Based on Love

24. We do not think it essential to Our subject to cite at length passages from the Old Testament books which contain truths divinely revealed in ancient times. We consider it sufficient to call to mind that the covenant made between God and the people and sanctified by peace offerings—the first Law of which was written on two tablets, made known by Moses,[17] and explained by the prophets—was an agreement established not only on the strong foun-

dation of God's supreme dominion and of man's duty of obedience but was also based and nourished on more noble considerations of love. The ultimate reason for obeying God, for the people of Israel, was not the fear of divine vengeance which the rumble of thunder and the lightning flashing from the top of Mount Sinai struck into their souls, but was rather the love they owed to God. "Hear, O Israel: the Lord our God is one Lord. Thou shalt love the Lord thy God with thy whole heart, and with thy whole soul, and with thy whole strength. And these words which I command thee this day, shall be in thy heart."[18]

5. Examples from Moses, Osee, Isaias, and Jeremias

25. We do not wonder then, that Moses and the prophets, whom the Angelic Doctor rightly names the "elders" of the chosen people,[19] perceived clearly that the foundation of the whole Law lay on this commandment of love, and described all the circumstances and relationships which should exist between God and His people by metaphors drawn from the mutual love of a father and his children, or a man and his wife, rather than from the harsh imagery derived from the supreme dominion of God or the obligation of subjecting ourselves in fear. And so, to take an example, when Moses himself was singing his famous hymn in honor of the people restored to freedom from the slavery of Egypt, and wished to indicate that it had come about by the power of God, he used these symbolic and touching expressions: "As the eagle enticing her young to fly, and hovering over them, he (God) spread his wings, and hath taken him (Israel) and carried him on his shoulders."[20]

26. But perhaps none of the holy prophets has expressed and revealed as clearly and vividly as Osee the love with which God always watches over His people. In the writings of this prophet, who is outstanding among the minor

prophets for the sublimity of his concise language, God declares that His love for the chosen people, combining justice and a holy anxiety, is like the love of a merciful and loving father or of a husband whose honor is offended. This love is not diminished or withdrawn in the face of the perfidy or the horrible crimes of those who betray it. If it inflicts just chastisements on the guilty, it is not for the purpose of rejecting them or of abandoning them to themselves, but rather to bring about the repentance and the purification of the unfaithful spouse and ungrateful children, and to bind them once more to itself with renewed and yet stronger bonds of love. "Because Israel was a child, and I loved him: and I called my son out of Egypt. . . . And I was like a foster father to Ephraim, I carried them in my arms, and they knew not that I healed them, I will draw them with the cords of Adam, with the bands of love . . . I will heal their wounds, I will love them freely: for my wrath is turned away from them. I will be as the dew: Israel shall spring as the lily, and his root shall shoot forth as that of Libanus."[21]

27. Similar sentiments are uttered by the prophet Isaias when he introduces a conversation in the form of question and answer, as it were, between God and the chosen people: "And Sion said, The Lord hath forsaken me, and the Lord hath forgotten me. Can a woman forget her infant, so as not to have pity on the son of her womb? And if she should forget, yet will not I forget thee."[22]

28. No less moving are the words with which the author of the Canticle of Canticles, employing comparisons from conjugal affection, describes symbolically the bonds of mutual love by which God and His chosen people are united to each other: "As the lily among thorns, so is my love among the daughters. . . . I to my beloved, and my beloved to me, who feedeth among the lilies. . . . Put me as a seal upon thy heart, as a seal upon thy arm: for love is

strong as death, jealousy as hard as hell. The lamps thereof are fire and flames."[23]

29. This most tender, forgiving and patient love of God, though it deems unworthy the people of Israel as they add sin to sin, nevertheless at no time casts them off entirely. And though it seems strong and exalted indeed, yet it was only an advance symbol of that burning charity which mankind's promised Redeemer, from His most loving Heart, was destined to open to all, and which was to be the type of His love for us and the foundation of the new Covenant.

30. Assuredly, when He who is the only-begotten of the Father, and the Word made flesh, "full of grace and truth,"[24] had come to men, weighed down with many sins and miseries, it was He alone, from that human nature united hypostatically to the divine Person, who could open to the human race the "fountain of living water" which would irrigate the parched land and transform it into a fruitful and flourishing garden.

31. That this most wondrous effect would come to pass as a result of the merciful love of God, the prophet Jeremias seems to foretell in a manner in these words: "I have loved thee with an everlasting love: therefore have I drawn thee, taking pity on thee. . . . Behold the days shall come, saith the Lord, and I will make a new covenant with the house of Israel and with the house of Juda . . . this shall be the covenant that I will make with the house of Israel, after those days, saith the Lord: I will give my law in their bowels and I will write it in their heart: and I will be their God and they shall be my people . . . for I will forgive their iniquity and I will remember their sin no more."[25]

Part II: *Devotion to the Sacred Heart in the Light of the New Testament and Tradition*

A. GOD'S LOVE IN THE MYSTERY OF THE REDEMPTION, AS REVEALED IN THE GOSPELS

1. *The Superiority of the New Testament over the Old*

32. But it is only in the Gospels that we find definitely and clearly set out the new covenant between God and man; for that covenant which Moses had made between the people of Israel and God was a mere symbol and a sign of the covenant foretold by the prophet Jeremias. We say that this new covenant is that very thing which was established and effected by the work of the Incarnate Word, who is the source of divine grace. This covenant is therefore to be considered incomparably more excellent and more solid, because it was ratified, not as in the past by the blood of goats and calves, but by the most Precious Blood of Him whom these same innocent animals, devoid of reason, had already prefigured: "The lamb of God, who takes away the sin of the world."[26]

33. The Christian covenant, much more than that of the old, clearly appears as an agreement based not on slavery or on fear, but as one ratified by that friendship which ought to exist between a father and his children; as one nourished and strengthened by a more generous outpouring of divine grace and truth, according to the saying of St. John the Evangelist: "And of his fullness we have all received, grace for grace. For the Law was given *through* Moses; grace and truth came *through* Jesus Christ."[27]

34. Since we have been introduced, venerable brethren, to the innermost mystery of the infinite charity of the Word Incarnate, by these words of the disciple "whom Jesus loved, the one who, at the supper, had leaned back upon his breast,"[28] it seems meet and just, right and avail-

ing unto salvation, to pause for a short time in sweet contemplation of this mystery, so that enlightened by that
light which shines from the Gospel and makes clearer the
mystery itself, we also may be able to obtain the realization of the desire of which the Apostle of the Gentiles
speaks in writing to the Ephesians: "to have Christ dwelling through faith in your hearts: so that, being rooted and
grounded in love, you may be able to comprehend with
all the saints what is the breadth and length and height
and depth, and to know Christ's love which surpasses
knowledge, in order that you may be filled unto all the
fullness of God."[29]

2. A Twofold Love in the Mystery of the Redemption

35. The mystery of the divine redemption is primarily
and by its very nature a mystery of love, that is, of the perfect love of Christ for His heavenly Father to whom the
sacrifice of the cross, offered in a spirit of love and obedience, presents the most abundant and infinite satisfaction
due for the sins of the human race: "By suffering out of
love and obedience, Christ gave more to God than was required to compensate for the offense of the whole human
race."[30]

36. It is also a mystery of the love of the Most Holy
Trinity and of the divine Redeemer towards all men. Because they were entirely unable to make adequate satisfaction for their sins,[31] Christ, through the infinite treasure of
His merits acquired for us by the shedding of His Precious
Blood, was able to restore completely that pact of friendship between God and man which had been broken, first
by the grievous fall of Adam in the earthly paradise and
then by the countless sins of the chosen people.

37. Since our divine Redeemer as our lawful and perfect Mediator, out of His ardent love for us, restored complete harmony between the duties and obligations of the

human race and the rights of God, He is therefore responsible for the existence of that wonderful reconciliation of
divine justice and divine mercy which constitutes the sublime mystery of our salvation. On this point the Angelic
Doctor wisely comments: "That man should be delivered
by Christ's Passion was in keeping with both His mercy
and His justice. With His justice, because by His Passion
Christ made satisfaction for the sins of the human race,
and so man was set free by Christ's justice; and with His
mercy, for since man of himself could not satisfy for the
sin of all human nature, God gave him His Son to satisfy
for him. And this came of a more copious mercy than if
He had forgiven sins without satisfaction. Hence St. Paul
says: 'God, who is rich in mercy, by reason of his very great
love wherewith he has loved us even when we were dead
by reason of our sins, brought us to life together with
Christ.' "[32]

3. The Nature of Christ's Love

38. But in order that we really may be able, so far as it
is permitted to mortal men, "to comprehend with all the
saints what is the breadth and length and height and
depth"[33] of the hidden love of the Incarnate Word for His
heavenly Father and for men infected by the taint of sins,
we must note well that His love was not entirely the spiritual love proper to God inasmuch as "God is a spirit."[34]
Undoubtedly the love with which God loved our forefa-
thers and the Hebrew people was of this nature. For this
reason the expressions of human, intimate, and paternal
love which we find in the Psalms, the writings of the
prophets, and in the Canticle of Canticles are tokens and
symbols of the true but entirely spiritual love with which
God continued to sustain the human race. On the other
hand, the love which breathes from the Gospel, from the

letters of the apostles and the pages of the Apocalypse, all of which portray the love of the Heart of Jesus Christ, expresses not only divine love but also human sentiments of love. All who profess themselves Catholics accept this without question.

39. For the Word of God did not assume a feigned and unsubstantial body, as even in the first century of Christianity some heretics declared, who were condemned in these solemn words of St. John the Apostle: "For many deceivers have gone forth into the world who do not confess Jesus as the Christ coming in the flesh. This is the deceiver and the Antichrist,"[35] but He united to His divine Person a truly human nature, individual, whole and perfect, which was conceived in the most pure womb of the Virgin Mary by the power of the Holy Ghost.[36]

4. Christ Put on a Perfect Human Nature

40. Nothing, then, was wanting to the human nature which the Word of God united to Himself. Consequently He assumed it in no diminished way, in no different sense concerning the spiritual and the corporeal: that is, it was endowed with intellect and will and the other internal and external faculties of perception, and likewise with the desires and all the natural impulses of the senses. All this the Catholic Church teaches as solemnly defined and ratified by the Roman Pontiffs and the general councils. "Whole and entire in what is His own, whole and entire in what is ours."[37] "Perfect in His Godhead and likewise perfect in His humanity."[38] "Complete God is man, complete man is God."[39]

. . . with a Heart Capable of Suffering

41. Hence, since there can be no doubt that Jesus Christ received a true body and had all the affections proper to the same, among which love surpassed all the rest, it is

likewise beyond doubt that He was endowed with a physical heart like ours; for without this noblest part of the body the ordinary emotions of human life are impossible. Therefore the Heart of Jesus Christ, hypostatically united to the divine Person of the Word, certainly beat with love and with the other emotions; but these, joined to a human will full of divine charity and to the infinite love itself which the Son shares with the Father and the Holy Spirit, were in such complete unity and agreement that never among these three loves was there any contradiction or disharmony.[40]

42. However, even though the Word of God took to Himself a true and perfect human nature, and made and fashioned for Himself a heart of flesh, which, no less than ours, could suffer and be pierced, unless this fact is considered in the light of the hypostatic and substantial union and in the light of its complement, the fact of man's redemption, it can be a stumbling block and foolishness to some, just as Jesus Christ, nailed to the Cross, actually was to the Jewish race and to the Gentiles.[41]

43. The official teachings of the Catholic faith, in complete agreement with Scripture, assure us that the only-begotten Son of God took a human nature capable of suffering and death especially because He desired, as He hung from the Cross, to offer a bloody sacrifice in order to complete the work of man's salvation. This the Apostle of the Gentiles teaches in another way: "For both he who sanctifies and they who are sanctified are all from one. For which cause he is not ashamed to call them brethren, saying, 'I will declare thy name to my brethren'. . . . And again, 'Behold, I and my children whom God has given me.' Therefore because children have blood and flesh in common, so he in like manner has shared in these. . . . Wherefore it was right that he should in all things be made like unto His brethren, that he might become a merciful

and faithful high priest before God to expiate the sins of the people. For in that he himself has suffered and has been tempted, he is able to help those who are tempted."[42]

B. THE TEACHING OF THE FATHERS OF THE CHURCH

1. The Mystery of Love is the Foundation and Culmination of the Incarnation and Redemption

44. The holy fathers, true witnesses of the divinely revealed doctrine, wonderfully understood what St. Paul the Apostle had quite clearly declared: namely, that the mystery of love was, as it were, both the foundation and the culmination of the Incarnation and the Redemption. For frequently and clearly we can read in their writings that Jesus Christ took a perfect human nature and our weak and perishable human body with the object of providing for our eternal salvation, and of revealing to us in the clearest possible manner that His infinite love for us could express itself in human terms.

45. St. Justin, almost echoing the voice of the Apostle of the Gentiles, writes: "We adore and love the Word born of the unbegotten and ineffable God since He became man for our sake, so that having become a partaker of our sufferings He might provide a remedy for them."[43]

46. St. Basil, the first of the three Cappadocian Fathers, declares that the activities of the senses in Christ were at once true and holy: "It is clear that the Lord did indeed put on natural affections as a proof of His real and not imaginary Incarnation, and that He rejected as unworthy of the Godhead those corrupt affections which defile the purity of our life."[44]

47. Similarly that light of the Church of Antioch, St. John Chrysostom, admits that the emotion to which the divine Redeemer was subject made obvious the fact that He assumed a human nature complete in all respects: "For

if He had not shared our nature He would not have re-peatedly been seized with grief."[45]

48. Among the Latin Fathers one may cite those whom the Church today honors as the greatest doctors. Thus St. Ambrose bears witness that the movements and disposi-tions of the senses, from which the Incarnate Word of God was not exempt, flow from the hypostatic union as from their natural source: "And therefore He put on a soul and the passions of the soul; for God, precisely because He is God, could not have been disturbed nor could He have died."[46]

49. It was from these very emotions that St. Jerome de-rived His chief proof that Christ had really put on human nature: "Our Lord, to prove the truth of the manhood He had assumed, experienced real sadness."[47]

50. St. Augustine notices in a special manner the con-nections that exist between the sentiments of the Incar-nate Word and their purpose, man's redemption. "These affections of human infirmity, even as the human body itself, and death, the Lord Jesus put on not out of necessity, but freely, out of compassion, so that He might transform in Himself His body, which is the Church of which He deigned to be the Head, that is, His members who are among the faithful and the saints, so that if any of them in the trials of this life should be saddened and afflicted they should not therefore think that they are de-prived of His grace. Nor should they consider this sorrow a sin, but a sign of human weakness. Like a choir singing in harmony with the note that has been sounded, so should His body learn from its Head."[48]

51. More briefly, but no less effectively, do the follow-ing passages from St. John Damascene set out the teaching of the Church: "Complete God assumed me completely, and complete man is united to complete God so that He might bring salvation to complete man. For what was not

assumed could not be healed."[49] "He therefore assumed all that He might sanctify all."[50]

52. It must be noted, however, that although these selected passages from Scripture and the fathers, and many similar ones that We have not cited, give clear testimony that Jesus Christ was endowed with affections and sense perceptions, and hence that He assumed human nature in order to work for our eternal salvation, yet they never refer those affections to His physical heart in such a way as to point to it clearly as the symbol of His infinite love.

2. Christ Put on Human Nature to Manifest His Love in a Human Way

53. Granted that the evangelists and other sacred writers do not explicitly describe the heart of our Redeemer, living and throbbing like our own with the power of feeling, and ever throbbing with the emotions and affections of His soul and the glowing charity of His twofold will, yet they often set in their proper light His divine love and the sense emotions which accompany it: that is, desire, joy, weakness, fear, and anger, as shown by His face, words or gestures. The face of our adorable Saviour was especially the guide, and a kind of faithful reflection, of those emotions which moved His soul in various ways, and like recurrent waves touched His Sacred Heart and excited its beating. For what is true of human psychology and its effects is valid here also. The Angelic Doctor, relying on ordinary experience, notes: "An emotion caused by anger is conveyed to the external members, and particularly to those members in which the heart's imprint is more obviously reflected, such as the eyes, the face, and the tongue."[51]

C. THE HEART OF THE INCARNATE WORD IS THE SYMBOL OF HIS THREEFOLD LOVE

54. For these reasons, the Heart of the Incarnate Word

is deservedly and rightly considered the chief sign and symbol of that threefold love with which the divine Redeemer unceasingly loves His eternal Father and all mankind.

55. It is a symbol of that divine love which He shares with the Father and the Holy Spirit but which He, the Word made flesh, alone manifests through a weak and perishable body, since "in him dwells the fullness of the Godhead bodily."[52]

56. It is, besides, the symbol of that burning love which, infused into His soul, enriches the human will of Christ and enlightens and governs its acts by the most perfect knowledge both derived from the beatific vision and directly infused.[53]

57. Finally—and this is a more natural and direct way —it is the symbol also of sensible love, since the body of Jesus Christ, formed by the Holy Ghost in the womb of the Virgin Mary, possesses full powers of feelings and perception, in fact, more so than any other human body.[54]

D. CONCLUSIONS

1. Ways in Which We Can Honor the Heart of Our Redeemer

58. Since, therefore, Sacred Scripture and the official teaching of the Catholic faith instruct us that all things find their complete harmony and order in the most holy person of Jesus Christ, and that He has manifestly directed His threefold love for the securing of our redemption, it unquestionably follows that we can contemplate and honor the Heart of the divine Redeemer as a symbolic image of His love, a witness of our redemption, and, at the same time, as a sort of mystical ladder by which we mount to the embrace of "God our Saviour."[55]

2. Everything He Did Was a Proof of His Threefold Love

59. Hence His words, actions, commands, miracles, and especially those works which manifest more clearly His love for us (such as the institution of the Eucharist, His most bitter sufferings and death, the loving gift of His holy Mother to us, the founding of the Church for us, and finally, the sending of the Holy Spirit upon the apostles and upon us)—all these, We say, ought to be looked upon as proofs of His threefold love.

3. We Should Meditate on the Beatings of His Heart

60. Likewise we ought to meditate most lovingly on the beating of His Sacred Heart by which He seemed, as it were, to measure the time of His sojourn on earth until that final moment when, as the evangelists testify, "Jesus . . . cried out with a loud voice 'It is consummated!' And bowing his head, he gave up his spirit."[56] Then it was that His heart ceased to beat and His sensible love was interrupted until the time when, triumphing over death, He rose from the tomb.

4. His Heart Will Never Cease to Symbolize His Threefold Love

61. But after His glorified body had been reunited to the soul of the divine Redeemer, conqueror of death, His most Sacred Heart never ceased, and never will cease, to beat with calm and imperturbable pulsations. Likewise, it will never cease to symbolize the threefold love with which He is bound to His heavenly Father and to the entire human race, of which He has every claim to be the mystical Head.

PART III: *The Profound Influence of the Heart of Jesus
in His Redemptive Mission*

A. MANIFESTATIONS OF DIVINE AND HUMAN LOVE
IN THE GOSPELS

62. And now, venerable brethren, in order that we may
be able to gather from these holy considerations abundant
and salutary fruits, We desire to reflect on and briefly
contemplate the manifold affections, human and divine, of
our Saviour Jesus Christ, which His Heart made known to
us during the course of His mortal life and which it still
does and will continue to do for all eternity. From the
pages of the Gospel particularly there shines forth for us
the light, by the brightness and strength of which we can
enter into the secret places of this divine Heart and, with
the Apostle of the Gentiles, gaze at "the abundant riches
of (God's) grace, in His bounty towards us in Christ
Jesus."[57]

1. . . . *in His Hidden Life*

63. The adorable Heart of Jesus Christ began to beat
with a love at once human and divine after the Virgin
Mary generously pronounced her *Fiat;* and the Word of
God, as the apostle remarks: "coming into the world, saith,
'Sacrifice and oblation thou wouldst not, but a body thou
hast fitted to me; in holocausts and sin-offerings thou hast
had no pleasure. Then said I, Behold I come—(in the
head of the book it is written of me) to do thy will, O
God!' . . . It is in this "will" that we have been sanctified through the offering of the body of Jesus Christ once
for all."[58]

64. Likewise was He moved by love, completely in harmony with the affections of His human will and the divine
love, when, in the house at Nazareth, He conversed with
His most sweet mother and His foster-father, St. Joseph,

in obedience to whom He performed laborious tasks in the trade of a carpenter.

2. . . . in His Public Life

65. Again, He was influenced by that threefold love, of which We spoke, during His public life: in long apostolic journeys; in the working of innumerable miracles, by which He summoned back from the grave or granted health to all manner of sick persons; in enduring labors; in bearing fatigue, hunger and thirst; in the nightly watchings during which He prayed most lovingly to His Father; and finally, in His preaching and in setting forth and explaining His parables, in those particularly which deal with mercy—the lost drachma, the lost sheep, the prodigal son. By these indeed, both by act and by word, as St. Gregory the Great notes, the Heart of God Itself is revealed: "Learn the Heart of God in the words of God, that you may long more ardently for things eternal."[59]

66. But the Heart of Jesus Christ was moved by a more urgent charity when from His lips were drawn words breathing the most ardent love. Thus, to give examples: when He was gazing at the crowds weary and hungry, He exclaimed, "I have compassion on the crowd";[60] when He looked down on His beloved city of Jerusalem, blinded by its sins, and so destined for final ruin, He uttered this sentence: "Jerusalem, Jerusalem, thou who killest the prophets, and stonest those who are sent to thee! How often would I have gathered thy children together, as a hen gathers her young under her wings, but thou wouldst not!"[61] And His Heart beat with love for His Father and with a holy anger when, seeing the sacrilegious buying and selling taking place in the temple, He rebuked the violators with these words: "It is written, 'My house shall be called a house of prayer'; but you have made it a den of thieves."[62]

3. . . . in His Passion and Death

67. But His Heart was moved by a particularly intense love mingled with fear as He perceived the hour of His bitter torments drawing near and, expressing a natural repugnance for the approaching pains and death, He cried out: "Father, if it is possible, let this cup pass away from me."[63] And when He was greeted by the traitor with a kiss, in love triumphant united to deepest grief, He addressed to him those words which seem to be the final invitation of His most merciful Heart to the friend who, obdurate in his wicked treachery, was about to hand Him over to His executioners: "Friend, for what purpose hast thou come? Dost thou betray the Son of Man with a kiss?"[64] It was out of pity and the depths of His love that He spoke to the devout women as they wept for Him on His way to the unmerited penalty of the cross: "Daughters of Jerusalem, do not weep for me, but weep for yourselves and for your children . . . For if in the case of green wood they do these things, what is to happen in the case of the dry?"[65]

68. And when the divine Redeemer was hanging on the cross, He showed that His Heart was strongly moved by different emotions—burning love, desolation, pity, longing desire, unruffled peace. The words spoken plainly indicate these emotions: "Father, forgive them; they know not what they do!"[66] "My God, my God, why hast thou forsaken me?"[67] "Amen I say to thee, this day thou shalt be with me in paradise."[68] "I thirst."[69] "Father, into thy hands I commend my spirit."[70]

B. GIFTS OF THE HEART OF JESUS TO MEN

69. But who can worthily depict those beatings of the divine Heart, the signs of His infinite love, at those moments when He granted men His greatest gifts: Himself

in the sacrament of the Eucharist, His most holy Mother, and the office of the priesthood shared with us?

1. The Eucharist and the Priesthood

70. Even before He ate the Last Supper with His disciples, Christ our Lord, since He knew He was about to institute the sacrament of His body and blood by the shedding of which the new covenant was to be consecrated, felt His heart roused by strong emotions, which He revealed to the apostles in these words: "I have greatly desired to eat this passover with you before I suffer."[71] And these emotions were doubtless even stronger when "having taken bread, he gave thanks and broke, and gave it to them, saying, 'This is my body which is being given for you; do this in remembrance of me.' In like manner he took also the cup after the supper, saying, 'This cup is the new covenant in my blood, which shall be shed for you.' "[72]

71. It can therefore rightly be declared that the divine Eucharist, both the sacrament which He gives to men and the sacrifice in which He unceasingly offers Himself "from the rising of the sun till the going down thereof,"[73] and likewise the priesthood, are indeed gifts of the Sacred Heart of Jesus.

2. The Gift of His Mother

72. Another most precious gift of His Sacred Heart is, as We have said, Mary, the beloved mother of God and the most loving mother of us all. She who gave birth to our Saviour according to the flesh, and was associated with Him in recalling the children of Eve to the life of divine grace, has deservedly been hailed as the spiritual mother of the whole human race. And so St. Augustine writes of her: "Clearly she is mother of the members of the Saviour (which is what we are), because she labored with Him in

love that the faithful who are members of the Head might be born in the Church."[74]

73. To the unbloody gift of Himself, under the appearance of bread and wine, our Saviour Jesus Christ wished to join, as the chief proof of His deep and infinite love, the bloody sacrifice of the cross. By this manner of acting, He gave an example of His supreme charity, which He had proposed to His disciples as the highest point of love in these words: "Greater love than this no one has, that one lay down his life for his friends."[75]

74. Thus the love of Jesus Christ the Son of God, by the sacrifice of Golgotha, cast a flood of light on the meaning of the love of God Himself: "In this we have come to know his love, that he laid down his life for us; and we likewise ought to lay down our life for the brethren."[76] And in truth it was more by love than by the violence of the executioners that our divine Redeemer was fixed to the cross, and His voluntary total offering is the supreme gift which He gave to each man, according to that terse saying of the apostle: "He loved me, and gave Himself up for me."[77]

C. THE SYMBOLISM OF THE PIERCED HEART OF JESUS

75. The Sacred Heart of Jesus shares in a most intimate way in the life of the Incarnate Word, and has been thus assumed as a kind of instrument of the Divinity. It is therefore beyond all doubt that, in the carrying out of works of grace and divine omnipotence, His Heart, no less than the other members of His human nature, is also a legitimate symbol of that unbounded love.[78]

1. *His Mystical Marriage with His Church*

76. Under the influence of this love, our Saviour, by the

outpouring of His blood, became wedded to His Church: "By love, He allowed Himself to be espoused to His Church."[79] Hence, from the wounded Heart of the Redeemer was born the Church, the dispenser of the blood of the Redemption, whence flows that plentiful stream of sacramental grace from which the children of the Church drink of eternal life, as we read in the sacred liturgy: "From the pierced Heart the Church, the Bride of Christ, is born . . . And He pours forth grace from His Heart."[80]

2. The Image of God's Love for Us

77. Concerning the meaning of this symbol, which was known even to the earliest Fathers and ecclesiastical writers, St. Thomas Aquinas, echoing something of their words, writes as follows: "From the side of Christ, there flowed water for cleansing, blood for redeeming. Hence blood is associated with the sacrament of the Eucharist, water with the sacrament of baptism, which has its cleansing power by virtue of the blood of Christ."[81]

78. What is here written of the side of Christ, opened by the wound from the soldier, should also be said of the Heart which was certainly reached by the stab of the lance, since the soldier pierced it precisely to make certain that Jesus Christ crucified was really dead. Hence the wound of the Most Sacred Heart of Jesus, now that He has completed His mortal life, remains through the course of the ages a striking image of that spontaneous charity by which God gave His only-begotten Son for the redemption of men, and by which Christ expressed such passionate love for us that He offered Himself as a bleeding victim on Calvary for our sake: "Christ also loved us and delivered himself up for us an offering and a sacrifice to God to ascend in a fragrant odor."[82]

D. IN HEAVEN THE HEART OF JESUS CONTINUES TO LOVE HIS CHURCH

79. After our Lord had ascended into heaven, His body adorned with the splendors of eternal glory, and had taken His place by the right hand of the Father, He did not cease to remain with His Spouse, the Church, by means of the burning love with which His Heart beats. For He bears in His hands, feet, and side, the glorious marks of the wounds which manifest the threefold victory won over the devil, sin, and death.

80. He likewise keeps in His Heart, locked as it were in a most precious shrine, the unlimited treasure of His merits, the fruits of that same threefold triumph, which He generously bestows on the redeemed human race. This is a truth full of consolation, which the Apostle of the Gentiles expresses in these words: " 'Ascending on high, he led away captives; he gave gifts to men.' . . . He who descended, he it is who ascended also above all the heavens, that he might fill all things."[83]

1. *The Gift of the Holy Spirit*

81. The gift of the Holy Spirit, sent to His disciples, is the first notable sign of His abounding charity after His triumphant ascent to the right hand of His Father. For after ten days the Holy Spirit, given by the heavenly Father, came down upon them in the upper room in accordance with the promise made at the Last Supper: "I will ask the Father and he will give you another Advocate to dwell with you forever."[84] And this Advocate, who is the mutual personal love between the Father and the Son, is sent by both. Under the adopted appearance of tongues of fire, He poured into their souls an abundance of divine charity and the other heavenly gifts.

2. *Divine Love, a Gift of the Heart of Jesus*

82. The infusion of this divine charity also has its origin in the heart of the Saviour, in which "are hidden all the treasures of wisdom and knowledge."[85] For this charity is the gift of Jesus Christ and of His Spirit; for He is indeed the spirit of the Father and the Son from whom the origin of the Church and its marvelous extension are revealed to all the pagan races which had been defiled by idolatry, family hatred, corrupt morals, and violence.

3. *Divine Love, the Source of All Graces*

83. This divine charity is the most precious gift of the Heart of Christ and of His Spirit: it is this which imparted to the apostles and martyrs that fortitude, by the strength of which they fought their battles like heroes until death, in order to preach the truth of the Gospel and bear witness to it by the shedding of their blood; it is this which implanted in the doctors of the Church their intense zeal for explaining and defending the Catholic faith; this nourished the virtues of the confessors, and roused them to those marvelous works useful for their own salvation, and beneficial to the salvation of others both in this life and in the next; this, finally, moved the virgins to a free and joyful withdrawal from the pleasures of the senses, and to complete dedication of themselves to the love of their heavenly Spouse.

84. It was to pay honor to this divine charity which, overflowing from the Heart of the Incarnate Word, is poured out by the aid of the Holy Spirit into the souls of all believers, that the Apostle of the Gentiles uttered this hymn of triumph, which proclaims the victory of Christ the Head, and of the members of His mystical body, over all which might in any way impede the establishment of the Kingdom of Love among men: "Who shall separate

us from the love of Christ? Shall tribulation, or distress, or persecution, or hunger, or nakedness, or danger, or the sword? . . . But in all these things we overcome because of him who has loved us. For I am sure that neither death, nor life, nor angels, nor principalities, nor things present, nor things to come, nor powers, nor height, nor depth, nor any other creature will be able to separate us from the love of God, which is in Christ Jesus our Lord."[86]

E. CONCLUSIONS

1. We May Adore the Sacred Heart as the Symbol and Source of Love

85. Nothing therefore prevents our adoring the Sacred Heart of Jesus Christ, as having a part in and being the natural and expressive symbol of the abiding love with which the Divine Redeemer is still on fire for mankind. Though it is no longer subject to the varying emotions of this mortal life, yet it lives and beats, and is united inseparably with the Person of the Divine Word, and, in Him and through Him, with the Divine Will. Since, then, the Heart of Christ is overflowing with love both human and divine, and rich with the treasures of all graces which our Redeemer acquired by His life, sufferings and death, it is therefore the enduring source of that charity which His Spirit pours forth on all the members of His mystical body.

2. The Sacred Heart Is a Summary of the Mystery of Redemption

86. And so the Heart of our Saviour reflects in some way the image of the divine Person of the Word, and, at the same time, of His twofold nature, the human and the divine; in it we can consider not only the symbol, but, in

a sense, the summary of the whole mystery of our Redemption. When we adore the Sacred Heart of Jesus Christ, we adore, in it and through it, both the uncreated love of the Divine Word and also its human love and its other emotions and virtues, since both loves moved our Redeemer to sacrifice Himself for us and for His Spouse, the Universal Church, as the apostle declares: "Christ . . . loved the Church, and delivered himself up for her, that he might sanctify her, cleansing her in the bath of water by means of the word; in order that he might present to Himself the Church in all her glory, not having spot or wrinkle or any such thing, but that she might be holy and without blemish."[87]

3. The Heart of Jesus Is a Powerful Advocate with His Father

87. Just as Christ loved the Church, so He still loves it most intensely with that threefold love of which we spoke, which moved Him as our Advocate,[88] "always living to make intercession for us,"[89] to win grace and mercy for us from His Father. The prayers which are drawn from that unfailing love, and are directed to the Father, never cease. As "in the days of His earthly life,"[90] so now victorious in heaven, He makes His petition to His heavenly Father with equal efficacy, to Him who "so loved the world that he gave his only-begotten Son, that those who believe in him may not perish, but may have life everlasting."[91] He shows His living Heart, wounded as it were, and throbbing with a love yet more intense than when it was wounded in death by the Roman soldier's lance: "[Thy Heart] has been wounded so that through the visible wound we may behold the invisible wound of love."[92]

88. It is beyond doubt, then, that His heavenly Father, "who has not spared even His own Son, but has delivered him for us all,"[93] when appealed to with such loving ur-

gency by so powerful an Advocate, will, through Him, send down on all men an abundance of divine graces.

PART IV: *The Origin and Development of This Devotion*

89. It was Our wish, venerable brethren, by this general outline, to set before you and the faithful the inner nature of the devotion to the Sacred Heart of Jesus Christ and the endless riches which spring from it as they are made clear by the primary source of doctrine, divine revelation. We think that Our comments, which are guided by the light of the Gospel, have proved that this devotion, summarily expressed, is nothing else than devotion to the divine and human love of the Incarnate Word and to the love by which the heavenly Father and the Holy Spirit exercise their care over sinful men. For as the Angelic Doctor, St. Thomas Aquinas, teaches, the love of the Most Holy Trinity is the origin of man's redemption; it overflowed into the human will of Jesus Christ and into His adorable Heart with full efficacy, and led Him, under the impulse of that love, to pour forth His blood to redeem us from captivity of sin:[94] "I have a baptism to be baptized with, and how distressed I am until it be accomplished!"[95]

A. THIS DEVOTION IS NOT ENTIRELY NEW

90. We are convinced, then, that the devotion which We are fostering to the love of God and Jesus Christ for the human race, by means of the revered symbol of the pierced Heart of the crucified Redeemer, has never been altogether unknown to the piety of the faithful, although it has become more clearly known and spread in a remarkable manner throughout the Church in quite recent times. Particularly was this so after our Lord Himself had privately revealed this divine secret to some of His children,

to whom He had granted an abundance of heavenly gifts, and whom He had chosen as His special messengers and heralds of this devotion.

1. *It Is an Outgrowth of Devotion to Christ's Sacred Humanity*

91. But, in fact, there have always been men specially dedicated to God who, following the example of the beloved Mother of God, of the apostles and the great fathers of the Church, have practiced the devotion of thanksgiving, adoration, and love toward the most sacred human nature of Christ, and especially toward the wounds by which His body was torn when He was enduring suffering for our salvation.

92. Moreover, is there not contained in those words "My Lord and My God"[96] which St. Thomas the apostle uttered, and which showed he had been changed from an unbeliever into a faithful follower, a profession of faith, adoration and love, mounting up from the wounded human nature of his Lord to the majesty of the divine Person?

93. But if men have always been deeply moved by the pierced Heart of the Saviour to a worship of that infinite love with which He embraces mankind—since the words of the prophet Zacharias "They shall look on him whom they have pierced,"[97] referred by St. John the Evangelist to Jesus nailed to the cross, have been spoken to Christians in all ages—it must yet be admitted that it was only by a very gradual advance that the honors of a special devotion were offered to that Heart as depicting the love, human and divine, which exists in the Incarnate Word.

2. *Forerunners of the Modern Devotion*

94. But for those who wish to touch on the more significant stages of this devotion through the centuries, if we consider outward practice, there immediately occur the

names of certain individuals who have won particular re-
nown in this matter as being the advance guard of a form
of piety which, privately and very gradually, had gained
more and more strength in religious congregations. To cite
some examples in establishing this devotion to the Sacred
Heart of Jesus and continuously promoting it, great service
was rendered by St. Bonaventure, St. Albert the Great,
St. Gertrude, St. Catherine of Siena, Blessed Henry Suso,
St. Peter Canisius, and St. Francis of Sales. St. John Eudes
was responsible for the first liturgical office celebrated in
honor of the Sacred Heart of Jesus, whose solemn feast,
with the approval of many bishops in France, was observed
for the first time on October 20, 1672.

3. St. Margaret Mary Alacoque

95. But surely the most distinguished place among those
who have fostered this most excellent type of devotion is
held by St. Margaret Mary Alacoque. She, under the spiritual direction of Blessed Claude de la Colombiére, who
assisted her work, was on fire with an unusual zeal to see
to it that the real meaning of the devotion which had had
such extensive development—to the great edification of the
faithful—should be established and be distinguished from
other forms of Christian piety by the special qualities of
love and reparation.[98]

B. ITS PROGRESS IS DUE TO ITS HARMONY WITH DOCTRINE

1. It Did Not Originate from a Private Revelation

96. It is enough to recall the record of that age in which
the devotion to the Sacred Heart of Jesus began to develop
to understand clearly that its marvelous progress has
stemmed from the fact that it agreed entirely with the
nature of Christian piety, since it was a devotion of love.

It must not be said that this devotion has taken its origin from some private revelation of God and has suddenly appeared in the Church; rather, it has blossomed forth of its own accord as a result of that lively faith and burning devotion of men who were endowed with heavenly gifts, and who were drawn toward the adorable Redeemer and His glorious wounds, which they saw as irresistible proofs of that unbounded love.

2. The Importance of the Revelations to St. Margaret Mary Alacoque

97. Consequently, it is clear that the revelations made to St. Margaret Mary brought nothing new into Catholic doctrine. Their importance lay in this: that Christ our Lord, exposing His Sacred Heart, wished in a quite extraordinary way to invite the minds of men to a contemplation of, and a devotion to, the mystery of God's merciful love for the human race. In this special manifestation Christ pointed to His Heart, with definite and repeated words, as the symbol by which men should be attracted to a knowledge and recognition of His love. At the same time, He established it as a sign or pledge of mercy and grace for the needs of the Church of our times.

3. The Feast Was Approved before the Writings of the Saint

98. That this devotion flows from the very foundations of Christian teaching is clearly shown by the fact that the Apostolic See approved the liturgical feast before it approved the writings of St. Margaret Mary. Without exactly taking account of any private revelation from God, but rather graciously acceding to the petitions of the faithful, the Sacred Congregation of Rites—by a decree of the 25th of January, 1765, which was approved by Our predecessor, Clement XIII, on the 6th of February of the same year—

granted the liturgical celebration of the feast to the Polish bishops and to what was called the Archconfraternity of the Sacred Heart of Jesus at Rome. The Apostolic See acted in this way so that the devotion then existing and flourishing might be extended, since its purpose was "by this symbol to renew the memory of that divine love"[99] by which our Saviour was moved to offer Himself as a victim atoning for the sins of men.

4. The Extension of the Feast to the Universal Church

99. This first approval, granted as a privilege and restricted within limits, was followed about a century later by another of far greater importance and couched in more solemn terms. We mean the decree, which We referred to above, of the Sacred Congregation of Rites of the 23rd of August, 1856, by Our predecessor of immortal memory, Pius IX, in answer to the prayer of the French bishops and of almost the whole Catholic world, which extended the feast of the Sacred Heart of Jesus to the universal Church and ordered it to be fittingly observed.[100] This act richly deserves to be commended to the lasting memory of the faithful, for as we read in the liturgy of the same feast: "From that time the devotion to the Sacred Heart, like a stream in flood sweeping aside all obstacles, spread out over the whole world."

100. From what We have so far explained, venerable brethren, it is clear that the faithful must seek from Scripture, tradition and the sacred liturgy, as from a deep, untainted source, the devotion to the Sacred Heart of Jesus, if they desire to penetrate its inner nature and, by piously meditating on it, to receive the nourishment for the fostering and development of their religious fervor. If this devotion is constantly practiced with this knowledge and understanding, the souls of the faithful cannot but attain to the sweet knowledge of the love of Christ which is the

perfection of Christian life. As the apostle, who knew this from personal experience, teaches: "For this reason I bend my knees to the Father of our Lord Jesus Christ . . . that he may grant you from his glorious riches to be strengthened with power through his Spirit unto the progress of the inner man; and to have Christ dwelling through faith in your hearts: so that, being rooted and grounded in love you may be able . . . to know Christ's love which surpasses knowledge, in order that you may be filled unto all the fullness of God."[101] The clearest image of this all-embracing fullness of God is the Heart of Christ Jesus itself. We mean the fullness of mercy, which is proper to the New Testament, in which "the goodness and kindness of God our Saviour appeared,"[102] for "God did not send his Son into the world in order to judge the world, but that the world might be saved through him."[103]

C. THE SPIRITUAL CHARACTER OF THE WORSHIP OF THE SACRED HEART

1. *This Devotion Is Not Materialistic*

101. The Church, the teacher of men, has therefore always been convinced, from the time she first published official documents concerning the devotion to the Sacred Heart of Jesus, that its essential elements, namely, acts of love and reparation by which God's infinite love for the human race is honored, are in no sense tinged with so-called "materialism" or tainted with the poison of superstition. Rather, this devotion is a form of piety that fully corresponds to the true spiritual worship which the Saviour Himself foretold when speaking to the woman of Samaria: "The hour is coming, and is now here, when the true worshippers will worship the Father in spirit and in truth. For the Father also seeks such to worship him. God is a

spirit; and they who worship him must worship in spirit and in truth."[104]

2. *It Does Not Hinder an Interior Love for God*

102. It is wrong, therefore, to assert that the contemplation of the physical Heart of Jesus prevents an approach to a close love of God and holds back the soul on the way to the attainment of the highest virtues. This false mystical doctrine the Church emphatically rejects as, speaking through Our predecessor of happy memory, Innocent XI, she rejected the errors of those who foolishly declared: "[Souls of this interior way] ought not to make acts of love for the Blessed Virgin, the saints or the humanity of Christ; for love directed towards those is of the senses, since its objects are also of that kind. No creature, neither the Blessed Virgin nor the saints, ought to have a place in our heart, because God alone wishes to occupy it and possess it."[105] It is obvious that those who think in this way imagine that the image of the Heart of Jesus represents His human love alone, and that there is nothing in it on which, as on a new foundation, the worship of adoration—which is exclusively reserved to the divine nature—can be based. But everyone realizes that this interpretation of sacred images is entirely false, since it obviously restricts their broader meaning much too narrowly.

3. *A False Interpretation of Images Is Condemned*

103. Quite the contrary are the thought and teaching of Catholic theologians, among whom St. Thomas writes as follows: "Religious worship is not paid to images, considered in themselves, as things, but according as they are representations leading to God Incarnate. The approach which is made to the image as such does not stop there, but continue toward that which is represented. Hence,

because a religious honor is paid to the images of Christ, it does not therefore mean that there are different degrees of supreme worship or of the virtue of religion."[106] It is, then, to the Person of the Divine Word as to its final object that that devotion is directed which, in a relative sense, is observed toward the images—whether those images are relics of the bitter sufferings which our Saviour endured for our sake, or that particular image which surpasses all the rest in efficacy and meaning, namely the pierced Heart of the crucified Christ.

4. Through the Sacred Heart We Contemplate Divine Love

104. Thus, from something corporeal, such as the Heart of Jesus Christ with its natural meaning, it is both lawful and fitting for us, supported by Christian faith, to mount not only to its love as perceived by the senses but also higher, to a consideration and adoration of the infused heavenly love; and finally, by a movement of the soul at once sweet and sublime, to reflection on, and adoration of, the divine love of the Word Incarnate. We do so since, in accordance with the faith by which we believe that both natures—the human and the divine—are united in the Person of Christ, we can grasp in our minds those most intimate ties which unite the love of feeling of the physical Heart of Jesus with that twofold spiritual love, namely, the human love and the divine love. For these loves must be spoken of not only as existing side by side in the adorable Person of the divine Redeemer but also as being linked together by a natural bond insofar as the human love, including that of the feelings, is subject to the divine and, in due proportion, provides us with an image of the latter. We do not pretend, however, that we must contemplate and adore in the Heart of Jesus what is called the formal image, that is to say, the perfect and absolute symbol of

His divine love, for no created image is capable of expressing adequately the essence of this love. But a Christian in paying honor along with the Church to the Heart of Jesus is adoring the symbol and, as it were, the visible sign of the divine charity which went so far as to love intensely, through the Heart of the Word made flesh, the human race stained with so many sins.

105. It is therefore essential, at this point, in a doctrine of such importance and requiring such prudence, that each one constantly hold that the truth of the natural symbol, by which the physical Heart of Jesus is related to the Person of the Word, depends entirely upon the fundamental truth of the hypostatic union. Should anyone declare this to be untrue he would be reviving false opinions, more than once condemned by the Church, for they are opposed to the oneness of the Person of Christ even though the two natures are each complete and distinct.

D. THIS DEVOTION IS THE HIGHEST EXPRESSION OF PIETY

1. *It Is Centered in Jesus, Our Mediator*

106. Once this essential truth has been established, we understand that the Heart of Jesus is the heart of a divine Person, the Word Incarnate, and by it is represented and, as it were, placed before our gaze, all the love with which He has embraced and even now embraces us. Consequently, the honor to be paid to the Sacred Heart is such as to raise it to the rank—so far as external practice is concerned—of the highest expression of Christian piety. For this is the religion of Jesus, which is centered on the Mediator who is man and God, and in such a way that we cannot reach the Heart of God save through the Heart of Christ, as He Himself says: "I am the way, and the truth, and the life. No one comes to the Father but through me."[107]

2. *It Is a Devotion of Love*

107. And so we can easily understand that the devotion to the Sacred Heart of Jesus, of its very nature, is the worship of the love with which God, through Jesus, loved us. At the same time, it is an exercise of our own love, by which we are related to God and to other men. To express it in another way, devotion of this kind is directed toward the love of God for us, in order to adore it, give thanks for it, and live so as to imitate it. It has this in view, as the end to be attained, that we bring that love by which we are bound to God and to the rest of men to perfect fulfillment by carrying out daily more eagerly the new commandment which the divine Master gave to His apostles as a sacred legacy when He said: "A new commandment I give you, that you love one another . . . as I have loved you. . . . This is my commandment, that you love one another as I have loved you."[108] This commandment is really new and Christ's own, for as Aquinas says, "It is, in brief, the difference between the New and the Old Testament, for as Jeremias says, 'I will make a new covenant with the house of Israel.'[109] But that commandment which in the Old Testament was based on fear and reverential love was referring to the New Testament; hence, this commandment was in the old Law, not really belonging to it, but as a preparation for the new Law."[110]

Part V: *The Faithful are Urged to Study and Practice Devotion to the Sacred Heart*

A. THE IMPORTANCE OF THIS DEVOTION

108. Before We conclude Our treatment of the concept of this type of devotion and its excellence in Christian life, which We have offered for your consideration—a subject at once attractive and full of consolation—by virtue of the

apostolic office which was first entrusted to Blessed Peter after he had made his threefold profession of love, We think it opportune to exhort you once again, venerable brethren, and through you all those dear children of Ours in Christ, to continue to exercise an ever more vigorous zeal in promoting this most attractive form of piety; for from it in our times also We trust that very many benefits will arise.

1. No Ordinary Form of Piety

109. In truth, if the arguments brought forward, which form the foundation for the devotion to the pierced Heart of Jesus, are duly pondered, it is surely clear that there is no question here of some ordinary form of piety which anyone at his own whim may treat as of little consequence or set aside as inferior to others, but of a religious practice which helps very much toward the attaining of Christian perfection. For if "devotion"—according to the accepted theological notion which the Angelic Doctor gives us— "appears to be nothing else save a willingness to give one-self readily to what concerns the service of God,"[111] is it possible that there is any service of God more obligatory and necessary, and at the same time more excellent and attractive, than the one which is dedicated to love? For what is more pleasing and acceptable to God than service which pays homage to the divine love and is offered for the sake of that love, since any service freely offered is a gift in some sense, and love "has the position of the first gift, through which all other free gifts are made"?[112]

2. Proposed by Christ, Approved by Popes

110. That form of piety, then, should be held in highest esteem by means of which man honors and loves God more and dedicates himself with greater ease and promptness to

the divine charity; a form which our Redeemer Himself deigned to propose and commend to Christians, and which the Supreme Pontiffs in their turn have defended and praised highly in memorable published documents. Consequently, to consider of little worth this signal benefit conferred on the Church by Jesus Christ would be to do something both rash and harmful, and also deserving of God's displeasure.

3. Through Love We Fulfill Our Duties

111. This being so, there is no doubt that Christians, in paying homage to the Sacred Heart of the Redeemer, are fulfilling a serious part of their obligations in their service of God. At the same time, they are surrendering themselves to their Creator and Redeemer with regard to both the affections of the heart and the external activities of their life; in this way, they are obeying that divine commandment: "Thou shalt love the Lord thy God with thy whole heart, and with thy whole soul, and with thy whole mind, and with thy whole strength."[113]

4. External Acts of Piety Do Not Hold First Place

112. Besides, they have the firm conviction that they are moved to honor God not primarily for their own advantage in what concerns soul and body in this life and in the next, but for the sake of God's goodness they strive to render Him their homage, to give Him back love for love, to adore Him and offer Him due thanks. Were it not so, the devotion to the Sacred Heart of Jesus Christ would be out of harmony with the whole spirit of the Christian religion, since man would not direct his homage, in the first instance, to the divine Love. Not unreasonably, as sometimes happens, accusations of excessive self-love and self-interest are made against those who either misunder-

stand this excellent form of piety or practice it in the wrong way. Hence, let all be completely convinced that in showing devotion to the most Sacred Heart of Jesus, the external acts of piety have not the first or most important place; nor is its essence to be found primarily in the benefits to be obtained. For if Christ has solemnly promised these benefits in private revelations, it was for the purpose of encouraging men to perform with greater fervor the chief duties of the Catholic religion—namely, love and expiation—and thus to take all possible measures for their own spiritual advantage.

B. ALL ARE URGED TO PRACTICE THIS DEVOTION

1. *It Is Solid, Approved, and Fruitful*

113. We therefore urge all Our children in Christ, both those who are already accustomed to drinking the saving waters flowing from the Heart of the Redeemer and, more especially, those who look on from a distance like hesitant spectators, eagerly to embrace this devotion. Let them carefully consider, as We have said, that it is a question of a devotion which has long been powerful in the Church and is solidly founded on the Gospel narrative. It received clear support from tradition and the sacred liturgy, and has been frequently and generously praised by the Roman Pontiffs themselves. These were not satisfied with establishing a feast in honor of the Most Sacred Heart of the Redeemer and extending it to the Universal Church; they were also responsible for the solemn acts of dedication which consecrated the whole human race to the same Sacred Heart.[114]

114. Moreover, there are to be reckoned the abundant and joyous fruits which have flowed therefrom to the Church: countless souls returned to the Christian religion, the faith of many roused to greater activity, a closer tie between the faithful and our most loving Redeemer. All

these benefits, particularly in the most recent decades, have passed before Our eyes in greater numbers and more dazzling significance.

2. Gratitude of the Holy Father for Its Widespread Practice

115. While We gaze round at such a marvelous sight—namely, a devotion to the Sacred Heart of Jesus both warm and widespread among all ranks of the faithful—We are filled with a sense of gratitude and joy and consolation. And after We have offered thanks, as We ought, to our Redeemer who is the infinite treasury of goodness, We cannot help offering Our paternal congratulations to all those, whether of the clergy or of the laity, who have made active contributions to the extending of this devotion.

C. THE PRESSING NEED FOR THIS DEVOTION IN CHURCH AND SOCIETY

1. The Church Militant Lacks Necessary Perfection

116. But although, venerable brethren, devotion to the Sacred Heart of Jesus has everywhere brought forth fruits of salvation for the Christian life, all are aware that the Church militant on earth—and especially civil society—has not yet attained in a real sense to its essential perfection, which would correspond to the prayers and desires of Jesus Christ, the mystical Spouse of the Church and Redeemer of the human race. Not a few children of the Church mar, by their too many sins and imperfections, the beauty of this mother's features, which they reflect in themselves. Not all Christians are distinguished by that holiness of behavior to which God calls them; not all sinners have returned to the Father's house, which they unfortunately abandoned, that they may be clothed once again with the

"first robe"[115] and worthily receive on their finger the ring, the pledge of loyalty to the spouse of their soul; not all the heathen peoples have yet been gathered into the membership of the mystical body of Christ.

2. Militant Atheism Threatens Souls

117. And there is more. For if We experience bitter sorrow at the feeble loyalty of the good in whose souls, tricked by a deceptive desire for earthly possessions, the fire of divine charity grows cool and gradually dies out, much more is Our heart deeply grieved by the machinations of evil men who, as if instigated by Satan himself, are now more than ever zealous in their open and implacable hatred against God, against the Church and, above all, against him who on earth represents the person of the divine Redeemer and exhibits His love towards men, in accordance with that well-known saying of the Doctor of Milan: "For [Peter] is being questioned about that which is uncertain, though the Lord is not uncertain; He is questioning not that He may learn, but that He may teach the one whom, at His ascent into heaven, He was leaving to us as 'the representative of His love.' "[116]

118. But, in truth, hatred of God and of those who lawfully act in His place is the greatest kind of sin that can be committed by man created in the image and likeness of God and destined to enjoy His perfect and enduring friendship forever in heaven. Man, by hatred of God more than by anything else, is cut off from the Highest Good and is driven to cast aside from himself and from those near to him whatever has its origin in God, whatever is united with God, whatever leads to the enjoyment of God, that is, truth, virtue, peace and justice.[117]

D. DEVOTION TO THE SACRED HEART IS THE BEST ANTIDOTE FOR THESE EVILS

119. Since then, alas, one can see that the number of those whose boast is that they are God's enemies is in some places increasing, that the false slogans of materialism are being spread by act and argument, and that unbridled license for unlawful desires is everywhere being praised, is it remarkable that love, which is the supreme law of the Christian religion, the surest foundation of true and perfect justice and the chief source of peace and innocent pleasures, loses its warmth in the souls of many? For as our Saviour warned us: "Because iniquity will abound, the charity of the many will grow cold."[118]

1. *It Is Best Suited to Contemporary Needs*

120. When so many evils meet Our gaze—such as cause sharp conflict among individuals, families, nations and the whole world, today more than at any other time— where are We to seek a remedy, venerable brethren? Can a form of devotion surpassing that to the most Sacred Heart of Jesus be found which corresponds better to the essential character of the Catholic faith, which is more capable of assisting the present-day needs of the Church and the human race? What religious practice is more excellent, more attractive, more salutary than this, since the devotion in question is entirely directed toward the love of God itself?[119] Finally, what more effectively than the love of Christ—which devotion to the Sacred Heart of Jesus daily increases and fosters more and more—can move the faithful to bring into the activities of life the Law of the Gospel, the setting aside of which (as the words of the Holy Spirit plainly warn, "the work of justice shall be peace"[120]) makes peace worthy of the name completely impossible among men?

2. *It Is Best Suited to Save Souls and Society*

121. And so, following in the footsteps of Our immediate predecessor, We are pleased to address once again to all Our dear sons in Christ those words of exhortation which Leo XIII, of immortal memory, toward the close of the last century addressed to all the faithful and to all who were genuinely anxious about their own salvation and that of civil society: "Behold, today, another true sign of God's favor is presented to our gaze, namely the Sacred Heart of Jesus . . . shining forth with a wondrous splendor from amidst flames. In It must all our hopes be placed; from It salvation is to be sought and hoped for."[121]

E. THE SACRED HEART IS THE SYMBOL OF UNITY, SALVATION, AND PEACE

122. It is likewise Our most fervent desire that all who profess themselves Christians and who are seriously engaged in the effort to establish the kingdom of Christ on earth will consider the practice of devotion to the Heart of Jesus as the source and symbol of unity, salvation and peace. Let no one think, however, that by such a practice anything is taken from the other forms of piety with which Christian people, under the guidance of the Church, have honored the divine Redeemer. Quite the opposite. Fervent devotional practice towards the Heart of Jesus will beyond all doubt foster and advance devotion to the Holy Cross, in particular, and love for the Most Holy Sacrament of the Altar. We can even assert—as the revelations made by Jesus Christ to St. Gertrude and to St. Margaret Mary clearly show—that no one really has a proper understanding of Christ crucified, to whom the inner mysteries of His Heart have not been made known. Nor will it be easy to understand the strength of love, which moved Christ to give Himself to us as our spiritual food, save by fostering in a

special way the devotion to the eucharistic Heart of Jesus, the purpose of which is—to use the words of Our predecessor of happy memory, Leo XIII—"to call to mind the act of supreme love whereby our Redeemer, pouring forth all the treasures of His Heart, in order to remain with us until the end of time, instituted the adorable Sacrament of the Eucharist."[122] For "not the least part of the revelation of that Heart is the Eucharist, which He gave to us out of the great charity of His own Heart."[123]

1. *It Is the Best School of Divine Love*

123. Finally, moved by an earnest desire to set strong bulwarks against the wicked designs of those who hate God and the Church, and, at the same time, to lead men back again, in their private and public life, to a love of God and their neighbor, We do not hesitate to declare that devotion to the Sacred Heart of Jesus is the most effective school of the love of God; the love of God, We say, which must be the foundation on which to build the kingdom of God in the hearts of individuals, families, and nations. As that same predecessor of pious memory wisely reminds us: "The reign of Jesus Christ takes its strength and form from divine love: to love with holiness and order is its foundation and its perfection. From it these must flow: to perform duties without blame; to take away nothing of another's right; to guide the lower human affairs by heavenly principles; to give the love of God precedence over all other creatures."[124]

2. *It Must Be Joined with Devotion to the Immaculate Heart of Mary*

124. In order that favors in greater abundance may flow on all Christians, nay, on the whole human race, from the devotion to the most Sacred Heart of Jesus, let the faithful

see to it that this devotion is closely joined to that to the
Immaculate Heart of the Mother of God. For, by God's
will, the Blessed Virgin Mary was inseparably linked with
Christ in carrying out the work of the Redemption in such
a manner that our salvation sprang from the love and the
sufferings of Jesus Christ intimately united to the love and
sorrows of His Mother. It is, then, entirely fitting that the
Christian people—who received the divine life from Christ
through Mary—after they have paid their debt of honor to
the Sacred Heart of Jesus, should also offer to the most
loving Heart of their heavenly Mother the corresponding
acts of piety, affection, gratitude, and expiation. Entirely
in keeping with this most sweet and wise disposition of
Divine Providence is the memorable act of consecration by
which We Ourselves solemnly dedicated Holy Church and
the whole world to the spotless Heart of the Blessed Virgin
Mary.[125]

CONCLUSION OF ENCYCLICAL

125. Since in the course of this year there is completed,
as We mentioned above, the first hundred years since the
Universal Church, by order of Our predecessor of happy
memory, Pius IX, celebrated the feast of the Sacred Heart
of Jesus, We earnestly desire, venerable brethren, that the
memory of this centenary be everywhere observed by the
faithful in the making of public acts of adoration, thanksgiving and expiation to the divine Heart of Jesus. And
though all Christian peoples will be linked by the bonds
of charity and prayer in common, ceremonies of Christian
joy and piety will assuredly be carried out with a special
religious fervor in that nation in which, according to the
dispensation of the Divine Will, a holy virgin pointed the
way and was the untiring herald of that devotion.

126. Meanwhile, refreshed by sweet hope and foreseeing

already those spiritual fruits which We are confident will spring up in abundance in the Church from the devotion to the Sacred Heart of Jesus—provided it is correctly understood according to Our explanation and actively put into practice—We make Our prayer to God that He may graciously deign to assist these ardent desires of Ours by the strong help of His grace. May it come about, by the divine inspiration, as a token of His favor, that out of the celebration established for this year the love of the faithful may grow daily more and more towards the Sacred Heart of Jesus and its sweet and sovereign kingdom be extended more widely to all in every part of the world: the kingdom "of truth and life; the kingdom of grace and holiness; the kingdom of justice, love and peace."[126]

127. As a pledge of these favors with a full heart We impart to each one of you, venerable brethren, together with the clergy and faithful committed to your charge, to those in particular who by their devoted labors foster and promote the devotion to the Sacred Heart of Jesus, Our Apostolic Benediction.

Given at Rome, at St. Peter's, the 15th of May, 1956, the eighteenth year of Our Pontificate.

PIUS XII, POPE

Notes

1 Is. XII, 3.
2 Jac. I, 17.
3 John. VII, 37–39. (Translator's note: In this passage, Pope Pius uses the punctuation favored by St. Irenaeus, St. Cyprian, and some other ancient authorities. The translation therefore follows this and not the Douay version.)
4 Cfr. Is. XII, 3; Ez. XLVII, 1–12; Zach. XIII, 1; *Ex.* XVII, 1–7; *Num.* XX, 7–13; *I Cor.* X, 4; *Apoc.* VII, 17; XXII, 1.
5 *Rom.* V, 5.
6 *I Cor.* VI, 17.
7 John. IV, 10.
8 *Act.* IV, 12.
9 Enc. *Annum Sacrum,* 25 Maii 1899: *Acta Leonis,* vol. XIX, 1900, pp. 71, 77–78.
10 Enc. *Miserentissimus Redemptor,* 8 Maii 1928: A. A. S. XX, 1928, p. 167.
11 Cfr. Enc. *Summi Pontificatus,* 20 Oct., 1939: A. A. S. XXXI, 1939, p. 415.
12 Cfr. A. A. S. XXXII, 1940, p. 276; XXXV, 1943. p. 170; XXXVII, 1945, pp. 263–264; XL, 1948, p. 501; XLI, 1949, p. 331.
13 *Eph.* III, 20–21.
14 Is. XII, 3.
15 Conc. Ephes., can. 8; cfr. Mansi, *Sacrorum Conciliorum Ampliss. Collectio,* IV, 1083 C.; Conc. Const. II, can. 9; Cfr. *ibid.* IX, 382 E.
16 Cfr. Enc. *Annum sacrum: Acta Leonis,* vol. XIX, 1900, p. 76.
17 Cfr. *Ex.* XXXIV, 27–28.
18 *Deut,* VI, 4–6.
19 *Sum. Theol.,* II–II, q .2, a. 7: ed. Leon., tom. VIII, 1895, p. 34.
20 *Deut.* XXXII, 11.
21 *Os.* XI, 1, 3–4; XIV, 5–6.
22 Is. XLIX, 14–15.
23 *Cant.* II, 2; VI, 2; VIII, 6.
24 John. I, 14.
25 Jer. XXXI, 3; 31, 33–34.
26 Cfr. John. I, 29; *Hebr.* IX, 18–28; X, 1–17.
27 John. I, 16–17.
28 John. XXI, 20.
29 *Eph.* III, 17–19.
30 *Sum. Theol.,* III, q. 48, a. 2: ed. Leon., tom. XI, 1903, p. 464.
31 Cfr. Enc. *Miserentissimus Redemptor: A. A. S.* XX, 1928, p. 170.
32 *Eph.* II, 4; *Sum. Theol.,* III, q. 46, a. 1 ad 3: ed. Leon., tom. XI, 1903, p. 436.
33 *Eph.* III, 18.
34 John. IV, 24.
35 *II John.* 7.
36 Cfr. Luke. I, 35.

37 S. Leo Magnus, *Epist, dogm.* (*Lectis dilectionis tuae*) *ad Flavianum Const. Patr.*, 13 Iun., a. 449: *P. L.* LIV, 763.

38 Conc. Chalced., a. 451: Mansi, *Op. cit.* VII, 115 B.

39 S. Gelasius Papa, Tract. III: (*Necessarium*) *de duabus naturis in Christo:* cfr. A. Thiel, *Epist. Rom. Pont. a S. Hilaro usque ad Pelagium II*, p. 532.

40 Cfr. S. Thom., *Sum. Theol.*, III, q. 15, a. 4; q. 18, a. 6: ed. Leon., tom, XI, 1903, p. 189 et 237.

41 Cfr. *I Cor.* I, 23.

42 *Hebr.* II, 11–14; 17–18.

43 *Apol.* II, 13: *P. G.* VI, 465.

44 *Epist.* 261, 3: *P. G.* XXXII, 972.

45 In John., *Homil.* 63, 2: *P. G.* LIX, 350.

46 *De fide al Gratianum*, II, 7, 56: *P. L.* XVI, 594.

47 Cfr. *Super Matt.* XXVI, 37: *P. L.* XXVI, 205.

48 *Enarr. in Ps.* LXXXVII, 3: *P. L.* XXXVII, 1111.

49 *De Fide Orth.* III, 6: *P. G.* XCIV, 1006.

50 *Ibid.* III, 20: *P. G.* XCIV, 1081.

51 *Sum. Theol.*, I–II, q. 48, a. 4: ed. Leon., tom. VI, 1891, p. 306.

52 *Col.* II, 9.

53 Cfr. *Sum. Theol.*, III, q. 9, aa. 1–3: ed. Leon., tom. XI, 1903, p. 142.

54 Cfr. *Ibid.*, III, q. 33, a. 2, ad 3m; q. 46, a. 6: ed. Leon., tom. XI, 1903, pp. 342, 433.

55 *Tit.* III, 4.

56 Matt. XXVII, 50; John. XIX, 30.

57 *Eph.* II, 7.

58 *Hebr.* X, 5–7, 10.

59 *Registr. epist.*, lib. IV, ep. 31 ad Theodorum medicum: *P. L.* LXXVII, 706.

60 Mark. VIII, 2.

61 Matt. XXIII, 37.

62 Matt. XXI, 13.

63 Matt. XXVI, 39.

64 Matt. XXVI, 50; Luke, XXII, 48.

65 Luke. XXIII, 28, 31.

66 Luke. XXIII, 34.

67 Matt. XXVII, 46.

68 Luke. XXIII, 43.

69 John. XIX, 28.

70 Luke. XXIII, 46.

71 Luke. XXII, 15.

72 Luke. XXII, 19–20.

73 Mal. I, 11.

74 *De sancta virginitate*, VI: *P. L.* XL, 399.

75 John. XV, 13.

76 *I John.* III, 16.

77 Gal. II, 20.

78 Cfr. S. Thom., *Sum. Theol.*, III, q. 19, a. 1: ed Leon., tom. XI, 1903, p. 329.

220 APPENDIX

79 *Sum. Theol., Suppl.*, q. 42, a. 1 ad 3m; ed. Leon., tom. XII, 1906, p. 81.
80 Hymn. ad Vesp. Festi Ssmi Cordis Iesu.
81 *Sum. Theol.*, III, q. 66, a. 3, ad 3m: ed. Leon., tom. XII, 1906, p. 65.
82 *Eph.* V, 2.
83 *Eph.* IV, 8, 10.
84 John. XIV, 16.
85 *Col.* II, 3.
86 *Rom.* VIII, 35, 37–39.
87 *Eph.* V. 25–27.
88 Cfr. *I. John.* II, 1.
89 *Hebr.* VII, 25.
90 *Hebr.* V, 7.
91 John. III, 16.
92 S. Bonaventura, Opusc. X: *Vitis mystica*, c. III, n. 5; *Opera Omnia*. Ad Claras Aquas (Quaracchi) 1898, tom. VIII, p. 164; cfr. S. Thom., *Sum. Theol.*, III, q. 54, a. 4: ed. Leon., tom. XI, 1903, p. 513.
93 *Rom.* VIII, 32.
94 Cfr. *Sum. Theol.*, III, q. 48, a. 5: ed. Leon., tom. XI, 1903, p. 467.
95 Luke. XII, 50.
96 John. XX, 28.
97 John. XIX, 37; Cfr. Zach. XII, 10.
98 Cfr. Litt. Enc. *Miserentissimus Redemptor:* A. A. S. XX, 1928, pp. 167–168.
99 Cfr. A. Gardellini, *Decreta authentica*, 1857, n. 4579, tom. III, p. 174.
100 Cfr. *Decr. S. C. Rit.*, apud N. Nilles, *De rationibus festorum Sacratissimi Cordis Iesu et purissimi Cordis Mariae*, 5a ed., Innsbruck, 1885, tom. I. p. 167.
101 *Eph.* III, 14, 16–19.
102 *Tit.* III, 4.
103 John. III, 17.
104 John. IV, 23–24.
105 Innocentius XI, Constit. Ap. *Coelestis Pastor*, 19 Novembris 1687; *Bullarium Romanum*, Romae, 1734, tom. VIII, p. 443.
106 *Sum. Theol.*, II–II, q. 81 a. 3 ad 3m: ed. Leon., tom. IX, 1897, p. 189.
107 John. XIV, 6.
108 John. XIII, 34; XV, 12.
109 Jer. XXXI, 31.
110 *Comment. in Evang. S. Ioan.*, c. XIII, lect. VII, 3: ed. Parmae, 1860, tom. X, p. 541.
111 *Sum. Theol.*, II–II, q. 82, a. 1: ed. Leon., IX, 1897, p. 187.
112 *Ibid.* I, q. 38, a. 2: ed Leon, tom. IV, 1888, p. 393.
113 Mark. XII, 30; Matt. XXII, 37.
114 Cfr. Leo XIII, Enc. *Annum Sacrum: Acta Leonis*, vol. XIX, 1900, p. 71 sq.; *Decr. S. C. Rituum*, 28 Iun. 1899, in *Decr. Auth.* III, n. 3712; Pius XI, Enc. *Miserentissimus Redemptor:* A. A. S. XX, 1928, p. 177 sq.; *Decr. S. C. Rit.*, 29 Ian. 1929: A. A. S. XXI, 1929, p. 77.

115 Luke. XV, 22.
116 *Exposit. in Evang. sec. Lucam*, l. X, n. 175; *P. L.* XV, 1942.
117 Cfr. S. Thom., *Sum. Theol.*, II–II, q. 34, a. 2: ed Leon., tom. VIII, 1895, p. 274.
118 Matt. XXIV, 12.
119 Cfr. Enc. *Miserentissimus Redemptor: A. A. S.* XX, 1928, p. 166.
120 Is. XXXII, 17.
121 Enc. *Annum Sacrum: Acta Leonis*, vol. XIX, 1900, p. 79; Enc. *Miserentissimus Redemptor: A. A. S.*, XX, 1928, p. 167.
122 *Litt. Apost. quibus Archisodalitas a Corde Eucharistico Iesu ad S. Ioachim de Urbe erigitur*, 17 Febr. 1903: *Acta Leonis*, vol. XXII, 1903, p. 307 sq.; cfr. Enc. *Mirae caritatis*, 22 Maii 1902: *Acta Leonis*, vol. XXII, 1903, p. 116.
123 S. Albertus M., *De Eucharistia*, dist. VI, tr. 1, c. 1: *Opera Omnia*, ed. Borgnet, vol. XXXVIII, Parisiis, 1890, p. 358.
124 Enc. *Tametsi: Acta Leonis*, vol. XX, 1900, p. 303.
125 Cfr. *A. A. S.* XXXIV, 1942, p. 345 sq.
126 Ex Miss. Rom., *Praef. I. Christi Regis*.

Haurietis Aquas Outline

* The numbers refer to the paragraphs in the Encyclical.

Part II:

DEVOTION TO THE SACRED HEART IN THE LIGHT OF THE NEW TESTAMENT AND TRADITION (32–61)

A. GOD'S LOVE IN THE MYSTERY OF THE REDEMPTION, AS REVEALED IN THE GOSPELS (32–43)
1. The Superiority of the New Testament Over the Old (32–34)
2. A Twofold Love in the Mystery of the Redemption (35–37)
3. The Nature of Christ's Love (38–39)
4. Christ Put on a Perfect Human Nature (40)
5. . . . with a Heart Capable of Suffering (41–43)

B. THE TEACHING OF THE FATHERS OF THE CHURCH (44–53)
1. The Mystery of Love Is the Foundation and Culmination of the Incarnation and Redemption (44–52)
2. Christ Put on Human Nature to Manifest His Love in a Human Way (53)

C. THE HEART OF THE INCARNATE WORD IS THE SYMBOL OF HIS THREEFOLD LOVE (54–57)

D. CONCLUSIONS (58–61)
1. Ways in Which We Can Honor the Heart of Our Redeemer (58)
2. Everything He Did Was a Proof of His Threefold Love (59)
3. We Should Meditate on the Beatings of His Heart (60)
4. His Heart Will Never Cease to Symbolize His Threefold Love (61)

Part III:

THE PROFOUND INFLUENCE OF THE HEART OF JESUS IN HIS REDEMPTIVE MISSION (62–88)

A. MANIFESTATIONS OF DIVINE AND HUMAN LOVE IN THE GOSPELS (62–68)

Part IV:

THE ORIGIN AND DEVELOPMENT OF THIS DEVOTION (89–107)

Part V:

THE FAITHFUL ARE URGED TO STUDY AND PRACTICE DEVOTION TO THE SACRED HEART (108–124)

2. Indulgenced Prayers

LORD JESUS, who art our most loving Redeemer and a Priest forever, look mercifully on us, Thy humble suppliants, whom Thou hast been pleased to call Thy friends and partakers of Thy priesthood. We are Thine; we wish to be Thine forever: therefore to Thy Most Sacred Heart which Thou hast shown to oppressed humanity as their only safe refuge, we dedicate and devote ourselves wholly this day. Thou who hast promised plenteous fruit in the divine ministry to those priests who are devoted to Thy Sacred Heart, make us, we beseech Thee, fit workmen in Thy vineyard, truly meek and humble, filled with the spirit of devotion and patience, so fired with love of Thee that we shall never cease to enkindle and quicken the same fire of love in the hearts of the faithful. Renew our hearts, therefore, in the fire of Thy Heart, so that henceforth we shall desire nothing save to promote Thy glory and to win for Thee the souls whom Thou didst redeem by Thy Precious Blood. Show Thy mercy, good Shepherd, chiefly to those priests, our brethren, if there be any such, who, walking in the vanity of sense, have saddened Thee and Thy beloved Spouse, Holy Church, by their lamentable falling away from Thee. Grant us grace to bring them back to Thy embrace, or, at least, to atone for their crimes, to repair the harm they have done, and to lessen the sorrow they have caused Thee, by the consolation of our love. Allow each one of us, finally, to pray to Thee in the words of Saint Augustine: "O sweet Jesus, live Thou in me, and let the living coal of Thy love burn brightly in my spirit, and grow into a perfect conflagration; let it burn perpetually on the altar of my heart, let it glow in my marrow, let it blaze up in the most secret places of my soul; in the day of my consummation let me be found totally consumed thereby in Thy presence, who with the Father and the Holy Ghost livest and reignest one God for ever and ever, Amen."

An indulgence of 3 years.
An indulgence of 7 years on the day of the monthly retreat.
A plenary indulgence on the usual conditions at the end of a course of "Spiritual Exercises" (Pius X, Rescript in his own hand, Aug. 17, 1908, exhib. Nov. 14, 1908; S. P. Ap., Oct. 24, 1935).—The Raccolta, Official Edition, Benziger Brothers.

A PRAYER TO STIR UP THE GRACE OF THE PRIESTHOOD

Dearest Jesus, who of Thy great goodness hast called me to be Thy follower in preference to countless others and hast raised me to the high dignity of Thy priesthood, bestow upon me abundantly, I pray, Thy divine help in fulfilling my duties in a right spirit. I beseech Thee, Lord Jesus, to stir up in me Thy grace both today and always, that grace which is in me by reason of the laying on of hands of the bishop. O mighty Physician of souls, heal me in such wise that I may never be entangled in sinful habits, but that I may renounce them all and be enabled to please Thee even to the day of my death. Amen.

An indulgence of 500 days once a day. Raccolta, 733

A PRAYER FOR THE GRACE OF PREACHING HOLILY AND FRUITFULLY

Give me, O Lord, a mild and judicious eloquence which shall keep me from being puffed up and exalted above my brethren by reason of Thy gifts. Put into my mouth, I beseech Thee, words of consolation and edification and exhortation through Thy Holy Spirit, that I may be enabled to exhort the good to better things, and, by word and example, to recall to the straight way of Thy righteousness those who walk perversely. Let the words which Thou shalt give Thy servant, be like to sharp javelins and burning arrows that shall pierce and enkindle unto Thy fear and holy love the minds of all them that hear me. Amen (St. Anselm, Bishop, Confessor and Doctor).

An indulgence of 500 days, if this prayer is said before preaching the Word of God. Raccolta, 738

PRAYERS FOR HOLINESS OF LIFE

AN INVOCATION

O good Jesu, grant that I may be a priest after Thine own Heart.

An indulgence of 300 days. Raccolta, 739

PRAYER

Almighty and merciful God, graciously attend to my humble prayers; and make me, Thy servant, whom Thou hast appointed to dispense Thy heavenly mysteries, through no merits of mine own, but only of the infinite bounty of Thy mercy, a worthy minister at Thy sacred altar, that what is set forth by my voice, may be confirmed by Thy hallowing grace. Through Christ our Lord. Amen (Roman Missal).

An indulgence of 3 years. Raccolta, 740

PRAYER

O Almighty God, let Thy grace assist us, that we who have undertaken the office of Priesthood, may be able to wait upon Thee worthily and devoutly, in all purity, and with a good conscience. And if we cannot live in so great innocency of life as we ought to do, grant to us at least worthily to lament the sins that we have committed; and in the spirit of humility, and with the full purpose of a good will, to serve Thee more earnestly for the time to come. Through Christ our Lord. Amen (*The Imitation of Christ*, book IV, chap xi, n. 7).

An indulgence of 500 days. Raccolta, 741

3. Acts of Consecration
by Father Mateo

ACT OF CONSECRATION TO THE JUSTICE OF CHRIST,
THE ADORABLE JUDGE

I know whom I trust! My Judge as well as my Saviour!
Through Him, and with Him, and
in Him, is to Thee, God the
Father Almighty, in the Unity
of the Holy Ghost,
all honor and glory!
(three times)

To the Heart of the eternal Father and for the glory of
the most holy Paraclete, for the honor of the most august,
most adorable Trinity, Father, Son, and Holy Ghost, I
offer up my whole life with all my shortcomings.

Furthermore, in advance, I lovingly consecrate my agony
and my death to Christ, my Judge and my Lord, in a spirit
of perfect contrition and humility, as well as confident love
and thanksgiving. So may it be!

Mother of fair love and mercy;
Queen of the Cenacle and priests,
Mediatrix of all graces, pray for me, now
And at the hour of my death.

Saint Joseph, comfort and help me,

I beseech thee in my last hour. Amen.
My own dearest sister, Little Thérèse
Obtain from the Father that
I may live and die in perfect charity.

Guardian Angel, my beloved brother,
I trust in Thee, help me!

* * * *

To Christ, the Son of God, the most equitable Judge, be honor, praise, love, and glory in the unity of the Father and the Paraclete. Amen.

I believe that the Father judges no one, but that He reserves to His Son our judgment, and to Him alone belongs all power and true sanction.

I believe with the most steadfast faith in the infinite justice of Christ, my adorable judge.

I believe that He alone has the power to destroy my body and to sentence my soul to the eternal flames of hell.

If, then, love be the fulfillment of the Law, love for our Lord would not be true love unless I feared to offend the Lord and thereby to be deprived of God for an eternity of damnation. Hence, "the fear of the Lord is the beginning of wisdom."

Therefore, because I must and want to love God with all my heart, with all my soul, and with all my mind, I fear Jesus my Judge, but I fear Him with a filial fear, that is, with a fear suffused with love.

I fear indeed so that I may be able to love with a strong love for all eternity.

I fear the holiness of the Lord!
I fear the most just anger of the Lord!
I fear the adorable vengeance of the Lord!
I fear the irrevocable sentence of the Lord!

Grant, O Lord, that I may have a constant fear as well as love of Thy holy name.

I fear my most sweet Saviour in the crib in Bethlehem and I love my Judge coming in the clouds of heaven in majesty and glory; grant that both may find me prepared.

I fear Jesus my Judge because I have sinned exceedingly in thought, word, and deed, sins of ignorance and frailty, but especially sins of malice and ingratitude—have mercy on me!

Indeed, I fear my adorable Judge because I am a sinner, and I know that God's holiness cannot leave sin unpunished nor tolerate it to remain without reparation.

Jesus, Jesus, Judge most just, give to my eyes, I beseech Thee, a fountain of tears, and mixing them in the chalice with Thy Most Precious Blood, cleanse me yet more and redeem me.

I groan and tremble like one guilty, because—even though today, aided by the mercy and grace of God, I have good will—I humbly recognize my inconstancy and I fear my changeableness.

O God, come to my aid! O King of love, make haste to help me, have mercy on me!

> O Christ, Judge of the living and the dead,
>   most just and most wise, I love Thee!
> O Christ, Judge, most faithful and almighty,
>   I praise Thee!
> O Christ, Judge, truthful and omniscient,
>   I glorify Thee!
> O Christ, Judge, ineffable and infallible,
>   I adore Thee!
> O Christ, Judge, I fear Thee, for
>   Thou alone art holy—Holiness itself!

Jesus, Jesus, most just, prostrate before Thee, I beseech Thee for the glory of the Father and the Paraclete, through

Mary, thy most tender mother and my mother, do not forsake me in that dreadful day of judgment, do not cast me into everlasting fire.

Be my Saviour, not only my Judge, O Lord!

For the glory of the Father and the Paraclete, and for Thy glory, number me among the blessed and save me!

Yes, through the love of the Father, through the grace of the Paraclete, through the tenderness of the Mother of Sorrows, Jesus, Jesus, most just and most meek Judge, Thou who knowest all things, Thou who searchest the hearts and minds of men, turn Thy face from my sins, and do not take Thy Holy Spirit from me.

Jesus, Jesus, King and Saviour, Mediator and Victim, Jesus most just Judge, blot out all my faults, before I am called to stand before Thy tribunal to give an account of my stewardship.

I know whom I trust. I am certain that Thou, Lord Jesus, art able to preserve until that day of Thy visitation, when Thou shalt come to judge, the trust which Thou hast committed to me.

In that day of might, show me the Father and it will be sufficient.

Come, Lord Jesus, come and kindly grant me, not because of my merits, but because of Thy forgiveness and mercy, the crown promised to Thy most unworthy, yet penitent and confident servant, namely, *Thy great glory and Thy love.*

I will love Thee for all eternity with all my heart, with all my soul, and with all my mind.

Jesus, Jesus, grant that in that supreme hour I may be able to say to Thee, with St. Bonaventure, these words of confidence, of friendship, and of peace:

I have found the Heart of a King, I have found the Heart of a Brother, I have found the Heart of a Friend, most kind

Jesus! Oh, how good it is, how pleasing it is, to dwell and to die in this Heart.

It is good for me to be here forever.

I know whom I trust!

In Thy Heart, Jesus, most just Judge, I commend my heart to Thee. In Thy Hands, Saviour King and Judge, I commend my heart to Thee. In Thy Hands, Saviour King and Judge, I commend my spirit to the Father.

> Through Him, and with Him, and
> in Him, is to Thee, God the
> Father Almighty, in the Unity
> of the Holy Ghost,
> all honor and glory!

> *Salve Regina. . . .*
> *Confiteor. . . .*

ACT OF CONSECRATION TO THE
THREE PERSONS OF THE BLESSED TRINITY
TO THE FATHER

Abba, Abba, per Ipsum et cum Ipso et in Ipso, I consecrate my whole being to You, Creator and Father, whose omnipotence drew me from nothing through love and only through love.

Abba, Abba, Adonai, God of glory and majesty, I adore You with my heart and my mind.

> *Honor, praise and love to the*
> *eternal and beloved Father!*

Abba, Abba, Jehovah, God of mercy and charity, I adore You with my heart and my mind.

Honor, praise and love to the
eternal and beloved Father!

Abba, Abba, Elohim, God of wisdom and justice, I adore
You with my heart and my mind.

Honor, praise and love to the
eternal and beloved Father!

Adonai, Jehovah, Elohim, I adore and love You with
Israel and the Church; with Abraham, Isaac, Jacob; with
heaven, purgatory and earth.

Abba, Abba, *per Ipsum et cum Ipso et in Ipso*, I offer
You an infinite thanksgiving for the gift of the Word, Thy
Son, my Saviour, my Judge, my adorable Friend.

Abba, Abba, *per Ipsum et cum Ipso et in Ipso*, I offer
You a perfect reparation for my sins. I beg pardon for them
all, especially for the sin of ingratitude.

Parce, Pater adorande et dilectissime.
Parce, Abba et miserere.

Abba, Abba, *per Ipsum et cum Ipso et in Ipso*, I abandon
myself filially in life and in death to You, to Your Fatherly
Heart, asking only for one grace: to love You, Abba, *toto*
corde, tota anima, tota mente for all eternity.

TO THE MERCIFUL LOVE OF THE SACRED HEART

Per Ipsum et cum Ipso et in Ipso, I consecrate myself
to Your Sacred Heart, as through Your own adorable Hands
You gave Yourself to me on Holy Thursday.

With the simplicity of the Little Flower;
with the seraphic flame of St. Francis of Assisi;
with the apostolic fire of St. Francis Xavier;
with the perfect abandonment of St. Margaret Mary,

I deliver myself in life and in death, as a Christian, as a religious, and as a priest, with all the graces of my triple vocation, but also with all the shortcomings and sins of my life.

Yes, I consecrate myself to the infinite and merciful love of the Sacred Heart of Jesus: *diligam Te Domine, toto corde, tota anima, tota mente.*

And so that my oblation may be acceptable to the Father and for the glory of the Blessed Trinity, I offer it in the wound of the pierced side of my Saviour, the Victim of my daily Mass. I present it in the Precious Blood of my chalice.

And to render it less unworthy of the adorable King, I ask the Mother of fair love to offer this, my poor gift, in her Immaculate and Sorrowful Heart, for the glory of the Father and the Son and the Holy Ghost.

Through this consecration I intend to give thanks most especially for the ineffable gift of my priesthood and for the miracle of love of my daily Mass.

With my hands in the hands of the Immaculate Queen I promise to make the greatest effort to be a saint at the altar for the glory of the Blessed Trinity and the redemption of many priestly souls.

It is my explicit will to renew this consecration to the merciful Love of the Sacred Heart every morning during Holy Mass, humbly imploring the supreme grace of being, in time and in eternity, a saintly priest of the Blessed Trinity, and of Mary, the Immaculate and Sorrowful Queen, through a thrice holy daily Mass.

TO THE PARACLETE

Per Ipsum et cum Ipso et in Ipso, I consecrate myself to the Holy Ghost, substantial Light and Love; to the Paraclete sent by the Father to crown the work of Christ the Redeemer.

Holy Ghost, I adore You, in the Sacred Heart of the Man-God, and of the supreme and adorable Priest, created through Your inspiration in the womb of the Virgin Mary.

I adore You, O Paraclete, whose omnipotent breathing created the Christian Church in the Cenacle on Pentecost Sunday.

Accept, O Holy Ghost, the gift of my soul, of my heart and of my body, and transform my whole life into Yours for the glory of the Blessed Trinity.

Come, O Paraclete, come with Your sevenfold gifts and sanctify me.

Adorable Paraclete, in a special way I consecrate to You my priesthood.

O, infinite thanks for my priestly character!

Infinite thanks for my priestly powers!

Infinite thanks for my priestly saving mission!

O, infinite thanks particularly for the ineffable treasure of the Holy Sacrifice of the Mass!

As a proof that You deign to accept me, may my daily Mass, by Your grace, be really and truly a hymn of praise and glory to the Blessed Trinity, whose solemn feast I wish to celebrate every morning at the altar *cum omni militia coelesti*, that through You, O Paraclete, I may really be, in life and death, an *Alter Christus*.

Gloria Patri flagranti amore Filii; inflamma cor meum amore Filii!

Gloria Filio flagranti amore Patris, inflamma cor meum amore Patris!

Gloria Spiritui Sancto flagranti amore Patris et Filii: inflamma cor meum amore Patris et Filii et amore Tuo!

> *Per Te sciamus, da Patrem*
> *Noscamus atque Filium,*
> *Teque utriusque Spiritum*
> *Credamus omni tempore.*

Oremus:

Deus, qui corda fidelium Sancti Spiritus illustratione docuisti, da nobis in eodem Spiritu recta sapere; et de ejus semper consolatione gaudere. Per Christum Dominum. Amen.

CONSECRATION OF PRIESTS TO THE
SACRED HEART OF JESUS

Sacred Heart of Jesus, King of love, through the Immaculate Heart of Mary, Queen of the Clergy and Queen of Apostles, I consecrate forever to Your merciful love, my heart, my soul, and all my undertakings.

Adorable Friend of priests, ever faithful to Your promises, I entrust to You the work of my sanctification. Help me to become a saint. Grant me the grace to bring to You many souls, even those most hardened by sin, according to the promise You explicitly made to St. Margaret Mary.

O merciful Heart of Jesus, in order that I may love You with my whole heart, with my whole soul and with all my strength, and so that I may really make You better known and better loved, keep me in the wound of Your sacred side, and grant that, burning with love for You, I may dwell there in time and for eternity. Amen.

4. Doctrinal Practices Proposed by Father Mateo

LITTLE CHAPLET OF THE PARACLETE
As proposed by Father Mateo, SS.CC.

It is sad to realize, and indeed only too true, that the Holy Spirit does not play a prominent role in the spiritual life of most Christians. Those who have genuine devotion to Him are few and far between.

This is, undoubtedly, a great defect in our spiritual life. We are thereby deficient in understanding and holiness.

Let us react! It is never too late! Here is a practical way to honor the Holy Spirit and draw His sevenfold gifts upon us.

In the very first place, let us try to spread this doctrinal devotion, love for the Paraclete, suitable for the highest spiritual aspirations of the best among our Catholic people, and let us form the praiseworthy habit of reciting this chaplet as a homage to the Holy Spirit.

Come, Holy Spirit, enlighten my mind!
Come, inflame my heart!

Method of Reciting

1. Take your beads (the Blessed Virgin rosary) and recite the *Apostles' Creed*.

2. After the Creed, very slowly and devoutly say the *Glory be to the Father*.

3. Then say the *Our Father*.

4. Now, very fervently, say this ejaculation:

Father, Father, send us the promised Paraclete, through Jesus Christ our Lord. Amen.

5. On each bead, instead of the Hail Mary, say with a burning heart:

Come, Holy Spirit, fill the hearts of Thy faithful and kindle in them the fire of Thy love!

6. After the tenth bead recite the following official prayer:

Send forth Thy Spirit and they shall be created.

And Thou shalt renew the face of the earth.

LET US PRAY

O God, who didst instruct the hearts of Thy faithful by the light of the Holy Spirit, grant us by the same Spirit to be truly wise and evermore to rejoice in His consolation. Through Christ our Lord. Amen.

7. Then recite the second decade and all the others in the same way as explained (beginning at 3): *Our Father*

8. After the seventh and last decade, recite the *Hail, Holy Queen* in honor of the Blessed Virgin, our Heavenly Queen, who presided in the Cenacle on the great Sunday of Pentecost.

Suggested Reflections

A few short reflections may be made on the seven glorious mysteries relating to the seven wonderful operations of the Paraclete. These meditations should be made briefly, between each decade.

First Mystery: Let us honor the Holy Spirit and adore Him who is Substantial Love, proceeding from the Father and the Son, and uniting Them in infinite and eternal love.

Second Mystery: Let us honor the operation of the Holy Spirit and adore Him in the Immaculate Conception of Mary, sanctifying her from the first moment with the fullness of grace.

Third Mystery: Let us honor the operation of the Holy Spirit and adore Him in the Incarnation of the Word, the Son of God by His Divine nature, and the Son of the Virgin by the flesh.

Fourth Mystery: Let us honor the operation of the Holy Spirit and adore Him in the promulgation of the Church on the glorious day of Pentecost.

Fifth Mystery: Let us honor the operation of the Holy Spirit and adore Him dwelling in the Church and assisting her faithfully according to the Divine promise, even to the consummation of the world.

Sixth Mystery: Let us honor the wonderful operation of the Holy Spirit within the Church, creating other Christs, the priests, and bestowing the fullness of the priesthood on the bishops.

Seventh Mystery: Let us honor the operation of the Holy Spirit, the adorable Sanctifier, and adore Him in His hidden and marvelous work of the formation of saints in the Church.

Practices

Recite this little chaplet often, especially on Sundays, even every day.

Recite it: when some important decision must be made and when special help is needed; every day during recollections and retreats; as a preparation for the Feast of Pentecost.

This simple chaplet must become a familiar practice and one of our great Catholic devotions: We must have enlightened piety. The Blessed Virgin, Queen of Apostles and of the Cenacle, will bless you. You will thus win her heart "full of grace," for she is the masterpiece of the Holy Spirit's operation. In your devotions always keep in mind the essential. The first of all devotions must be to the Blessed Trinity, which of necessity includes the Holy Spirit.

THE MASS OF ST. JOHN

In keeping with his strong preaching on the "greatest of all doctrinal devotions," that of the Holy Sacrifice of the Mass, Father Mateo has promulgated far and wide what he calls "the Mass of St. John." It is not a new idea for it simply encourages Catholics to unite themselves frequently with the Mass being celebrated uninterruptedly throughout the world.

The title brings out the fact that this practice consists of the three essential parts of the Holy Sacrifice, namely, the Offertory, the Consecration and the Communion. Holy Mass as celebrated by St. John was much shorter than our present Mass formula, yet consisted of these three elements. Hence the title, "Mass of St. John."

It is particularly appealing to priests as it stresses the priestly practice of keeping oneself frequently united with the Holy Sacrifice. Here is an excellent and practical means of "living the Mass" in daily life. It is especially helpful on the occasion of a priest's private Holy Hour, visits to the Blessed Sacrament, and is sometimes used for public Holy Hours. It is available in leaflet form at the National Enthronement Center, 4900 S. Dakota Ave. N.E., Washington 17, D.C.

> For the glory of the Blessed Trinity,
> In union with all the priests in the
>   Church offering the Holy Sacrifice,
> I unite myself to them,
> *Per Ipsum, et cum Ipso et in Ipso.*

I

Receive, O holy Father, almighty and eternal God, this spotless host, which I, Thy unworthy servant, offer unto

Thee, my living and true God, for mine own countless sins, offenses and negligences, and for all here present; as also for all faithful Christians living and dead, that it may avail both for my own and their salvation unto life eternal. Amen.

We offer unto Thee, O Lord, the chalice of salvation, beseeching Thy clemency, that it may ascend in the sight of Thy divine majesty with a sweet savor, for our own salvation and for that of the whole world. Amen.

II

The day before He suffered He took bread into His holy and venerable hands, and with His eyes lifted up to heaven, unto Thee, God, His almighty Father, giving thanks to Thee, He blessed, broke and gave it to His disciples, saying: Take and eat ye all of this,

For This Is My Body

In like manner, after He had supped, taking also this excellent chalice into His holy and venerable hands, and giving thanks to Thee, He blessed and gave it to His disciples, saying: Take and drink ye all of this,

For this is the Chalice of My Blood, of the new and eternal testament: the mystery of faith: which shall be shed for you and for many unto the remission of sins.

As often as ye shall do these things, ye shall do them in remembrance of Me.

III

Lord, I am not worthy that Thou shouldst enter under my roof; say but the word and my soul shall be healed. (3 times)

May the Body of our Lord Jesus Christ preserve my soul to life everlasting. Amen.

May the Blood of our Lord Jesus Christ preserve my soul to life everlasting. Amen.

Here make a spiritual Communion (Indulgence—3 years; plenary if performed each day for a month R 164).

5. Ceremony for the Enthrone-
ment of the Sacred Heart of
Jesus in the Home

Before the Ceremony

Prepare for the Enthronement:

1. Learn *what* it is and how *important* it is.
2. Set a date for the Enthronement in agreement with the Pastor or another priest.
3. If possible have the Holy Sacrifice of the Mass offered that morning for the reign of the Sacred Heart in your home, and as an act of love and reparation to the Sacred Heart. The entire family should try to receive Communion at this Mass, or at another Mass.
4. Obtain as beautiful a picture or statue of the Sacred Heart as possible. If you already have a picture, use that one.
5. Below the place of honor reserved for the statue or picture, prepare a "throne" or "altar," that is to say, a table (or perhaps the mantelpiece), covered with a white cloth, beautifully decorated with flowers and candles.

The picture or statue should be placed on a small table near this "throne" before the ceremony.

6. Invite your relatives and friends to be present. Thus you will already begin to be an "apostle of the Sacred Heart." Have a family party after the ceremony, with a special treat for the children, who, of course, should be present at the ceremony, even the smallest.

7. Make this day one of the outstanding events of the family life—one long to be remembered. The greater the solemnity, the better.

NOTE: Even though your home has been consecrated to the Sacred Heart, you may still have the *Enthronement*, as the two are not the same.

The Ceremony

1. All gather around the image of the Sacred Heart; father, mother and children nearest to the priest.

2. Priest, in surplice and white stole, blesses the image. (If priest is not present, have the image blessed beforehand.)

The Blessing of the Picture or Statue

V. Adjutorium nostrum in nomine Domini.
R. Qui fecit coelum et terram.
V. Dominus vobiscum.
R. Et cum spiritu tuo.

Oremus. Omnipotens sempiterne Deus, qui Sanctorum tuorum imagines pingi non reprobas, ut quoties illas oculis corporis intuemur, toties eorum actus et sancti-

V. Our help is in the name of the Lord.
R. Who hath made heaven and earth.
V. The Lord be with you.
R. And with thy spirit.

Let us pray. Almighty and everlasting God, who dost approve the painting and sculpturing of the images of Thy saints, so that as often as we gaze upon them we tatem ad imitandum memoriae oculis meditemur, hanc quaesumus, imaginem in honorem et memoriam Sacratissimi Cordis Unigeniti Filii tui Domini Nostri Jesu Christi adaptatam bene † dicere et sancti † ficare digneris; et praesta ut quicumque coram illa, Cor Sacratissimum Unigeniti Filii tui suppliciter colere et honorare studuerit, illius meritis et obtentu a te gratiam in praesenti, et aeternam gloriam obtineat in futurum. Per Christum dominum nos-Per Christum Dominum nostrum. Amen.

are reminded to imitate their deeds and sanctity; vouchsafe, we implore Thee, to bless and sanctify this image made in honor and in memory of the Most Sacred Heart of Thy only begotten Son, our Lord Jesus Christ; and grant that whosoever in its presence will suppliantly worship and honor the Most Sacred Heart of Thy only begotten Son, may obtain through His merits and intercession grace in this life and everlasting glory in the world to come. Through Christ our Lord. Amen.

(*The priest here sprinkles the image with holy water.*)

3. Then the father (or in his absence, the mother or some other member of the family) enthrones the image in the place of honor prepared for it. This is the symbolic act of *Enthronement*.

4. All stand while the Apostles' Creed is recited as an act of faith on the part of the family.

5. Everyone is seated while the priest addresses a few words to those present, reminding the members of the family of what the Sacred Heart expects from families which have acknowledged Him as King; recalling the magnificent promises of the Sacred Heart; urging the family to *live* its Enthronement, and frequently to renew the act of consecration which they are about to make.

6. All kneel, while the priest and the father (or father

alone, or his representative) recite the official *Act of Consecration.*

Act of Consecration to the Sacred Heart

(Recited by the priest and the father together, or father alone—or representative—if priest is absent. This is the formula required for indulgences and may not be changed.)

O Sacred Heart of Jesus, * who didst make known to St. Margaret Mary Thy ardent desire to reign over Christian families, * behold us assembled here today * to proclaim Thy absolute dominion over our home.

Henceforth we propose to lead a life like unto Thine * so that among us may flourish the virtues * for which Thou didst promise peace on earth, * and for this end * we will banish from our midst * the spirit of the world which Thou dost abhor so much.

Thou wilt reign over our understanding * by the simplicity of our faith. Thou wilt reign over our hearts * by our ardent love for Thee; * and may the flame of this love * be ever kept burning in our hearts * by the frequent reception of the Holy Eucharist.

Deign, O Divine Heart, * to preside over our meetings, * to bless our undertakings both spiritual and temporal, * to banish all worry and care, * to sanctify our joys * and soothe our sorrows. * If any of us * should ever have the misfortune to grieve Thy Sacred Heart, * remind him of Thy goodness and mercy * toward the repentant sinner.

Lastly, * when the hour of separation will sound * and death will plunge our home into mourning, * then shall we all and every one of us * be resigned to Thy eternal decrees, * and seek consolation in the thought * that we shall one day be reunited in heaven, * where we shall sing the praises and blessings of Thy Sacred Heart * for all eternity.

May the Immaculate Heart of Mary * and the glorious

Patriarch St. Joseph * offer Thee this our Consecration *
and remind us of the same * all the days of our life.

Glory to the Divine Heart of Jesus, * our King and our
Father!

7. The priest here asks those present to say with him one
Our Father and Hail Mary for all the absent members,
both living and dead, so that all may share in the graces
of the Enthronement.

8. All recite with the priest (or head of the family) the
following:

Prayer of Thanksgiving

Glory be to Thee, * O Sacred Heart of Jesus, * for the
infinite mercy * Thou hast bestowed * upon the privileged
members * of this family. * Thou hast chosen it * from
thousands of others, * as a recipient of Thy love * and a
sanctuary of reparation * wherein Thy most loving Heart
* shall find consolation * for the ingratitude of men. *
How great, O Lord Jesus, * is the confusion * of this portion of Thy faithful flock * as we accept the unmerited
honor * of seeing Thee preside over our family! * Silently
we adore Thee, * overjoyed to see Thee sharing * under
the same roof * the toils, cares and joys * of Thy innocent
children! * It is true * we are not worthy * that Thou
shouldst enter our humble abode, * but Thou hast already
reassured us, * when Thou didst reveal Thy Sacred Heart
to us, * teaching us to find in the wound of Thy Sacred
Side * the source of grace and life everlasting. * In this
loving and trusting spirit * we give ourselves to Thee, *
Thou who art unchanging Life. * Remain with us, Most
Sacred Heart, * for we feel an irresistible desire * to love
Thee and make Thee loved.

May our home be for Thee * a haven as sweet as that
of Bethany, * where Thou canst find rest * in the midst
of loving friends, * who like Mary * have chosen the better

part * in the loving intimacy of Thy Heart! * May this home be for Thee, * O beloved Saviour, * a humble but hospitable refuge * during the exile * imposed on Thee by Thine enemies. *

Come, then Lord Jesus, come, * for here as at Nazareth, * we have a tender love * for the Virgin Mary * Thy sweet mother * whom Thou hast given us to be our mother. * Come, * to fill with Thy sweet presence the vacancies * which misfortune and death * have wrought in our midst.

O most faithful Friend, * hadst Thou been here * in the midst of sorrow, * our tears would have been less bitter; * the comforting balm of peace * would then have soothed these hidden wounds, * which are known to Thee alone. * Come, for even now perhaps, * there is drawing near for us * the twilight of tribulation, * and the decline of the passing days * of our youth and our illusions. * Stay with us, * for already it is late, * and a perverted world * seeks to envelop us * in the darkness of its denials * while we wish to adhere to Thee * who alone art the Way * the Truth * and the Life. * Repeat for us those words * Thou didst utter of old * "This day I must abide in this home".

Yes, dear Lord, * take up Thy abode with us, * so that we may live in Thy love * and in Thy presence, * we who proclaim Thee as our King * and wish no other! * May Thy triumphant Heart, O Jesus, * be forever loved, * blessed, * and glorified * in this home! * Thy Kingdom come! Amen!

9. (All stand) To thank the Immaculate Heart of Mary for the grace of the Enthronement, and to proclaim this loving mother as the queen of the home, all recite the Hail Holy Queen. (If so desired, an Act of Consecration to the Heart of Mary may be added, and her image installed near the Sacred Heart.)

10. Most Sacred Heart of Jesus: Have mercy on us! (3 times)

Immaculate Heart of Mary: *Pray for us.*

St. Joseph: *Pray for us.*

St. Margaret Mary: *Pray for us.*

(ALL) Glory to the Most Sacred Heart of Jesus forever and ever! Amen.

11. *The priest gives his blessing:* Benedictio Dei omnipotentis, Patris, et Filii, et Spiritus Sancti, descendat super vos et maneat semper. Amen. May the blessing of Almighty God, Father, Son and Holy Ghost, descend upon you and remain forever. Amen.

12. Then the members of the family and the priest sign the Certificate of the Enthronement, which should be framed and hung near the image of the Sacred Heart.

13. Then are announced the following indulgences to be gained by the members of the family (Raccolta 1952, page 560):

a. A plenary indulgence under the usual conditions, on the day of the Enthronement.

b. An indulgence of 7 years for all the members of the family who, at least contrite of heart, assist at the ceremony of the Enthronement in their home.

c. An indulgence of 3 years—once a year—on the day they renew their official act of consecration before the likeness of the Sacred Heart of Jesus.

d. A plenary indulgence on the same day under the usual conditions.

NOTE: *The CEREMONY of the Enthronement is only the beginning: the following practices of devotion will help you LIVE the Enthronement. This is the TRUE reign of the Sacred Heart in your family.*

Suggested Practices of Devotion

1. Frequent and even daily attendance at Mass by at least one member of the family, and Communion of Reparation. Recite the "Mass of St. John" during the day.

2. Observance of the First Friday of each month. (Holy Mass, Communion of Reparation: renewal of act of consecration before enthroned image.)

3. Daily morning offering to the Sacred Heart.

4. Daily Family Rosary before the enthroned image of the Sacred Heart, with renewal of the act of consecration.

5. Celebration of the Feast of the Sacred Heart by the entire family; attendance at Mass, Communion for the extension of the Reign of the Sacred Heart through the Enthronement; family gathering and celebration at home, with renewal of Enthronement; special party for the children.

6. Observe the month of June, the month of the Sacred Heart; keep flowers before the "throne." Mass and Communion as often as possible.

7. Assist at Holy Hour in Church.

8. Night adoration in the home. Any hour between 9:00 and 6:00, by any one or all the members of the family at least once a month. Special Family Holy Hour booklets available.

9. Celebrate the feast of the Immaculate Heart of Mary on the 22nd of August. Mass, Communion, Consecration of family to Immaculate Heart.

10. Make the five First Saturdays in reparation to the Immaculate Heart of Mary and for the conversion of Russia; Holy Mass and Communion of reparation; five decades of the Rosary plus a fifteen-minute meditation on the fifteen mysteries of the Rosary. The Rosary and meditation may be carried out at any hour on the First Saturday; a sermon in church will satisfy the obligation of the meditation.

Special Occasions on Which the Family Should Renew the Act of Consecration

(*Prayer of Thanksgiving may be added.*)

1. Feast of Sacred Heart; of Christ the King.
2. Anniversary of the Enthronement.
3. Anniversaries of parents and children.
4. At births; after baptism in the Church consecrate the children to the Sacred Heart before the "throne" in the home.
5. At First Communion: prepare the children before the image of the Sacred Heart in the home. When they return from Church, let the children renew the act of consecration made for them by parents at birth.
6. Before a departure from home: to join army, convent, seminary, before marriage, etc.
7. On the return of an absent member of family.
8. On days of great family joys: in times of sorrow, sickness and death.

   NOTE: *There is no more appropriate way for a young couple to begin their married life, than to enthrone the Sacred Heart in their new home.*

NOTE: If the above ceremonial is used for the Enthronement in a rectory, the indulgenced "Form of Consecrating Priests to the Sacred Heart of Jesus," to be found in Appendix 2, may be substituted for the "Prayer of Thanksgiving." Special ceremonials for religious communities, seminaries, and schools, as well as "Enthronement Certificates" for same are available at Enthronement Centers or from the National Enthronement Center, 4900 S. Dakota Ave. N.E., Washington 17, D.C. A complete Enthronement manual, containing a short history of Father Mateo's life, detailed explanations of the enthronement, night adoration in the home, the Tarcisians of the Sacred Heart, and many true examples of conversions and blessings through the Enthronement in American homes, is available at bookstores. (*Enthronement of the Sacred Heart* by Fr. Larkin, SS.CC. 416 pages. Stiff cover. 95¢)

Renewal of the Consecration of the Family

(To be said at night prayers in union with all families in which the Sacred Heart has been enthroned.)

Most sweet Jesus, humbly kneeling at Thy feet, we renew the consecration of our family to Thy Divine Heart. Be Thou our King forever! In Thee we have full and entire confidence. May Thy spirit penetrate our thoughts, our desires, our words and our works. Bless our undertakings, share in our joys, in our trials and in our labors. Grant us to know Thee better, to love Thee more, to serve Thee without faltering.

By the Immaculate Heart of Mary, Queen of Peace, set up Thy kingdom in our country. Enter closely into the midst of our families and make them Thine own through the solemn enthronement of Thy Sacred Heart, so that soon one cry may resound from home to home: "May the triumphant Heart of Jesus be everywhere loved, blessed and glorified forever!" Honor and glory to the Sacred Hearts of Jesus and Mary!

"Sacred Heart of Jesus, protect our families."

(300 days indulgence, Raccolta, p. 143.)

6. Message of the Sacred Heart to the Heart of the Priest[1]

"Cold, I am athirst and hungry. . . . Tell My dear priests to warm Me with their love, and to give Me souls, souls, and more souls! Did I not die for love of them?

"All the riches of My Heart lie open! The more the nations stray from Me and cast Me off, the more does My sweet mother press Me to unfold the wealth of love, of pity and of holiness stored up in My Heart.

"It is true that devotion to My Sacred Heart is widespread, and this consoles Me, and yields many souls to Me —to Me, the Saviour of souls. And yet how far men are from realizing the boundless treasures of My Heart! . . . My Mother urges Me, My own love constrains Me, to pour out these treasures, and to invite all worthy souls to plunge and lose themselves in this Ocean of mercy and of love. . . . Oh, bear My Heart's appeal to the utmost limits of the earth: bear it, above all, to My priests, whom I love so greatly. To My priests, My 'alter egos'—'My other selves.' Ah! if they did but understand how intense is my desire to

[1] This message, written in a strange hand, was found among the papers of a saintly Marist Father. He had been rector of the major seminary in Brittany, France, for twenty years, and after having labored zealously for the sanctification of the clergy died in Rome in 1900. It has been widely circulated throughout the world.

unite Myself intimately with each one of them! . . . Few
of them attain to this union in that degree of closeness
which My Heart designs for them on earth.

"And what is needed for its attainment? That they col-
lect together, and—as it were—gather up all their affections,
and center them wholly upon Me who am present there,
in the inmost depths of their souls. Ah! proclaim it to them
all—to those who toil for Me in the frozen North; to those
who scorch beneath the fiery Southern heats; to those brave
warriors who fight beneath My standard; to those who
spend themselves night and day in work for souls, who are
weighed down by persecutions, labors, contradictions and
disappointments met with in My service. Cry out to all
of these how much I love them: beseech them to hearken
to the appeal I make to them so lovingly, so pressingly—
My tender invitation to descend into their deep-most souls,
and there unite themselves to Me, never to leave Me: to
become in some sort, one with Me . . . and then how
great are the blessings I promise to them! . . . This mystic
and divine union will become the starting-point of a life
all different, in its sanctity and fruitfulness, from that which
they have led till now.

"Many a priest knows well the theory of this union of
the soul with Me. Some aspire to it. But how few there
are who know it by practice! how few among good and
earnest priests, although devoted friends of Mine, realize
that I am there, deep down in their souls, and all on fire
to make them one with Me.

"And why is this? Because they live, so to say, on the
outer surface of their souls. If only they would withdraw
themselves from the things of sense and from human influence, in order thus to dive down into the inner recesses
of their souls, even to their lowest depth, where I am, right
speedily would they find Me: and what a life of union,
light and love would then be theirs!

"Very many are well content with being on the right path and keeping a certain watch over themselves, and seek for nothing beyond. . . . But let them go in fullest confidence to My mother, who is also theirs. Oh! how dearly does she love My priests! How fond she is of pleading with Me in their behalf! It is she—I say it once again —it is she, My own sweet mother, who urges Me to unfold all the treasures of My Heart and make a fresh appeal to all good souls and especially to My dear priests.

"My gentle mother is My Heart's delight: make her also the delight of yours. Know that this Mother of Divine Love holds the secret of this wondrous union, which, by a vast outpouring of mercy and love, My Heart now offers to all its priests as a new and tremendous grace unto their sanctification."

A NOTE ON THE TYPE

IN WHICH THIS BOOK WAS SET

This book has been set in Electra, a type face created in 1935 by W. A. Dwiggins, the well-known Boston artist. This type falls within the "modern" family of type styles, but was drawn to avoid the extreme contrast between "thick and thin" elements that marks most "modern" type faces. The design is not based upon any traditional model, and is not an attempt to revive or to reconstruct any historic type. Since its birth, Electra has met with success because of its easy-to-read quality. This book was composed and printed by the York Composition Company, Inc., of York, Pa., and bound by Moore and Company of Baltimore, Md. The design and typography of this book are by Howard N. King.